MY DAMAGE

MY DAMAGE

The Story of a Punk Rock Survivor

By Keith Morris
with Jim Ruland

DA CAPO PRESS

Editorial Production by Lori Hobkirk at the Book Factory
Designed by Cynthia Young
Set in 11.75 point Minion

Morris, Keith (Vocalist), author. | Ruland, Jim, author.
My damage : the story of a punk rock survivor / By Keith Morris with Jim Ruland.
Boston : Da Capo Press, [2016] | Includes bibliographical references and index.
LCCN 2016014833 (print) | LCCN 2016015099 (ebook) | ISBN 9780306824067
(hardcover : alk. paper) | ISBN 9780306824074 (ebook)
Morris, Keith (Vocalist) | Singers—United States—Biography. |
Punk rock musicians—United States—Biography.
LCC ML420.M6188 A3 2016 (print) | LCC ML420.M6188 (ebook)
| DDC 782.42166092 [B]—dc23
LC record available at https://lccn.loc.gov/2016014833

Published by Da Capo Press, an imprint of Perseus Books,
A Hachette Book Group company
www.dacapopress.com

Da Capo Press books are available at special discounts for bulk purchases
in the U.S. by corporations, institutions, and other organizations.
For more information, please contact the Special Markets Department,
2300 Chestnut Street, Suite 200, Philadelphia, PA 19103,
or call (800) 810-4145, ext. 5000,
or e-mail special.markets@perseusbooks.com.

10 9 8 7 6 5 4 3 2

For my mom, Maudena Morris,
Brendan Mullen, and all of my friends
who have put up with my shit over the years

Author's Note

This book is a collection of memories about my life in music and some of the shit that went on before I was in a band. I haven't changed the names of any people or places. The events described in this book are exactly as I remember them, but because no one's memory is 100 percent accurate and I was under the influence for many of these stories, my recollection of events may differ from others who were there. Welcome to my world. I don't mean to throw anybody under the bus, but what else are buses for?

Contents

Crash   1

Thug   3

Hermosa Beach   8

Bait   15

Wasted   20

Black Seeds   25

Panic   31

Chuck the Duke   36

The Church   39

They Kept Playing   43

Moose Lodge   49

Nervous Breakthrough   56

Ground Zero   63

Brain Fry   67

Polliwog Park   73

LAPD   77

Not Having Fun   82

What's Next?   88

Inglegood   91

It's a Small World After All   98

The Pink House   105

Gin Ling Way   108

TDOWC   113

New York Calling   118

Wild in the Streets   124

World Up My Ass   130

Golden Shower of Hits   136

I Can't Believe I Used to Like These Guys   141

You Don't Belong Here   146

Bud Club   154

Ultra Megadeath   158

Not So Wönderful   162

It's the Monster . . .   167

Last Straw   174

V   181

Hangmen   186

The Nymph   191

Screwed   196

Bug Lamp   202

Zapped   208

A Wandering Jew   214

The Last Jerk Off   219

Devil's Mess   226

Down   231

Midget Handjob   235

V2   241

Heart of Darkness   246

Blackout   253

Oslo Coma Situation   259

OFF!   271

Happy Ending   277

Acknowledgments   285

About the Authors   289

Index   291

CRASH

I came to in a state of panic, covered in sweat with blood dripping down my face. I was behind the wheel of my car and I'd crashed into something. But what did I hit? What the hell happened? Where was I?

My whole life has been like this: coming out of the darkness, trying to figure out where I was and who I was with, struggling to assess the damage. I needed to figure out the answers fast because the car *was still moving*, rolling through a red light and into rush hour traffic.

I slammed on the brakes, stopped the car, and got out. I was on Sunset Boulevard in Hollywood in the shadow of Amoeba Records. I could see the headlines now: *Punk Rocker Slams into Record Store.* A fitting epitaph for a guy who's been butting heads with the music business for forty years, first as the founding lead vocalist for Black Flag, then as the head party-meister in the Circle Jerks, and finally as the front man for a bunch of other bands and almost-bands from Bug Lamp to Midget Handjob. I've managed bands, produced records, and even worked as an A&R guy for a major label. I've had falling outs with band members and had my heart trampled by members of other bands. Now, as I write this at the age of sixty, I'm the vocalist of OFF! and still going after it.

That night in Hollywood I'd slipped into a diabetic blackout and lost control while on my way to see a show. I was able to figure out what had happened because it had happened to me before: crashing my car while loaded on pills in Hermosa Beach, losing control of the tour van after hitting some black ice in Texas, ending up in an emergency room in Norway after slipping into a diabetic coma. All my life I've pushed the limits and put myself in situations I had no business walking away from. As a recovering alcoholic, drug addict, and full-blown diabetic, damage is a fact of life.

This is my story as a punk rock survivor. My damage is always with me, a reminder that if I'm not careful, it will kill me . . .

Los Feliz, California, November 2015

THUG

My dad was a straight-up drinking, drugging, hard-living, motorcycle-riding, leather jacket–wearing, take-no-shit-off-of-anybody kind of guy. He was basically a thug.

When my dad was a teenager he got kicked out of Inglewood High for kidnapping the principal. One morning he busted into the principal's office while he was getting ready to play "The Star-Spangled Banner" and recite the Pledge of Allegiance over the PA system. My dad tied the principal and his secretary to some chairs and gagged them. He proceeded to get on the microphone and tell the whole school it was a holiday and everybody could go home.

That didn't go over so well with the authorities, and my old man was told, "Don't ever come back here!"

My mom, however, went to the other high school in town, Morningside, which was Inglewood High's rival. She was a cheerleader and a straight-A student. Friendly and beautiful and all that wonderful stuff. My dad was all leather and denim. Grease your hair back and get in a fight on Friday night. They were like Danny and Sandy from the musical *Grease* but without all of the singing, dancing, and nice vibes.

My dad was short, but he was a Golden Glove boxer. Because he was the smallest guy in the motorcycle gang, he would be the first one to pull up to the drive-in or the sock hop and start trouble. People wouldn't take him seriously because of his size, but, being a boxer, my dad could usually finish what he started. Then the rest of the gang would come roaring in, and the shit would really hit the fan.

There were exceptions. For his initiation into the gang, he had to go to the big annual football game between the Inglewood Sentinels and Morningside Monarchs. He had to stand among all the Morningside fans and tell them to go fuck themselves. There he was, dressed like the Fonz with his leather jacket and chains, screaming, "Fuck you!" to all the fans. You didn't see that kind of drama on *Happy Days*.

That night didn't end well for my dad. Someone clocked him with a pipe, and they chained him to the back of the bleachers. When he woke up, the sun was beating down on him and he was soaking wet. He thought it was moisture from the grass, but it wasn't dew. The Morningside guys had pissed all over him while he was unconscious and he was covered in urine. That was his initiation.

I'm not sure how long my dad lasted in the motorcycle gang. He would eventually have an epiphany and realize he couldn't keep living like that if he wanted to get married and start a family. It was time to grow up, but trouble was in his blood.

MY DAD WAS BORN in Chicago but grew up in Tennessee. One summer evening he and his two brothers were playing outside when one of them kicked a ball over a hedge. They climbed through the bushes, and on the other side a burning cross lit up the sky as bright as day. Some guys in white robes were stringing somebody up in the trees—my dad and his brothers had stumbled upon a KKK lynch mob.

They left the ball and ran back home to tell my grandfather Saul what they'd seen. If my grandparents hadn't been aware of the secret white societies that ruled the South, they were now. Shortly afterward my grandparents changed their name from Goldstein to Morris, packed up all of their belongings, and moved to California.

MY MOM, MAUDENA CALDWELL, was eighteen when she had me on September 18, 1955. I was born on Sunset Boulevard—just a few blocks from where I've lived in Los Feliz for the last twenty years or so. My parents were living in Gardena at the time. My dad was supposed to go away to fight in the Korean War, but he was turned away because he had lead poisoning. So instead of going to war, he went to work for his dad. Saul owned a scrap yard and garbage dump in the desert outside of Palm Springs. We moved out to the desert, and my dad worked construction and did a lot of odd jobs for my grandfather, who was another tough guy. He was one of the few Jews who worked for Al Capone.

I saw a lot of weird shit out there in the desert. One time my dad and I were driving along one of the back roads when he hit the brakes and pointed up at the sky. The sun was flashing on these silver objects that were moving horizontally and vertically at incredibly high speeds. There was a naval air base out there, and I'd seen the Blue Angels doing maneuvers on a couple of occasions, but this was nothing like that—this was a flying saucer situation. When they disappeared my dad said, "We'll probably never see anything like that again."

He worked with a lot of rough characters at the scrap yard and got himself into some hairy situations. At one point my dad and my grandfather decided to dig a pit in the middle of the dump and hold dog fights there. My dad thought it would be good idea to put his Doberman in the ring with a pit bull. He thought the Doberman could hang. He learned almost immediately that he was wrong. Within a matter of minutes the pit bull had bitten off all four of the Doberman's legs and was thrashing him around by the throat, spraying blood everywhere. My dad told me it was one of the most brutal things he'd ever seen.

Our time in the desert was rough for everyone. When I was five or six years old a teenager molested me. She was a freckle-faced redhead with blue eyes. A cute, normal-looking girl. She took me behind one of the garages in the neighborhood, and that's where it went down. I don't really remember what happened. I just know that it was something completely foreign to me. The traumatic part was afterward, when she told me that I would get in big trouble if I told anyone what had happened, that it was our secret. That was really confusing to me because I didn't know what I'd done that was wrong. I thought we were just playing. It was a heavy thing for a kid to have to deal with. In fact, I've never told anyone about this, but maybe it explains my fascination with redheads.

I was smaller than the rest of the kids in the neighborhood—a lot smaller—and people were always messing with me. I was the shrimp, the runt of the litter. Got some anger or aggression you need to get out? Take it out on the little guy—everyone else did. I don't want to paint a picture that I didn't have any friends or that I was constantly getting picked on, because that wasn't the case, but sometimes people went too far.

One afternoon I was playing in front of the house with some local kids when the neighborhood bully decided he was going to mess with me. He grabbed me by my ankle and my wrist and swung me around like an airplane. I wasn't too cool with that and told him to put me down. Well, he put me down all right. He let me go.

I went flying through the air and crash-landed in the driveway and cracked my head open on the cement. My mom came outside and freaked out. She didn't even take me inside the house. She put me in the car and drove straight to the emergency room, where they stitched me up.

When kids picked on me, there wasn't much I could do. I could have run to my dad and told him what was happening, but even then I knew that wasn't a good idea. My dad didn't take shit from anybody, and I didn't want to sic him on my friends or their parents—that wouldn't have been a good situation for anyone. I think my dad knew what was going on, and he probably allowed some of it to happen to toughen me up; he wasn't going to step in and fight my battles for me. I had to learn how to take care of myself. If that meant a few scrapes and bruises along the way, so be it.

Unfortunately it didn't work. Being tough didn't make me weigh more or stand taller. What's a kid who weighs 40 pounds going to do to someone who weighs 120? Bruce Lee could have taught me the Monkey Paw or the Golden Sparrow or the Donkey Death Kick to defend myself, but it wouldn't have made much of a difference.

MY DAD WASN'T CUT OUT FOR working at a garbage dump. He was dabbling in drugs and got addicted to heroin. One of his high school buddies had moved to Puerto Vallarta with another friend and had started a pot farm. They reached out to my dad and concocted a scheme to smuggle a flatbed truck full of marijuana across the Mexico-California border. My dad flew to Puerto Vallarta and started driving. He made it all the way up to the US border in Tijuana before he was caught. He was arrested and sent to county jail for a year. The story they told my sister Trudy and me was that our dad was up in Northern California dredging for gold on the Klamath River.

It was actually a good thing for my dad. While he was in jail he got cleaned up and never did heroin again. It wasn't something he was proud of, but he was able to prove he wasn't a slave to his past. He made mistakes, but he outlived them. He was always trying to do better, and he was never satisfied.

After being cooped up in jail for a year my dad wanted to work outside again, so we moved to Las Vegas, where he worked in construction. This was before Las Vegas had turned into the big corporate adult playground it is today. I used to walk to school past blocks of empty desert that eventually would be built up into hotel towers and casinos.

One of my dad's uncles, Howie, lived there and worked as a pit boss in a bunch of the casinos. When he was sixty years old and getting ready to retire, he married a twenty-year-old Playboy bunny. All of our relatives were shocked and concerned, but my mom thought it was great. Her motto was, "Do what you want and have a great time." She's always been a real open-minded person.

I had my first public performance in Las Vegas when I was seven years old. I had to sing a solo performance of "Red River Valley" at an elementary school show in front of about five hundred people. It was an evening performance in an outdoor setting, and I was really nervous. The piano started up, and I started singing and almost immediately forgot my words. I was so terrified that I pissed my pants. It was an inauspicious beginning to my illustrious musical career.

HERMOSA BEACH

We didn't last in Las Vegas very long, and eventually my mom and dad moved back to California. I was really excited because the town we moved to was right on the ocean. One of my earliest memories of Hermosa Beach is walking to South Elementary School on Monterey with my sister and a neighborhood kid named Morgan.

We used to walk down the alleyway that ran parallel to the street. We were in this alley twice a day, five days a week. We started to notice a really foul odor, like rotting meat, only much stronger. We were on our way to school when we came across this yellow tape blocking the alley. *Police line. Do not cross.* Something was going on in one of the garages. We were looking around, wondering what to do. We were little kids, and this was our route to school. Now what?

I took it upon myself to walk into the taped-off garage. The place was packed with policemen, but being the curious kid I was, I was able to squeeze in next to the car. The window was rolled down, and it really stank in there. I looked over to see what was making this horrible smell and saw a dead body behind the wheel. Apparently the guy had tried to asphyxiate himself but got impatient and decided to blow his brains out with some kind of a gun instead.

It turned out the guy had been in there for weeks, and no one knew until someone who lived nearby complained about the odor. I was checking it out, thinking, *Wow, this is something you don't get to see every day!* when a cop noticed me and yelled at me to get out of there.

I didn't really understand what I saw that day. I had no concept of death and what it meant to the dead guy's friends and family. It was my first glimpse of death up close and personal.

HERMOSA BEACH is located in LA's South Bay, which stretches from the LA River just below the marina in Playa del Rey all the way to Palos Verdes. It includes all of the beach cities, like El Segundo, Manhattan Beach, Hermosa Beach, and Redondo Beach, and dozens of densely packed quasi-urban suburban towns like Hawthorne, Gardena, and Torrance, each with its own history.

The South Bay provided me with some of my earliest musical experiences. When I was ten years old I saw Arthur Lee and Love play a matinee show at a theater in Palos Verdes, the Beverly Hills of the South Bay. You bought your ticket and saw two movies, and in between a band would play a short set for fifteen or twenty minutes. Love played in between two movies, one of which was *Skaterdater*, one of the very first skateboarding movies, and it was actually filmed in places like Redondo Beach and Torrance with real skaters who were from the South Bay, so it was kind of a big deal. But it was Love who made the biggest impression on me that day.

Two weeks later I saw the Barbarians at the Fox Hermosa Theater on Hermosa Avenue. The Barbarians had a hit in 1965 called "Are You a Boy or Are You a Girl?" and their drummer had only one hand. He fixed a drumstick in his clasp, and away he went. It was really something to see.

I got to see a live band play when my Aunt Frances had a party in her backyard in North Redondo Beach right across the street from Mira Costa High School, which I would eventually attend. She unhooked the plumbing to her antique bathtub, dragged it out to the backyard, and filled it with ice and red wine—the party was ready to rage.

She got some friends of hers who were in a band to play. They were called Smokestack Lightning, after the Howlin' Wolf song the Yardbirds and the Grateful Dead covered, and they played up and down the Sunset Strip. They wanted to be a psychedelic blues band, but I didn't think they very inspiring, probably because of the mediocre PA system they were working with. I was only about twelve years old, and I was already a music critic.

Nevertheless, it was an unforgettable party. Somebody spiked the tub with LSD. All the adults, including my grandparents, drank the wine. Everybody was dancing around and getting their groove on. Normally when there's a live band playing in your backyard, the older folks are covering their ears and shaking their heads. "What is this shit? This is horrible!" Not this time. Everybody was laughing and smiling and having the time of their lives.

Many years later my mom told me what happened. Naturally, my dad wasn't there. He was working.

My Aunt Frances was a free spirit. She was a teen model and a go-go dancer at the Hollywood Palladium. She was also the president of the Elvis Presley Fan Club in Los Angeles, which was no small thing. I remember they had a meeting at my grandparent's house in Inglewood that turned into a slumber party. I walked in, and all of the girls were in their nighties and pajamas and sleeping gowns. Naturally, I wanted to see what was going on with all of these cute girls. The next thing I knew, they'd stripped me out of my pajamas and tossed me naked into the backyard, which wasn't so terrible, all things considered, but it was still embarrassing.

One of the things you need to understand about me is that, being a small kid, I was always told I couldn't do things. I was never part of the most popular crowd. I never had a girlfriend. In high school I stood five-foot-five and weighed 76 pounds, so you can imagine what I weighed when I was in elementary school and junior high. I wanted to play sports. I have a passion for football and baseball that persists to this day. I have great memories of going to the Coliseum with my grandfather Bob to see the LA Rams play. I'd go to the May Company and buy a pair of tickets at the Ticketron counter for $20. Fifty-yard line, fifty rows up. We wouldn't even have to get on the freeway—just drive up Hoover and park a few blocks away from the Coliseum.

I never got to be the quarterback or the running back or the wide receiver. I never really had an opportunity to be the guy who makes a play and gets a little glory. I was always picked last. I had to be the guy who stayed in and blocked so that the bigger kids would have an excuse to push me around some more.

I was surrounded by guys who played Pop Warner football or Little League over at Clark Stadium or basketball at the junior high gymnasium on Pier Avenue. Hermosa Beach was your typical Southern California town where kids played sports year round. I wanted to play too, but there was no place for me. I was constantly being told, "You're too small."

I wanted to play so bad that I tried out for the Mira Costa football team. This was like the D team, junior-junior varsity, the absolute bottom level. The players were all laughing, but it wasn't a joke to me. The coaches left a uniform out for me in the locker room, the smallest one they could find, and told me to get suited up. None of the equipment fit me. The helmet was three or four sizes too big. It started to sink in that I wasn't going to be able to play. If I went out on the field, I was going to get crushed. My dream of playing football wasn't realistic. Even with all the pads and the protection, I wouldn't have stood a chance. Maybe you have a vision of this little guy darting between the legs of all of these enormous dudes like something out of a Three Stooges comedy skit, but that wasn't going to happen. I would have been destroyed.

These disappointments were burned into my memory.

AFTER WE'D MOVED to Hermosa Beach my dad started working for one of his friends as a salesman for one of the biggest fence companies in Southern California. A lot of his customers were available only on weekends, so rather than leave me with my grandparents, my dad would take me with him on his sales calls. He wasn't above using me as part of his pitch, and it didn't hurt that I looked a lot younger than I really was because of my small size. My dad closed a lot of deals with me as his sympathetic sidekick. As a consequence, rather than making friends at the beach, I was being dragged by my dad all over Southern California.

Eventually my dad saved up enough money to start his own business: a bait and tackle shop at 21 Pier Avenue. I started working for him right away. I'd pack bait, count hooks, stock sinkers, and sweep the floor and the sidewalk in front of the store. I hated sweeping the fucking floor!

My dad had an uneasy relationship with Hermosa Beach, but he got along really well with the other business owners on Pier Avenue. It was a bait shop, so it opened early for the fishermen, but it was also an unofficial hangout for an older generation of pro surfers. Hap Jacobs, Greg Noll, and Dewey Weber would hang out at the shop and drink coffee and shoot the shit with my dad. Then in the evening the jazz club across the street would come to life, and my dad would hang out with the musicians. My dad was friends with Dez Cadena's dad long before his son and I became friends, though I'm sure we must have bumped into each other when we were kids. Dez, of course, would become a vocalist and guitar player for Black Flag.

Even though my dad went legit with his business, he didn't stop being a tough guy. While he was locking up the store one night, five guys accosted him in the alley behind the store. Down by the beach, when the marine layer crept in, it could get dark and dank and downright spooky, but my dad wasn't intimidated.

"Give us your wallet and your keys," one of the guys said.

"Come on and take it," my dad replied.

That's how my dad rolled. That's the kind of confidence he had. He wasn't going to let anyone take what belonged to him without a fight. He stood his ground and proceeded to teach them one of life's hard lessons, and every single one of those guys ended up in the hospital.

LIKE ANY BUSINESS OWNER, my dad had his ups and downs. On the corner of Hermosa Avenue and Pier Avenue my dad rented a ballroom above a men's clothing store and ice cream parlor. He'd bought out a company in Gardena that manufactured fishing equipment and used the ballroom as storage. One night one of the freezers in the ice cream store shorted out, started a fire, and burned most of the building down. The ballroom was filled with airtight wooden crates packed with parts for fishing rods and reels. When I say airtight, I mean vacuum sealed. So when these crates caught fire, that's when the real fireworks started.

We were living on 10th and Monterey, right up the hill, so we had a great view of the inferno. Each time one of these wooden crates caught fire it exploded and shot into the air like something you would see in a war movie. There were about fifty of them in all. It was four or five in the morning, shortly before dawn, and my dad and I stood on the porch watching the show.

"You're watching your college money go up in flames," my dad said.

I didn't really know what that meant. I just knew that my dad was really bummed. A couple of days later, my best friend Chuck Underwood, a couple of our buddies, and I stole Chuck's dad's car and drove down to where the fire had gutted the building. They hopped over the wooden wall that had been erected around the scene while I watched out for cops. They went into the clothing store and starting throwing clothes over the fence, and I stuffed everything in the trunk. This was on a Saturday morning in broad daylight—a pretty brazen maneuver on our part. We definitely had some hair on our balls.

We got in the car and drove away. We were all so proud of ourselves because we were going to give the clothes to our dads. We were all thinking about how much they were going to love us for this, that they were going to think we were the greatest. It turned out all the clothes were scorched and smoked and sodden beyond repair, and all of it had to go in the trash.

Not too long after that Chuck Underwood had an epileptic seizure while he was surfing one morning before school. He went under and didn't come back up. He got caught in a riptide and was sucked out to sea. He washed up a week later. All the sea creatures had eaten away his skin. His nose and eyelids were missing, and he didn't have any ears. They had to have a closed-casket funeral for him. He was the first person I was close to who died way too soon, but he wasn't the last.

BAIT

As I got older my dad gave me more and more responsibilities until I could run the bait shop on my own, but I was starting to explore my own interests—namely, booze, drugs, and rock and roll.

I was fourteen years old the first time I got drunk. Two of my best friends were twins named Ted and Dave. I'd go over to their house and watch live broadcasts of boxing, wrestling, and roller derby from the Olympic Auditorium. These events would inevitably inspire the twins to try out some new moves, and a fight would break out. Fists flying, bodies rolling on the floor—I always got pulled into it. Their mom would come in and say, "You guys can't do that in here. You're gonna have to take it outside."

On one particular night they scored a big bottle of Blue Nun, which was a cheap wine that wasn't going to give you a religious experience. We drank the wine and listened to Black Sabbath on an eight-track player. I'd always liked Black Sabbath, but this time they sounded heavier and more intense. There was a hippie couple who lived down the street from the twins, and they smoked us out. It was my first time for that too.

When I came home it was still early. I went into my room to crash, and the bed started spinning. I got nauseous and ran for the bathroom. I made it in time but missed the toilet and puked on the floor. That happened like five or six times, and I missed the toilet every single time. My dad was out, but my mom was home, and her response was pretty comical. She came down the hall with a mop. "You made this mess. You get to clean it up."

Despite my gruesome hangover the next day, I continued to experiment. I loved the feeling drugs and alcohol gave me when listening to music. It just made the whole experience more enjoyable, even if I occasionally overdid it.

My dad smoked pot, drank a lot of coffee, and took tons of pills. When I was in middle school I'd dip into my dad's stash of weed and speed and do little deals with my friends behind the building where they kept all the janitorial supplies. I'd sell crisscross for fifty cents a pop. I'd give my friends a pinch of pot here and there. I'd fill a flask with my dad's vodka and replace it with water. I never got caught by the school or by my old man, but I'm pretty sure he knew what I was doing.

THE FIRST BIG CONCERT I attended was at the Los Angeles Forum in Inglewood. It was my fifteenth birthday, and the bands on the bill were the Grass Roots, who had a couple of AM radio hits, Three Dog Night, and Steppenwolf, who had just released *Monster*, which tells the story of American history leading up to the Vietnam War. I still hold that album in high regard.

After that first experience of seeing live music I was hooked, and I witnessed some unbelievable performances that had a lasting impact on me. When I was seventeen years old I saw Iggy and the Stooges on the Raw Power tour, the record that David Bowie produced with James Williamson, at the Whisky A Go Go. Iggy came out wearing a pair of pants and nothing else—no shirt, no socks, no shoes. The first thing he did was dump a bucket of ice cold water on his head. He was standing barefoot on stage with all these live wires running everywhere. All he had to do was grab the mic the wrong way, and he would have been blasted through the roof. The band sounded amazing even though they were just a couple of weeks away from breaking up.

Speaking of Bowie, I saw him on the Ziggy Stardust tour in 1972 with Mick Ronson, Trevor Bolder, and Mick "Woody" Woodmansey, aka the Spiders from Mars. I was in the seventh row with a nugget of hashish in my pocket. An unbelievable show—just mind-bogglingly genius. Don't take my word for it: there's a live album of that show called *Santa Monica '72*.

Around this time I saw the Kinks for the first time at the Hollywood Palladium. The Davies brothers got into a fight, though it was a one-sided affair. Ray just hauled off and sucker punched Dave and knocked him down. Dave kept playing his guitar until a pair of roadies came out to lift him up. Dave just shrugged it off like all he wanted to do was lie there in his misery and play guitar. Ray had some kind of breakdown not too long after that show.

My friends and I loved to see live music but couldn't always afford to go, so I got really good at sneaking into places. That was one advantage to being short: I was able to sneak into places I didn't belong. One night I snuck into the dressing room at the Starwood when the Runaways were doing a photo shoot with Led Zeppelin. I was able to sneak past the guy at the door and finagle my way in. However, my first brush with rock and roll superstardom didn't work out so well. In fact, it ended pretty abruptly when Kim Fowley, one of the most hated men in the music business, spotted me. "Get him out of here!" he shouted.

A bouncer picked me up off my feet and threw me against the wall. When I slumped to the ground he grabbed me by the neck, lifted me up by my belt loop, and tossed me out the door like a piece of garbage. I was a little groggy from my crash landing and all the beer I'd been drinking that day, but when I lifted my head up, there was a hand reaching down to help me up. I grabbed the hand and got to my feet and found myself standing in front of a man with long blonde hair and platform shoes and dressed in some outrageous glam costume. I recognized him immediately: Arthur Killer Kane of the New York Dolls.

"I hate that motherfucking Kim Fowley, that motherfucker," he growled.

Killer Kane made a big impression on me. Here he was, a bona fide rock star, but he wasn't too big to lend a helping hand to a scrawny kid. Although the lesson to be learned from the whole experience was obviously "Don't fuck around in someone else's dressing room," that episode planted a seed with respect to how to be a decent human being. If I ever got famous, I wouldn't be like Kim Fowley and step on people just because I could. I'd be like Arthur Killer Kane.

Sometimes my friends and I would sneak into the Hollywood Bowl. Even though it's an outdoor venue, it wasn't as easy as it sounds. A lot of people thought the best way to get into the Hollywood Bowl without paying was to come over the hills and sneak in the back way. But the security staff at the Hollywood Bowl was particularly brutal. They liked to climb up in the trees behind the venue and hide out until someone tried to sneak in. Then they'd jump out of the trees with bats and pipes and start swinging. We heard stories about people getting hospitalized just for trying to catch a free show.

We took a more direct approach. Right behind the will call booth near the front entrance to the Hollywood Bowl there was a cement drainage ditch that cut underneath the fence. If you were up for a super-secret underground banzai mission, it was the best way in. We'd act all nonchalant and then someone would whisper, "Go!" and we'd make a break for it.

Adding to the danger was the fact that these friends of mine were all into hardcore drugs. If they couldn't get heroin, they'd get prescription cough syrup because of its over-the-top codeine content. We'd sit in the parking lot outside the Hollywood Bowl drinking peach-flavored cough syrup until it was time for the show to start. If we got caught, at least it would dull the pain.

The ditch let us off to the side about twenty rows up from the orchestra pit. Then we'd split up and look for open seats. If we couldn't find seats, we could always go up to the grassy area where the people drinking wine and eating stinky cheese would hang out.

We saw a fair amount of shows this way. The Allman Brothers Band, Procol Harum with the LA Philharmonic, and Pink Floyd around the time of *Atom Heart Mother*. Thankfully the goons at the Hollywood Bowl never caught on to what we were doing, because we were in no condition to defend ourselves.

When I was a teenager I had posters of all of my favorite musicians up on my bedroom walls—David Bowie, Marc Bolan, Edgar Winter's *They Only Come Out at Night*, and the first KISS album. My dad didn't really know what to make of it. One time he came into my room while I was listening to music and looked at all the posters and said, "You're a fag, aren't you?"

This was an actual one-sided conversation we had.

I think it was hard for him because he liked music too, but jazz was his genre of choice. To him it was this exciting, creative thing, and he just didn't understand the appeal of these strange-looking gender-bending rock stars. To him they were all a bunch of queers. It wasn't just the way the bands looked; he had a genuine dislike for the music. The harder the music, the more he disliked it. One afternoon I was listening to Sham 69, and he came into my room and said, "I'm going to a jazz festival today, and they won't be playing any of this shit!"

Okay, Dad. You do your thing, and I'll do mine.

WASTED

My partying started off with hanging out with friends on the weekends, trying to cram as much action and adventure between Friday and Monday as possible. Pretty soon I was partying after school and then sometimes before class or even during school hours. There was never a bad time to get wasted.

I had a friend who worked at the zoo and would steal elephant tranquilizer, rhino tranquilizer, hippo tranquilizer—you name it. If there was an animal that needed to be tranquilized, he could get the drugs. A couple of lines of that stuff, and we were flying out of our minds. One night we walked up and down the Strand. We walked from the breakwater in Redondo Beach all the way to El Porto in Manhattan Beach and back. We must have walked it seven or eight times. I felt so fucking high, I thought, *Man, I'm never coming down from this.*

That, I thought, was a good thing.

I remember one Christmas morning my friends and I decided to smoke some angel dust. We'd just gotten new wet suits and surfboards for Christmas, and we wanted to break them in, but first we got really high. We went down to the beach, and there were, like, three hundred surfers in the water because there was no school and everyone had the same plan. The surf conditions were really bad. There was no surf—just walls.

To be honest, I was never that big into surfing. The guys I hung out with had been surfing their whole lives, but it was still pretty new to me. The water was freezing cold. I paddled out and somehow made it past the wall. The waves had no shape. They were nonexistent.

Someone said, "Go!" And I went. I was immediately clobbered. I got tossed around the surf. I couldn't tell what was up and what was down. I thought I was going to die. I thought about my friend Chuck Underwood, who'd died in these waves. All these things were going through my mind while I was tumbling around in the surf. It was definitely not an ideal time to be dusted. When I dragged myself out of the water I said, "Fuck this. I'm not doing this anymore!" And by that I meant surfing, not PCP.

My friends and I had a knack for putting ourselves in difficult situations. We decided it would be a great idea to get really wasted and attend a dance party at Myron's Ballroom in downtown Los Angeles. We'd purchased a couple of eight-packs of Norwegian beer that was on special. Horrible stuff, like drinking Viking piss. We didn't have any cocaine, so we took a bunch of Tuinals, which were sedatives, the opposite of coke. I picked everyone up, drank most of the beer on the way to the dance, took a bunch of pills, and passed out in the back of my dad's Ford Falcon station wagon.

At the end of the night my friends woke me up and—my friends being my friends—put me behind the wheel so I could drive. I was in no condition to be on the road, but they guided me to their houses, and I got everyone home safely.

On the way back to my house, somewhere in Manhattan Beach, I blacked out and hit a car parked in the driveway in front of someone's house. I hit the car so hard that I drove it all the way through the garage and up into the guy's living room. My car rolled back onto Manhattan Beach Boulevard with smoke pouring out of the engine. I wasn't in much better shape. My face was all beat up, and I'd broken off three-quarters of my front tooth so that the nerve was dangling, but I didn't feel a thing because of all the Tuinals I'd taken earlier.

The cops came, hauled me off to the police station, and called my dad. It was around three in the morning, and he was pissed.

"I'd fuck you up if you weren't so fucked up!"

I ended up pleading no contest to reckless driving. I wasn't arrested or put in handcuffs or anything like that. I guess it was one of the perks of being the son of a local business owner, but he was so pissed off that when we left the police station he wouldn't talk to me or look at me. He kept me on a tight leash at the bait shop for a while, but when things calmed down I pinched a couple of bucks from the cash register and went back to partying with my friends.

WHEN I GOT OLD ENOUGH to work a full shift at the bait shop I'd open the store on weekends, turn on the lights and the radio, get some coffee going, and put in a day's work. I did the banking on Mondays and Fridays. I dealt with the Department of Fish and Game for our fishing licenses. I was in charge of inventory and invoicing. I handled shipments with UPS and the US Postal Service. I'd package squid and shrimp and clams and send them off to our customers. If it swims in the ocean, chances are I've boxed it, sold it, and shipped it.

The best part about working for my dad was I used the store as my own personal bank. If I needed some money, I'd ring up a sale and pocket the cash or I'd just take it from the safe at the end of the day.

The worst thing about working in the bait shop was how early I had to get up in the morning. I kept fisherman's hours and had to get up super early to open the store. My dad hated it when I came in late, obviously hungover and reeking of booze. He would take one look at me and say, "Your eyes look like two piss holes in the snow!"

My dad didn't look like he was in a motorcycle gang anymore, but he was the same guy. He dressed like a square, but he still used speed and coffee to get up for the day and alcohol and marijuana to come down. So when I came stumbling into the shop in the morning he knew what was happening. I never tried to hide what I was doing from him. Why lie when he'd see right through it?

My dad told me again and again not to make drugs a regular part of my life, especially heroin. Unlike a lot of my friends, I was fortunate that I never developed a taste for it, probably because my dad had warned me about it so many times. But the rest of my dad's advice went out the window. I wanted to do what most teenagers want to do: have a good time. He wanted me to get serious about my life. He wanted me to be more responsible. I wanted him to get off my back.

I warned my friends not to hang around the store when they were high, but they wouldn't listen. They'd come in drunk and stoned and loaded on heroin. My old man would walk into the store and see these guys, and he'd know *exactly* what they were up to. He had that junkie intuition. He just knew. When they'd leave to go nod out on the beach my dad would confront me.

"These guys are your friends? You make terrible choices!"

He was determined to give me the opportunities he never had growing up, but I had zero interest in becoming the Bait King of the South Bay. I was thinking about becoming an artist.

My senior year in high school I was presented with a scholarship to attend Pasadena Art Center. I'd blazed my way through the art department at Mira Costa, from painting to sculpture to jewelry making. Ten of my paintings were on display at the LA County Fair and won a couple of gold medals. One of those paintings was even featured on the cover of *Westways* magazine. That got the attention of the people at Pasadena Art Center.

As part of my requirement for graduating, I had to critique all of the art classes I had taken my senior year in high school. I had no problem getting up in front of the class and talking about all of the things I'd learned—those art teachers were my heroes. They saw something in me and cultivated what little talent I had to the point where I was making some cool stuff. One teacher called me "fearless" because I always took on the most challenging projects, and that meant a lot to me.

But there was one art class that a lot of the stoners took because all you had to do to get a C was show up. The quality of the work produced in that class wasn't up to par. I got up in front of all the students and told the teacher that I thought the art being created in her class was no better than what would have come out of the zoo if you gave the monkeys and elephants some brushes and paint. The teacher didn't like that. She cut me off and called me a name in front of all of the kids in the class, which I didn't think was very cool.

"You don't get to call me that in front of my friends, you bitch!" I said, and that was the end of my scholarship. Instead of going to Pasadena Art Center, I enrolled at El Camino Community College and worked at my dad's store. The sad thing about all of that is, I don't even like fishing.

A FEW YEARS AFTER I GRADUATED from high school my parents split up. They had it all worked out. They were just waiting for my younger sister to turn eighteen. For a couple of years my parents lived together to keep the house stable. After all the moving around we did they didn't want to uproot us and start all over again at new schools when we were so close to finishing. So we all lived a lie, like the Ramones' song, "We're a Happy Family."

I would later learn that the reason why Mom wanted to divorce my dad is because he turned down an opportunity to buy a piece of property down at the beach. It was a big house with a huge lot half a block long with a three-car garage and a little bachelor pad attached for $70,000. I don't know why my dad didn't jump on it, but it probably had something to do with the bait and tackle shop. That property would be worth multiple millions today, and my mom knew it.

Maybe it's a good thing my dad didn't buy it: I probably wouldn't have left home. I'd still be down there, getting wasted on the Strand with the rest of the burnouts and soaking up the California sun.

BLACK SEEDS

The seeds of Black Flag were planted at a Journey concert. That's right: the seminal American hardcore punk rock band got its start at an arena rock concert at the Santa Monica Civic in Los Angeles, California.

Journey was playing with Thin Lizzy on their Jailbreak tour, and we drove up from Hermosa Beach in a bright red Chevy Impala my dad had given to me that I would later sell for only a few grams of cocaine. I hated driving (and still do) but we had to get to the show, and this was a concert I wasn't going to miss. It was a Wednesday night in June in 1976. I was twenty years old and in addition to working at the bait shop, I'd picked up a few shifts at a record store on Pier Avenue in Hermosa Beach called Rubicon run by a guy named Michael Piper.

If you liked Joni Mitchell, Stevie Nicks, and Linda Ronstadt, Rubicon was the place for you. The record store was located right across from the mortuary, and the vibe at the Rubicon wasn't all that different from what was going down across the street. It sometimes felt like Michael was trying to brainwash his customers and employees with Buckingham-Nicks. Michael's idea of a wild time was playing the first three Bruce Springsteen records back-to-back-to-back. He played that combo so many times, I never wanted to hear the Boss again.

Michael was dating Erika Ginn, and sometimes she would come into the store with her older brother Greg. He was this really tall, dark-haired skinny guy who was into electronics and liked to listen to the

Grateful Dead and other kinds of weird music. I recognized Erika and Greg from Mira Costa High. He was a year older than me, so we were never classmates, but he was definitely hard to miss. Erika and Greg had two other siblings, and their dad was an air force veteran and an English professor who'd met their mom in Europe at the end of World War II.

Every time Michael left with Erika to grab some lunch or hang out on the pier, he'd leave me in charge of the record store, and the first thing I'd do is take off whatever crap was on the turntable and play some music *I* wanted to hear. I was into music that was heavier, like Deep Purple, Aerosmith, Ted Nugent, Alice Cooper, and Iggy and the Stooges—anything that would make my parents cringe.

In this process of hanging out and listening to music together at Rubicon, Greg and I got to know each other a little bit. We shared an interest in music that was outside the mainstream. He subscribed to the *Village Voice*, where he learned about the burgeoning punk rock scene in New York, and I was a faithful reader of the rock zine *Back Door Man*, the South Bay music bible, but we didn't really become friends until we went with Michael to see Journey at the Santa Monica Civic.

Steve Perry, aka the Guy with No Testicles, hadn't signed on yet, so Journey was still a prog rock band, which wasn't really my thing. We were there to see Phil Lynott and Thin Lizzy jamming "The Boys Are Back in Town." I'm not going to lie: they didn't blow me away or change my life. It wasn't the best rock concert I'd ever seen—not even close. I'd seen some amazing shows, and this wouldn't even rank in the top one hundred.

But something about the Thin Lizzy show took me outside my usual headspace and got me wondering whether there was a place for me in the rock and roll universe. Greg and I didn't say anything to each other that night. There was no magical moment I can point to and say, "That was the night we knew we were going to make music history together." But on the way back to Hermosa Beach the idea started to take shape: we wanted to get in a room together and bash on some equipment.

Greg told me he had some songs. I didn't know what that meant. I've always been a pessimist—it's my nature to stay on the cynical side of the street. So when Greg told me he'd written some stuff he wanted to play for me, I hoped for the best but expected the worst. I kept reminding myself that he was a Deadhead. I don't hate the Grateful Dead, but they don't do anything for me musically. I kept telling myself to be patient and see what happens.

The first time I heard Greg play I was absolutely floored. I didn't expect what I heard blasting out of the speakers to be coming from *him*. The energy, the tempo, and, most of all, the *anger* were completely unexpected. He threw me for a loop. What Greg was doing with his guitar had this totally different kind of energy. It was exciting and aggressive. You couldn't ignore it. Here was this tall, goofy-looking guy just wailing away on his guitar in a way I'd never seen before. It was extremely physical, and the way he went after it seemed *personal.* There weren't any vocals. No bass line. No beat. Even though it was just Greg and his guitar, the songs were thrilling to listen to. It clearly meant something to him. My reaction was instantaneous: *How in the world did he come up with this stuff?*

We knew about punk rock. We knew about the Clash and the Sex Pistols, the New York Dolls and the Ramones. We'd both attended the same Ramones show at the Roxy before we got to know each other, and we'd later go see the Sex Pistols final show together in San Francisco. Punk may have already had its moment in New York and was bottoming out in London, but in Southern California it was this strange new thing that was alive with possibility.

We were an odd couple—Greg stands six-foot-two; I'm five-foot-five on a good day—but my relationship with Greg consisted of hanging out and listening to records and going to see live music. We really didn't have much else in common. Greg had a college degree from UCLA and ran his own mail-order business selling electronics equipment. I worked for my dad in his bait shop. Greg was bright, intelligent, and extremely well read, and I . . . worked for my dad in his bait shop.

Our friendship was based on our passion for music. Lots of people liked music, but we were just a bit more intense about it, and we brought that intensity to the performances and to the practice space. Later Greg would become business minded about the band in a lock-step kind of way, but in the beginning it was very organic. Nothing we did was calculated. There wasn't a map for the territory we were about to explore.

Today there's a blueprint: first you form a band, then you lay down some tracks, then you get the word out on social media. There was none of that back then. There wasn't a punk rock manual like there is today. There wasn't a reason for us to be together doing what we were doing except that we loved doing it. We didn't talk about it and we didn't overthink it, but it felt like everything was laid out for us to be in a band together, like it was the thing we were supposed to do.

It had never been like that for me before. I was always picked last in PE class. I was the guy at the party who didn't know how to mingle with the popular people. I surfed and skated because that was part of the culture I grew up in, but I no longer hung out with surfers and skaters. I was an outsider. I wasn't the kind of person you wanted to spend time with on a Friday or Saturday night.

When Greg and I took the next step in forming the band, somehow it was decided that I was going to be the drummer. Greg played guitar, and he needed someone to hold down the beat. I didn't know how to play drums, but that didn't matter—we weren't going to let our lack of experience slow us down. Just like Greg had taught himself how to play guitar, I'd teach myself how to bang on some drums. How hard could it be?

My dad was a jazz fanatic who liked to fool around on the drums. Sometimes he'd sit in with bands at the Lighthouse, a legendary jazz club right across the street from my dad's shop on Pier Avenue. He got to play with Elvin Jones, one of the top jazz drummers of all time. If you were into jazz in the fifties and sixties, the Lighthouse was the place to be with guys like Chet Baker, Miles Davis, Max Roach, and many others playing and recording there.

But this was the seventies, and what we were doing sure as hell wasn't jazz. I needed some drums. I knew a guy who had a kit he wasn't using. I called him up and told him he should sell his drums to me. He said he'd give me the drum kit for two hundred bucks, and I told him he had a deal. It turned out the kit didn't belong to him; it belonged to this other friend of ours. So I narrowly avoided getting my ass kicked from one end of Hermosa to the other for purchasing a set of hot drums.

One day I was hanging out with Greg and a few other people at the workspace for his mail-order business, which was called Solid State Transmitters. Greg modified attenuators and shipped them off to ham radio operators around the country, and he hired me to help out. We did all the soldering and distribution in a rented room inside a community art space on Manhattan Avenue that used to be a church, so that's what everyone called it: the Church.

It was a weekend afternoon, and as usual, I'd spent my morning consuming some chilled adult beverages. I was ready to go wander down to the beach and sleep it off under the pier when Iggy and the Stooges' "Search and Destroy" came blasting out of the radio. I started to pogo around, jumping up on Greg's desk and springing into the air, screaming the lyrics to the song. I totally lost it and did what felt like a triple-flip in the air and bounced onto the sofa. I wasn't done yet. I jumped off the arm of the sofa and did a swan dive across the floor, which I'd timed perfectly to the end of the song, crash-landing on my face. I didn't care what happened to me. All I cared about was the song and putting on a show for my friends.

After the music stopped and I picked myself off the floor, Greg looked at me in disbelief and said, "You're not playing drums in the band!"

"What?" I thought he was going to kick me out of the shop for being a total spaz. I thought he was booting me out of the band.

"You're the vocalist!" Greg said.

And with that, out of a friendship between a tall guitar player and a short vocalist, the seeds for Black Flag were sown.

PANIC

We called ourselves Panic.

The name fit the feeling of Greg's guitar playing, this unstoppable nervous energy he created when he attacked his guitar. We didn't know there was a French band already using the name. We just wanted to plug in and blast off.

Greg and I had no idea what we were doing. We didn't have a plan. We hardly had any equipment. For our first rehearsals I sang through the same amp and speaker cabinet that Greg played his guitar through.

I recruited our first drummer, Bryan Migdol. He had two things going for him: he was the younger brother of my best friend in high school, and he was the only guy I knew who had a drum kit. We didn't know any other drummers. He was our best option. That doesn't mean he was into what we were doing, because he wasn't—at least not musically. If you asked him who he modeled his drumming after, he would say Marc Droubay, the drummer for Survivor, and Bobby Blotzer, who would later play with Ratt. Both guys were from Redondo Beach, and that was enough for Bryan. He had a better handle on his equipment than we did on ours, so I guess you could say we lucked out.

Bryan and I had developed a friendship through his older brother Jeff, but Bryan wasn't really part of our scene. He wasn't interested in any of the bands we liked. He only wanted to play drums in a band because he thought he'd meet girls, get directions to the party, and find out who had the drugs. It was something to do and gave him something to talk about with his friends. Bryan liked to party, just like his older brother, Jeff.

One day Jeff went to a department store on Hawthorne Boulevard in Torrance with his girlfriend. They were both high on loads, aka Doors and Fours, fake opium gel caps that were filled with a sedative called Doriden and Tylenol. They walked into the store looking like a couple of freaks. He had this wild hair that was like a lion's mane and wasn't wearing any shoes. Jeff's girlfriend knew what she wanted and went straight to the cosmetics department while Jeff wandered around. I don't know if he suddenly realized he wasn't wearing any shoes or if he found a pair that he really liked, but he sat down on the floor and put on a pair of shoes and walked out the door without paying for them. He didn't even bother to rip off a pair of socks. He just laced them up and went on his merry way. Security gave chase, and he took off in the Volkswagen. The police showed up right as he was turning onto Hawthorne Boulevard, and now the chase was on. He somehow managed to make his way onto the Harbor Freeway. He tried to turn off and get onto the 405, but he hit the ramp and went up and over the guardrail. His neck snapped on impact. He was killed immediately. He probably didn't feel a thing. I wrote a song about Jeff for OFF! called "Harbor Freeway Blues."

I wasn't a teenager anymore. I'd graduated from high school and had taken a few classes at El Camino Community College, which we called Crenshaw Trade Tech as a joke. When I wasn't working at my dad's bait and tackle shop I'd hang out at the record store or head down to the beach. I was always saving up to buy tickets to this show or that show. I was getting my party going on a regular basis. I was starting to get down with a coke dealer who lived down the street.

In those days Greg wasn't really a partyer. He was more of a dabbler, so most of the time he was the designated driver when we went to shows together. He grew up in a Bohemian household. Greg's parents owned two houses. His parents lived in a place near Mira Costa High School, and Greg lived in a house at Fourteenth and Owosso, just six blocks up the hill from my dad's shop. That's where our first band rehearsals took place while we learned Greg's songs and figured out what we were going to do.

It wasn't a very big place. They'd converted their garage into a library that was filled with books. Some belonged to Greg's parents and some belonged to Greg. He had already graduated from UCLA, where I imagine he received a degree in screwing people over and becoming an all-powerful dictator. Greg rented out the library to a guy, I forget his name, but I'd drink with him every now again, surrounded by all of those books.

Greg's younger brother Raymond was a regular who would hang out with us, and he would eventually become our first bass player. Raymond had already reinvented himself as Raymond Pettibon when he started getting serious about his artwork. It was a name his father had given him, and he used it when signing his art. Or maybe he had a feeling that he would need to distance himself from Greg someday.

Raymond was a partyer too. Whenever we'd go somewhere the first thing we'd do is hit the liquor store. I would try to get as much booze as I could for as little money as possible. Raymond would always get the weirdest, most exotic thing on the shelf. Whatever it was—tequila brandy, piña colada in a can—Raymond had a knack for finding the thing that was guaranteed to give you the worst hangover possible. It was like he had a radar for bad booze.

Raymond would do strange things when he was drunk. One time at a party he smashed a bunch of beer bottles in the sink and thrust his hands into the glass like it was soapsuds. Another time we all went to the Whisky to see John Cale and the Zeros, who were nicknamed the Mexican Ramones and were one of our favorite bands. About halfway through John Cale's performance there was a disturbance on the checkerboard dance floor. I went to check out what was going on, and there was Raymond and a young woman he'd met, dry humping on the floor. We got a large charge out of that one.

Although Raymond is one of my all-time favorite visual artists, he was a terrible bass player. He learned all the songs, but it was understood that he was just filling in until we could find someone who actually knew how to play. To this day he doesn't consider himself a former member of the band, but I do. Raymond remained part of our crew and would continue to exert a huge influence on the band even though he was no longer playing with us.

Bass player number two was a tall blonde-haired guy named Kansas who was friends with Bryan Migdol. I don't remember his last name—or his first name for that matter. Everyone called him Kansas. What else are you going to call someone from Kansas? He and his older brother lived around the corner from the house on Owosso Street.

Kansas would have fit right in with Jeff Spicoli. He was your classic stoner surfer type—only he didn't possess enough brain cells. Think *Slow Times at Ridgemont High*, and you've got the right idea. He used to eat mushrooms he would find growing on people's lawns. One day Kansas took it upon himself to steal a marijuana plant growing in Greg's neighbor's yard. He and his brother hopped the fence, uprooted this huge twenty-foot-tall marijuana tree, and dragged it up Fourteenth Street to Greg's backyard. When the guy came home and discovered his marijuana was missing, all he had to do was follow the trail of dirt to Greg's house. Any four-year-old could have figured it out. He banged on Greg's door and completely wigged out. Greg caught a ration of shit for that one. Needless to say, Kansas didn't last in the band very long, and eventually that episode would lead to Bryan being told to leave the band as well.

Our third bass player was a kid named Glen Lockett, but everybody called him Spot. He was maybe sixteen or seventeen years old when he started jamming with us. He didn't last very long as a member of the band but, like Raymond, was part of our crew and had a lasting influence on both the band and the scene. Spot worked closely with Greg and became the in-house producer for the first wave of records put out by SST. He worked on all of the early Black Flag albums and EPs. He would also have a hand in producing records by the Big Boys, the Descendents, Hüsker Dü, the Meat Puppets, the Minutemen, the Misfits, and more.

Spot was—and still is—an amazing photographer who documented Hermosa Beach. From the Strand to punk shows, Spot was there with his camera. You could make the case that no one captured the sights and sounds of the South Bay like Spot.

The thing you have to understand about our scene in Hermosa Beach is that we all lived a few blocks away from each other. From my parents' house on Ninth Street and Beach Drive it was just a couple of blocks from the beach or the record store, Greg's house or my dad's shop. I didn't need a car to get around. Everything was so close, I could walk to anywhere I needed to be in a couple of minutes.

In spite of the fact that we all basically lived in the same neighborhood, it took a while for the band to get going. It didn't happen all at once. Sometimes it barely felt like it was happening at all. Panic didn't play any shows, but it's not like we were turning anybody down. It was all very low key. Greg would throw these Saturday afternoon parties, and there would be a half dozen people hanging out at his house while we practiced. Little jam sessions. Public rehearsals. People would come over, hang out, watch us play. It was very loose, very informal. We probably goofed around like that for about nine months—just enough time to give birth to this thing that would become Black Flag.

That's what I mean when I say the band evolved organically. I'd be at the beach or eating a taco burrito or walking back from somewhere and would run into one of the guys, and we'd decide to go jam for a while. It wasn't this super-disciplined military operation where everybody had to be on the same schedule. Those days were coming. In the beginning we just took things as they came.

CHUCK THE DUKE

We didn't become a real band until Gary McDaniel, aka Chuck Dukowski, became our bass player. Chuck had two things going for him: he was in a local power trio called Würm and he had a van. His condition for playing with us was that we had to start taking the band more seriously, which was exactly what we wanted to hear. For me it was a classic case of "Be careful what you wish for because you just might get it."

"We're gonna start rehearsing," Chuck announced. "A lot."

He meant it. Practice was never a priority before Chuck came along. Chuck changed that. He transformed our work ethic, our whole mentality. We started practicing five, six, seven nights a week. The other guys we'd had on bass would just kind of slip-slide around, learning to play as they went along. But Chuck was a real bass player, and he was ready to grind.

A lot of people consider Greg the mastermind of Black Flag because he wrote all of these amazing songs. People put him up on this pedestal. But a band is only as good as the people playing the songs. Having great songs is an excellent place to start, but everybody has to contribute. We never would have gotten out of the garage without Chuck. If Greg was the brains behind the band, Chuck was its heart and soul. That's what he brought to the table.

We decided we needed a real space where we could practice and rehearse. Greg's house up on Owosso wasn't cutting it anymore. If we were going to take the next step forward as a band, we needed a space to call our own. That's when we started practicing at the Würmhole.

Once upon a time Hermosa Beach was a bona fide beach resort that had its own stop on the Red Car line, the electric streetcar system that connected Los Angeles with over a thousand miles of tracks. Back in the old days, when you stepped off the Red Car in Hermosa Beach, you were a few blocks from the entranceway to the Hermosa Pier and the Biltmore Hotel.

The pier is still there, but they demolished the Biltmore. Between the pier and the vacant lot where the hotel used to be was a two-story building that had shops, rooms to rent, and a public bathhouse. This place had a lot of names: the Tropic Shop (the name of one of the local businesses owned by former NFL athlete Joe Young who played for the New York Giants), the Bath House (after the public shower and changing room on the ground floor right on the Strand), and the Würmhole (because Chuck's band rehearsed there). We moved right in.

We rented a rehearsal space inside the building, and a bunch of us even lived in the rooms upstairs for a while. The rooms weren't very big, and we didn't have any furniture. We pooled our money together and crashed out on the floor. Not bad for beachfront property!

The Würmhole was right around the corner from my dad's store, which was super convenient on those occasions when I woke up with a hangover and only had to walk about a hundred steps to go to work in the morning—I'd get a taco burrito from Taco Bill's and be good to go.

We had a lot of fun at the Würmhole. Maybe too much fun. There was a gal we knew who was in the Germs army, and sometimes she would come hang out with us at our rehearsal space. She lived in North Redondo three or four blocks past Mira Costa High. She brought Darby Crash, the Germs vocalist, to one of our parties. It was your typical beach party with lots of drinking, carrying on, and rolling around in the sand. Darby was into what we were doing but thought we needed cooler-sounding names. So we came up with some

Hollywood punk names, and I was christened Johnny Bob Goldstein. Thankfully the name didn't stick.

Chuck found a Zippo lighter in the sand that had been engraved, "The Duke," which seemed like something a guy named Chuck Du-kowski would do, and a new nickname was born. It definitely suited Gary. He had strong opinions and was open-minded about a lot of things, but he was very strict when it came to band business, which rubbed me the wrong way at times.

If Duke was a dictator, I was the joker, the jester, the party animal. I was always trying to get the guys to cut band practice short so we could go up to Hollywood, check out some bands, and have a little fun. Here was this amazing scene unfolding right in front of our eyes, and I wanted to be a part of it.

Sometimes I succeeded. At the end of the summer I was able to talk the guys into going to see AC/DC. It was their first US tour, and they were doing three nights at the Whisky. The radio was just starting to play their music. I felt that not only did *I* need to see this band; we all did. We got in Duke's van and went on a field trip. It was an amazing show. "Let there be rock!" What else needs to be said?

After the show I was so blown away I went to see what mischief I could get into and ended up hanging out in the dressing room with Bon Scott, Phil Rudd, Cliff Jones, and Malcolm and Angus Young. I must have spent an hour with them drinking beer and smoking ciga-rettes. I still have the poster from that show hanging on my bathroom wall. The funny thing is I was the only one who was able to sneak backstage, while the rest of the guys waited for me outside.

Unfortunately our time at the Würmhole was short lived. It ended abruptly when the police busted in one day and told everyone to get out. We were upstairs tossing stuff out of the second-story windows as the cops were kicking in the door. I guess the city officials thought of the space as some kind of cultural center, and we didn't fit into their program. We were on the wrong end of the cultural scale. We man-aged to get everything out, but now the band needed a new place to practice.

THE CHURCH

After the cops kicked us out of the Würmhole, we hauled our gear up to the Church. Instead of looking for another place to rehearse, we decided to rent out more space in the place where Greg had his mail-order electronics business. The first thing we did was convert one of the rooms in the back into a proper rehearsal space. We chose the janitorial supply room, not unlike the place where I used to get wasted at my old junior high.

On Saturday morning we all piled into Chuck's van and went over to Hawthorne. We ducked into an alley off of Artesia Boulevard behind Carpeteria, which was a local carpet warehouse. We needed some carpet to soundproof our new rehearsal space. We weren't going to pay full price for brand-new carpet—we didn't have that kind of money. We went dumpster diving instead.

We found all this nasty old carpet that had been ripped out of people's homes and apartments with all kinds of disgusting stains. Cat piss and dog shit. Blood, beer, and bong water. Rancid milk, kids' vomit, and stuff we didn't want to know about. We took ten large pieces of this crap, no matter how much wear and tear it had, and tossed it in the van.

We didn't sweep or vacuum the carpets like we probably should have, and we certainly didn't get in there with shampoo and stain remover—and believe me, they needed it. At that time my pants were hand-me-down Levi's from my cousins and were all too big on me.

My jeans were always falling down. I'd use belts and duct tape and bits of rope to hold them up. On this particular Saturday my pants were drooping. As we were nailing the carpet to the walls inside the Church, whatever was in the shag would shake down into my pants. I had beach sand, bits of broken glass, and who knows what kind of hair falling into my underwear. Imagine the stuff that comes flying out when you shake a rug. All that junk was going down my pants.

A couple of days later I had a serious itch down there. It was like nothing I'd ever felt before. I went to the doctor, and he told me what I already suspected: I had a brutal case of carpet crabs!

With the rehearsal space ready to go, we all started spending a lot more time at the Church. It was located up the hill from the beach on Manhattan Avenue, right down the street from the library, where I'd logged lots of hours as a kid, and the police station, where thankfully I've never been a guest. As many times as we were harassed by the folks at the Hermosa Beach Police Department, we never got thrown in jail.

The Church was a massive place with about ten rooms that took up the entire corner of the block. From the rooms on the western side you could see the ocean. We could actually check out the surf without having to leave the Church. The space that Greg rented out in the back where he ran his business was the biggest in the building. Chuck had a job working for a pool table manufacturer and was able to get a good deal on a pool table that we kept in one of the front spaces. He would sleep under the table or on top of it, depending on his mood. My room was in the northwest corner, a real skinny room that had a stairwell and a loft space that I would sometimes share if someone needed a place to crash for a little while. It sounds like an anarchic scene, but it was actually pretty well organized and everybody stayed on top of things. I've been to a lot of punk houses over the years that were much, much worse. We paid our rent and looked out for each other's stuff—with at least one notable exception.

In the beginning the Church was an arts commune run by a hippie named Red. He was this little guy who wore plaid shirts and sold LSD to bands like the Grateful Dead and Jefferson Airplane. If you were in a band that was coming to play at the Shrine in Los Angeles, Red was the guy to talk to for hallucinogens. He was in charge of the day-to-day operation of the Church, but I don't know if it was all on the up and up.

He rode this big Indian motorcycle, and one night after rehearsal we were having a couple of beers on the porch when a pick-up truck pulled up and these two massive-looking guys got out and lifted up the motorcycle and put it in the back of the truck. They didn't say anything to us, and we didn't say anything to them. What were we going to do? Run out there with baseball bats? Was there even a baseball bat to run out there with? Would baseball bats slow these dudes down?

When Red came home we told him what happened. There was nothing he could do. He couldn't call the police. The last thing he wanted was a bunch of cops over at the Church asking him questions. Red didn't stick around for too much longer after that. As more of our band members and friends came into the building, the artists started to vacate the premises, opening space for more punks until we had the Church to ourselves.

Hermosa Beach was—and still is—a pretty conservative place, but there were a few freethinkers in the neighborhood. Right down the street from the Church there was a vegetarian restaurant that didn't have any prices on the menu. You ordered your food and paid what you wanted. It was a pretty amazing concept. Greg and I would eat there all the time. Plop down five bucks and get a really great vegetarian meal. Needless to say, it didn't last very long.

There was also a drive-thru dairy that doubled as a convenience store that we were in and out of all the time, and one of the kids who worked there was Jim Lindberg, who would go on to be the lead vocalist of Pennywise. The dairy is still there, but now it's on the other side of Pier Avenue.

Down on the corner was Greeko's, a place where you'd get your rock posters and assorted paraphernalia. They always had the most beautiful hippie chicks working there. The rumor was they were running a prostitution ring out of the store.

Across the street was the Either/Or Bookstore, which was a great place to get books that were out of step with the mainstream. Sex, drugs, and political anarchy. Over the years, as it became more popular, it expanded from one space to two spaces to three, which enraged the conservative establishment, who were always trying to figure out how to get these acid-dropping, heroin-addicted, commie-preaching homosexuals out of town. I guess they eventually succeeded because, like so many other things I used to love about Hermosa Beach, it's gone now.

THEY KEPT PLAYING

We played every chance we could get. One of our early shows was at a party over on Inglewood Avenue in North Redondo. A friend of Bryan's was having a party, and Bryan talked him into letting us be the live entertainment. This guy had a detached garage in the backyard, and he had this brilliant idea to put us in there and make it our stage. When we were ready to play, he'd open the garage door like a curtain. The idea was we'd be blasting away, and the guys would be drinking and the girls would be dancing and everybody would be into it. It didn't quite work out that way. The orgy didn't unfold as planned.

The party was this weird mix of bikers and jocks and surfers and drug dealers and the misfits we'd brought with us. Everybody was on edge. It felt like a fight could break out at any second. We were worried because our set was so short. We decided that if there was an encore, we'd just play the first three or four songs over again. But we didn't get an encore that night.

When the garage door opened we started playing songs like "Revenge," "No Values," and "I Don't Care." Our set-up was pretty crude. I sang through a shitty Peavey public address system that you might find at your local square dance. (I think one of the guys in the Shrine still has it.) There wasn't a sound check. No one was on the same level. We sounded muddy and raw and not in a good way. Maybe the drums were muffled or maybe they couldn't hear my vocals, but as soon as we started playing everybody focused their negativity on us. People started throwing things at us, which seemed to be the typical response whenever we played in the community. "What is this shit? Get them out of here!"

We had a group of friends who were into what we were doing and there to check us out, but everyone else wanted to hear covers by the Eagles and Fleetwood Mac. They were not into what we were trying to put out there, and they went ape shit. The guy who was having the party actually had to close the garage door while we were still inside to prevent us from getting killed. We could hear the beer cans thunking and bottles smashing against the big wooden garage door. Somebody even threw a brick at us. It was like we were at the zoo, only the animals were on the outside.

We were too much for them. They didn't want to hear us. They didn't want to know about us. They hated us, and it was like that for a long time.

WE WOULD DO ANYTHING TO PLAY. We were so desperate, it nearly killed me.

I was at the Hermosa Pier talking to a guy whose friends were throwing a keg party in a basement over on Inglewood Avenue near LAX. "Do you want to play our party?" he asked me.

"Hell yeah, we'll play!"

That's how desperate we were. It could have been a divorce party or somebody's wife having a kid. It didn't matter. A basement keg party was the best offer we'd had in weeks.

We grabbed our gear, went to the party, and loaded in. There wasn't a stage, and it felt like 100 degrees in the basement. Whoever was throwing the party had their own PA system, and it was set up right next to the keg, which was convenient for me. I'd been drinking all day, and I helped myself to some suds. I huffed some happy powder. I was feeling really good and excited to play.

There were so many people packed in the basement, I wasn't really aware that the ice in the tub that the keg was sitting in had melted and the water had spread all over the floor. So when the show was getting ready to start, I was basically standing in a giant puddle.

When the band hit the first note I grabbed the mic, and the next thing I knew there was a big white flash of light in front of me that knocked me back into the drum kit. I didn't see God, or if I did, he wasn't a fan. I'd just been given the shock of my life, and it wasn't fun. I wasn't injured, but ever since then I've been very leery about playing around water. Puddles, pools, rain—I don't want anything to do with it. As Frank Zappa would say, I almost got myself into a burnt weenie sandwich situation, and I was paranoid about it happening again.

WE WERE STILL PLAYING UNDER the name Panic when we went into the studio, but by then it was obvious that we couldn't keep using the name. Greg wanted to rename the band Rope, which nobody was very excited about. His brother Raymond was the one who came up with the name Black Flag. As soon as he said it everybody came to attention. We didn't need to go any further.

Raymond also created the band's logo: a stylized flag represented by four black bars, which remains one of the most iconic symbols to emerge from the hardcore movement and one that punk rockers of all ages continue to tattoo onto their bodies as a symbol of their dedication to the anarchic spirit that inspired the band.

Raymond did all of the artwork for our flyers and album covers. His combination of black and white images and words was so incendiary that kids would steal the flyers as soon as we stapled them to the telephone pole, and if the kids missed them, squares tore them down in disgust. Raymond's artwork set the bar for a whole generation of rock and roll artists. If Black Flag had a mastermind, one could make a case that it was Raymond, not Greg.

When we felt like we had a pretty good vibe going, we recorded some songs. We didn't have to go far. We recorded the *Nervous Breakdown* EP at Media Art Studios right on Pier Avenue. I think our old bass player Spot turned us on to the place because he worked there as an engineer.

The studio was on the second floor. We booked a late-night session because it was cheaper that way. As we were bringing our equipment up, the Plimsouls were coming down the stairs, having just finished recording some tracks.

It was an incredible session. The guy working at the studio didn't know what to make of us. We could hear music from the bar below. Our solution was to play so loud that we just drowned them out. We absolutely killed it. Our songs were so short and so brutal and intense, I think the producer, Dave Tarling, thought we were playing the same song over and over again.

"They just kept playing and playing," he said. "They wouldn't stop!"

Actually, we were just getting started.

Nervous Breakdown is four songs, five minutes of unvarnished punk rock fury. "Nervous Breakdown" was backed with "Fix Me," "I've Had It," and "Wasted," which I cowrote. I'm not going to pretend it's some great contribution to songwriting, but no one else could have written that song. It's basically my autobiography distilled into sixty seconds of feedback and frenzy. I didn't just write the lyrics to "Wasted"—I lived it. I spent a good chunk of my life in Hermosa Beach. If I wasn't at my dad's shop at the foot of the pier, I was down on the Strand. It's pretty self-explanatory. Take a walk down the Strand in the summertime and tell me what you see.

Even though there are only four songs on the EP, we recorded a few more that night, including "Gimme, Gimme, Gimme," "I Don't Care," "No Values," and "White Minority." These would be released much later on *Everything Went Black*.

"I Don't Care" is just me spouting nonsense off the top of my head and nothing to be proud of. But because we're on the subject of those early songs, there's a rumor I need to put to rest about the song "White Minority."

"White Minority" is the reason we attracted the attention of a lot of racist knuckleheads back in the early days even though Black Flag has never been about racism. Because we played with such aggression, people sometimes missed the sarcasm and humor of the lyrics. We were never just one thing. Sometimes we tackled serious subjects, and sometimes we wrote about lighthearted situations, but it could be hard to tell when we were joking around because we were always so loud and so intense.

Greg and I were eating lunch in the neighborhood, and because it was such a beautiful summer day, we went down to the beach to do some body surfing, which is one of the greatest ways to spend the day when you live at the beach. You don't need to wax your board or bust out a wet suit; you just get in the water and go with the flow.

We went down to the south side of the pier, and the beach was completely filled with people. There were so many bodies, we couldn't even see the water. We were looking around, and there were all kinds of people at the beach: blacks, Latinos, Asians, and Caucasians. People of every color. For whatever reason, on that particular stretch of beach, the white people were in the minority. As the realization that we weren't going to be able to go body surfing slowly started to dawn on us, we saw something incredible: in the middle of this sea of humanity there was a man and a woman fucking on a blanket. Incredibly, no one seemed to be paying any attention to them. One of us said to the other, "Well, it looks like we're gonna be a white minority." It was simply a reaction to the scene we stumbled upon at the beach that day. End of story.

"White Minority" isn't on the *Nervous Breakdown* EP, but it was part of our live set. I can see how someone with a racist mindset might hear the chorus of the song and mistakenly assume we shared the same values. Here we were, these angry white guys screaming and yelling about a "White Minority." There were no racists in Black Flag. No one in the band felt that way. We identified with outsiders of every class, gender, and race. It's always a dangerous thing to take lyrics out of context and then assume they speak for the members of the band.

We were just a bunch of beach punks. There were places in Hermosa Beach where the "My beach" and "My wave" mentality prevailed. I'd experienced that, and I didn't participate in that "us versus them" kind of thinking. When the beach was crowded or the surf conditions were less than ideal, I skipped it and saved it for another day. I lived two blocks away. If I didn't like the scene at the beach, I could wait until the crowds cleared or the surf improved or whatever. I could get up early or stay out late and have the whole fucking beach to myself. It wasn't that big of a deal. But people fucking on the beach? That's not something you see every day.

GREG AND I DIDN'T ALWAYS see eye-to-eye when it came to music. I didn't have a whole lot of input over our set because Greg wrote the music and the majority of the songs, but that changed when we decided to do a cover song.

Greg had it in his head that he wanted to play "Femme Fatale" by the Velvet Underground. That was kind of ironic to me because I wasn't that familiar with their music and the songs I did know were from other bands covering their songs. For instance, my introduction to the Velvet Underground was through Mott the Hoople playing "Sweet Jane," and of course I'd heard David Bowie's version of "Waiting for the Man." I finally listened to Lou Reed after he left the Velvet Underground doing "White Light, White Heat" and so on. When I finally got around to listening to "Femme Fatale" I was like, "No fucking way am I singing *that!*"

As far as I was concerned, there were plenty of Velvet Underground songs that were a better fit for us. But for Greg it wasn't about the music so much as the lyrics. "Femme Fatale" hit the nail on the head with regards to the way he felt about the women in the Hollywood scene that wanted nothing to do with him. His answer was to attack his feelings with his guitar playing, which was fine, but I wasn't in Black Flag to be his mouthpiece.

At the time I was completely enamored with the Stooges. My suggestion was to do "Louie Louie" because I had a copy of *Metallic K.O.*, which includes an amazing live version of the song. The best thing about "Louie Louie" is that, like so many other vocalists before me, I took some liberties with the lyrics and the song took on a life of its own. It's a fun song that was a popular part of our set that showed we weren't super serious all of the time.

MOOSE LODGE

We started 1979 with our first proper Black Flag show at an actual venue.

The Moose Lodge in Redondo Beach wasn't a place where we'd go to hang out. It was a place for veterans who'd fought in Vietnam, Korea, and World War II. There might have been some guys left over from the First World War. This was their clubhouse where they'd gather to drink and tell stories and watch TV.

The Moose Lodge had a decent-sized hall that they rented out for cheap. So Black Flag booked the venue for a Saturday night gig and tapped a couple of local bands to play with us—the Alley Cats from Lomita and Rhino 39 from Long Beach. Both of those bands had released seven-inch singles on Dangerhouse, which at the time was *the* punk rock label in Southern California.

Because our set was so short, we decided to play twice. We were the opening act and the closing band. That way if you went outside for a smoke or had to use the bathroom and missed half our set, you could stick around for the second one.

We were super excited to be playing our first real gig. It was an evening show, and we arrived early to load in all of our equipment and make sure everything was kosher with the venue. As part of my Saturday routine I'd started drinking immediately after breakfast. I was a couple of six-packs in, and when I showed up I was already in party mode and raring to go.

The Moose Lodge had a giant American flag, one of the biggest flags I'd ever seen. In between sets I took it upon myself to grab hold of this flag and swing from it like I was punk rock Tarzan. The members of the mighty Moose Lodge weren't down with that. That's not how you're supposed to act when you're a guest in someone else's establishment, and these guys were seriously pissed. They weren't interested in my explanation or an apology—they wanted my unpatriotic, un-American ass out of there, and they didn't care if it was in one piece. I didn't stick around to see what would happen, and the senior citizens brigade ran me out the back door and into the parking lot. They didn't take it any farther than that and went back inside to their drinks.

I started to freak out. We'd finally gotten a gig, and I'd been kicked out. How would I play our second set? What was I going to do?

Chuck came out to the parking lot, and I explained the situation to him. "They kicked me out. I can't go back in there!"

Chuck thought it was hilarious, but he had an idea. He gave me one of his T-shirts to wear and rummaged around in his trunk for something to complete the disguise.

"Here, put this on."

He tossed me a black wig that belonged to his girlfriend. She had short blonde hair and every once in a while would wear a wig when she went out. I hoped it looked better on her than it did on me. With long black hair I looked like I could have played guitar in Jefferson Airplane at Woodstock. After being accused of being a hippie by Hollywood scenesters, I was going to play a Black Flag gig looking like one.

Some people thought it was funny, while others bitched and moaned.

"That's not punk rock."

"What's that knucklehead up to?"

"Fuck these guys!"

It didn't matter what people thought because it fooled the veterans. I walked right in, and nobody batted an eye.

The show was pretty well attended, with a couple of hundred people in the audience, including Rodney Bingenheimer, an influential disc jockey and tastemaker at KROQ, one of LA's most popular radio stations. Rodney brought Stiv Bators along with him, the lead vocalist from the Dead Boys. They were both completely blown away by our performance. Rodney had heard about us but didn't know who we were or what we were about. Now he knew. That proved to be a big turning point for us.

For whatever reason I happened to have the first Dead Boys record in my car, and I ran out to get it so Stiv could sign it. I still have it somewhere.

Another souvenir from the show: a photo of Ron Reyes and Dez Cadena sitting next to each other on the side of the stage and watching us play like the ghosts of Black Flag's future.

AFTER THE SUCCESS OF THE SHOW at the Moose Lodge, we were hungry for more, but no one was asking us to play. The only way we could get a gig was by making it happen ourselves. We set up another show a few weeks later down in San Pedro.

Someone tipped us off about a vacant theater in San Pedro that the owners occasionally rented out for special functions. Our plan was to rent out the theater, invite some bands to play, charge a couple of bucks, and hope for the best. We knew the owner of the theater would never agree to it if he knew we were a punk band, so when Greg called him up, he told him we were having a teen dance. The owner agreed.

We went to San Pedro to check it out. The theater was perfect, and the owner was totally into it. While Greg was talking to him we took it upon ourselves to start moving the rows of seats in front of the stage.

The owner didn't like that. "What are you doing?" he demanded.

Greg explained that we needed space in front of the stage so teens would be able to dance. What was the point having a teen dance if the teens couldn't dance?

"Oh, no. That's not going to work. I can't have that in here." The owner asked us to leave.

We were dumbfounded and didn't know what to do. We were standing out on the sidewalk in front of the theater in a seriously negative mind space. One of the guys pointed to a sign at the end of the block for a teen center. We decided to investigate. What better place to throw a teen dance than a teen center?

The show ended up being pretty successful and was a lot of fun. The Alley Cats, the Descendents, the Last, and the Plugz all played. I don't think the Last were officially on the bill, but that never stopped the Nolte brothers from making an appearance. The opening band was the Reactionaries, and it was their first show. The lead vocalist was studying to be a pharmacologist and was getting ready to leave. That ended up being a good thing, as the remaining members went on to become the Minutemen. So that was our first run in with D. Boon, George Hurley, and Mike Watt.

It was a great mix of bands from one end of the Harbor Freeway to another. It was the kind of night that made all the rehearsals worth it. Why couldn't we do this every weekend?

A LOT OF BANDS WILL TELL YOU, "We'll play anywhere!" But not a lot of bands would play some of the gigs we played.

A friend of a friend hooked us up with a show at a tiny little bar on the grounds of the Standard Oil refinery in El Segundo. It was a place where the oil workers would hang out after their shift. It had a pool table, a kitchen area, and a corner with just enough room for Black Flag to set up. I don't think there were any opening bands. It was just us that night, playing for our friends and a bunch of oil workers. What could go wrong?

To say that the oil workers were a less-than-friendly crowd would be an understatement. They didn't know us, and we didn't know them.

"Who the fuck are these guys?"

"They have no business being here!"

"Go back to Hermosa Beach!"

It was that kind of jerk-ass mentality. None of us could remember why we thought this was a good idea. We played the show and managed to piss everybody off before we were halfway through the first song. These people didn't understand what we were doing and didn't want to have anything to do with us, which would have been fine except they wanted to smash our guitars and bash our drums. They wanted to punch holes in our faces and set our speaker cabinets on fire. They threatened to kill us, and I, for one, believed them.

When we were finished playing, there was no reason for us to stick around. We packed up our gear as quickly as possible so we could get out of there. Everyone was hustling when I stupidly struck up a conversation with the most beautiful woman in the bar, maybe in all of El Segundo. She wanted to know more about what we were about, and I was happy to tell her when all of the sudden this gnarly-looking gorilla lifted me off the ground and slammed me against the wall. He cocked his arm back so he could rearrange my face. He was grinning from ear to ear like he knew he was about to destroy me. The guy easily outweighed me by a hundred pounds. It wasn't even close to being a competition.

The woman I was speaking with started yelling at the gorilla. "You can't hit him! We were just having a friendly conversation! He wasn't making any moves on me!"

That wasn't exactly true, but it was my window of opportunity to get the fuck out of there. She tugged at his arm and urged him to calm down and be nice. He loosened his grip just enough for me to wriggle away and haul ass down the hallway. I got about halfway down the hall when he decided he wasn't going to listen to his girlfriend anymore. He started chasing after me, and a bunch of his buddies came along with him.

I hit the door and saw that the guys were already driving away. Maybe they figured they'd let me fend for myself and pick me up at the hospital later. I wasn't having any of that. I started running after the van. It was like a chase scene out of a movie—these oil workers wanted to tar and feather me.

One of the guys had the wherewithal to flip open the back doors and reach out a hand. I don't remember who it was, but I grabbed on, and he pulled me into the van and away we went. These guys who were chasing us started throwing rocks and bottles as we peeled out of the parking lot and pulled away from the refinery. As my grandfather Bob would say, "They didn't need to burn that place down to get us out of there."

You'd think that we would be like, "Fuck that! We're never doing that again!" But that was never our outlook. Honestly, it was pretty exciting. Playing in front of a hostile crowd brought a different kind of intensity to the show.

There was rarely a stage. There were no bouncers. No security. No separation between us and the crowd. It was part of breaking down the barriers between the people and the music. I didn't have a mic stand or anything like that. If someone didn't like what we were doing, there was nothing to stop him from coming after us. We were lucky we didn't get our heads torn off. But if a kid hearing "Depression" or "Nervous Breakdown" for the first time thought the song matched the feeling in his head, he could move to the front, sing along with us, and become a part of the experience.

We would change our songs around, but we didn't tailor our sets to the crowd. It wasn't rocket science. We weren't there to discuss the beginning of mankind or split atoms—these were parties. We'd be playing to South Bay surfers, California beach bunnies, grungy drug dealers, rock and roll burnouts, art crowd weirdoes, bikers crazy enough to mix it up with the Hell's Angels, and the kids on the Strand who were looking for something to do on Friday and Saturday night, a little bit of fun, the right kind of trouble.

Typically the highlight of a big rock and roll concert might be watching someone get into it with a bouncer. During a Black Oak Arkansas concert I attended at the Long Beach Arena on New Year's Eve the bouncers kicked someone out, and the guy climbed up in a tree and waited for the show to end. When the bouncer came out, the guy jumped out of the tree and stabbed the bouncer in the heart, which was terrible but pretty exciting.

To experience that kind of vibe firsthand because you're up on stage—even if there wasn't a stage—took the energy and excitement to a whole other level. I used to feed on it. Plus, I was drinking and taking pills and snorting coke, which just added to the fun. Even after a bad show, we just wanted to go out and do it again. Being the kind of guys we were, we didn't reach out to bookers and promoters—you know, the people who actually book the shows—and say, "This is who we are. This what we do—let us play!" We did things the hard way, the only way we knew how. Sometimes it felt like we were our own worst enemies.

NERVOUS BREAKTHROUGH

Even though there were plenty of punk rock bands in Hollywood who were doing amazing things and playing gigs all over the city, being from the South Bay was a big disadvantage.

If you were into music like we were, there wasn't a whole lot going on in the South Bay, so whenever someone started doing something interesting, you paid attention. One of the bands that had the biggest influence on us was the Last. If you put the Last on your turntable and listened to what they were about, you'd probably be scratching your head, thinking, *No way these guys influenced Black Flag!*

The Last was a pop band, plain and simple, with hooks and melodies that were slightly out of step with the times. The Last consisted of the Nolte brothers—Joe, Mike, and Dave Nolte—who all lived in Hermosa Beach. I'd put them in the same category as the Plimsouls, the Bangles, and the Knack. They played with aggression, and when they took the stage they had an attitude I really connected with. Even today it's hard to define. They stood out. They had a spark. They were one of a handful of bands in the South Bay that were truly doing something original. In a sea of bar bands, they were a breath of fresh air, so it was natural for us to gravitate toward them.

Arena rock had a stranglehold on the music industry to such a degree that it limited opportunities for musicians to perform and affected the way bands thought about themselves. In the seventies there were two ways to play music in front of a live audience: either you had a major label record deal or you were a cover band. Bars and clubs wouldn't book acts that played their own music unless they had a label behind them. This practice was entrenched for nearly a decade, undoing the creativity of the fifties folk acts and sixties garage bands. So just the idea of writing your own songs and having the audacity to want to play them in front of people was rebellious because nine times out of ten, people weren't interested. You really had to want to do it.

If we went into a bar or club on a Friday night, we were going to hear some band playing the Doobie Brothers or whatever was on the Top Forty that week. We might see someone massacring "Hotel California" by the Eagles. We didn't want anything to do with that scene. Some of these guys were probably really good musicians who couldn't write their own music. Maybe they didn't have their shit together. Maybe they felt inferior to the bands who played in the clubs on the Sunset Strip. I don't know why the South Bay was such a dead zone when there was so much going on in Hollywood. When I met someone in the South Bay who was doing something interesting, doing something different, I took notice. The Last's attitude played a big role in influencing Black Flag and, later on, the Circle Jerks—even though we sounded nothing like them.

Another South Bay musician who was a big influence on me that might surprise a few readers was rockin' Don Dokken. I wasn't the biggest fan of his music, but we shared similar interests. I used to hang out with him and Bobby Blotzer and Juan Croucier. They were all South Bay guys who played together in various bands as they came up and honed their skills. In 1978 Bobby and Juan left Dokken and eventually went on to join Ratt. The one and only time I saw Metallica was when they opened for Ratt at Doug Weston's Troubadour in West Hollywood.

Juan was a classically trained violinist and very down to earth. I played some music for him while we were partying a little bit. I put on the Ramones' first album, and he was taken aback by their brutal simplicity. He was like, "Anyone can do this!" which was kind of the point. I also played some Motörhead for him. That he understood because they were so heavy. On another occasion I was driving over to Don's to pick up some blow and was drinking out of a bottle that I'd swiped from my father's stash. I was so drunk that by the time I got to Don's place, I'd pissed my pants. Not one of my finer moments, but I didn't let it put a damper on the evening. I got what I came for and went on my merry way.

I LEARNED EARLY ON THAT THE PEOPLE in the Hollywood scene adhered to a pretty strict interpretation of the punk fashion that was coming out of the United Kingdom. There was a freedom to look and dress however you wanted—as long as you stuck to that paradigm. I didn't buy into that. I didn't change the way I looked or dressed just because I was in a band. So when I showed up at the Masque or the Starwood or the Whisky looking like I'd just fallen out of a van at a Grateful Dead concert, people scoffed at me. I had long hair and wore hand-me-down Levi's and flannel shirts and ripped up Vans tennis shoes, and people didn't like that. It's not that I didn't care how I looked; I didn't see the need to spend money on clothes when my cousins were kicking down shirts and pants I could wear. Why blow money on clothes that could be used for booze and drugs?

If I had to describe my look, I'd say I looked like someone you'd find in the front row of a Peter Frampton concert, and that didn't sit well with the scenesters competing in the Sid Vicious look-alike contest. Dutch, who worked the door at the Masque, would always give me shit.

"Why are you here? You're not part of this scene." Dutch looked like he was the fifth member of the Ramones with his leather jacket and bleach-blonde Prince Valiant hairstyle. He looked ridiculous, and yet *I* was the one with the image problem.

"I'm in a band," I'd say, and he'd laugh in my face.

One of the things that always bothered me about the scene was that once you got into punk rock music, all of the stuff you listened to before wasn't cool anymore and had to go. That was the attitude, but I didn't buy into it, just like I didn't buy into the idea that I needed to look a certain way to be a part of the punk music scene. Good music is good music. It doesn't matter where it comes from or what pedigree it has or doesn't have. I didn't throw away all of my Fleetwood Mac records just because they got seriously cheesy after Stevie Nicks joined the band; Peter Green, Danny Kirwan, and Jeremy Spencer made some brilliant music together. So what if I held on to those records? What we were doing had nothing to do with them.

People will tell you that the early days of punk rock in LA were open and free. It wasn't like that for me or for a lot of other people. If the musicians in the bands or the scenesters who worked for *Slash* or the kids who lived in the Canterbury Apartments didn't like the way you looked, the way you sounded, or the way you acted, they wouldn't let you into their little circles. No matter how many friends I made in Hollywood, I always felt like an outsider.

LIKE SO MANY OTHER THINGS ABOUT US, *Nervous Breakdown* was born out of frustration. We had a deal with Bomp!, a label that put out some amazing records. We dropped the recording off and waited to see what would happen. We were eager to get our songs out into the world. Black Flag was finally making some noise, but without a record, people weren't taking us seriously.

We were also going through some changes. Greg kicked Bryan out of the band, and he was replaced by Julio Roberto Valverde Valencia, aka Robo, a drummer who lived in El Segundo. He hadn't been playing drums for very long; in fact, Black Flag was his first band. We'd put "drummer wanted" ads in the *PennySaver*, *Easy Reader*, and on a couple of record-store bulletin boards, and he answered the call. Robo got his nickname due to his stiff, mechanical drumming style. He did have a secret weapon, though: being from Colombia, he brought Cumbia-influenced rhythms to his playing. He was very serious about the band, which was what we were looking for.

When we finally got tired of waiting for Bomp! Greg decided to release the record himself. That's when Greg's electronics company went from Solid State Transmitters to SST Records. Because of his experience running a mail-order business, Greg figured he could put the record out without too much difficulty. He simply looked up the number for a record-pressing plant in the phone book, and we were on our way.

Looking back, I probably could have been more involved in the process. Like Greg, I knew something about running a business. I could have gotten a loan from my dad and started a label out of the back room of the bait shop. I didn't have a degree from UCLA, but I had as much experience in the day-to-day operation of a business as Greg did.

But I didn't want to do any of those things. That was way too much responsibility for me. *Responsibility* and *Keith* were two words that didn't go together. I was having a great time being the front man of Black Flag. I wanted to go out and play. I didn't want to deal with the business end of being in a band. Sure, I wanted to do some adult things, but that didn't mean I was ready to *be* one.

One of things I didn't like about the EP was that Greg had put Robo down as the drummer. Although it was true Robo was our drummer and we loved playing with him, he didn't play drums on the *Nervous Breakdown* EP; Bryan Migdol did. I don't have any beef with Bryan. He was never that excited about being in Black Flag. He didn't think what we were doing was anything special. Black Flag was a way for Bryan to elevate himself from being a surf rat hanging out under the Hermosa Pier to a Friday night hero. Even though he wasn't into what we were doing, he stepped up and held it down on the *Nervous Breakdown* EP, and I will always give him respect for that.

Raymond did the artwork for the cover, the now iconic image of a male teacher backing a frustrated student into the corner with a chair, an early version of which appeared in his first zine, *Captive Chains*, sixty-four pages of pure Raymond Pettibon weirdness. The teacher resembles a lion tamer, and the kid in the corner looks like he's ready to tear the teacher's head off. That image is the perfect representation of what Black Flag was all about.

Once the record came out, Black Flag opened some ears. In fact, I can pinpoint the exact moment when people started to take us seriously.

We were at a party on Fountain Avenue in Hollywood. We'd all gone to see a band at the Whisky, and it was your typical after-concert vibe—people drinking and smoking and having fun. A lot of people from *Slash* magazine were there. You had the infamous Claude Bessy, aka Kickboy Face, a French transplant and writer who wrote searing reviews of everything he hated, which was almost everything. Jeffrey Lee Pierce was also there. He wrote about reggae and soul music for *Slash*. He was a big supporter of bands from the South Bay like the Alley Cats and the Last and would go on to found the Gun Club.

Also attending the party was Phast Phreddie Patterson, who, along with Don Waller, launched the influential music zine *Back Door Man*. He was from the South Bay too. My favorite story involving Phast Phreddie was the time he was playing DJ at a party in Hollywood. He was flipping through the records, and every time he found one he didn't like, he chucked it out the second-story window, jacket and all, into the swimming pool below. Naturally, this didn't sit well with the people who were throwing the party, but Phast Phreddie was unrepentant. "You can't have this in your collection!"

Of all the people in the Hollywood scene who were there that night, none was more influential than Brendan Mullen. Brendan was a Scotsman who'd immigrated to LA and immediately made a name for himself by opening the Masque, the most happening underground punk club in LA.

Someone was spinning records, and we had a copy of the *Nervous Breakdown* EP with us, so we busted it out. As soon as the music started to play all conversation in the room stopped. Jaws hit the floor. People were taken aback. They couldn't believe what they were hearing. Kickboy was incredulous: "You guys didn't record that!"

People were in shock because they'd written us off as stoners and beach hippies. They refused to accept that we could make something so ferocious. It messed with their perceptions of us. Brendan and Kickboy wanted to know more about us. For months Greg and I had been pestering Brendan about booking Black Flag to play at the Masque. We'd badgered him to the point that when he heard *Nervous Breakdown* at that party on Fountain, he already knew who we were. That night they realized we weren't just wannabes, that we had something to contribute. It was an ear-opening experience for a lot of people. That was the night people finally looked past where we came from and what we looked like and realized Black Flag was a force to be reckoned with.

GROUND ZERO

It's impossible to overstate the influence of the Masque on LA's punk rock scene. It was *the* place to go see punk rock music in LA. In many ways it was LA's version of CBGB, only it was way more under the radar—it was literally underground—and it lasted only for a short time. You can't tell the story of LA punk rock without the Masque.

It wasn't easy to find. The entrance was in an alley off of North Cherokee Avenue. I used to tell people to head down Hollywood Boulevard and turn at the Pussycat Theater. That was the landmark. Then you'd head south about half a block and turn right. You'd know you were in the right place by all the punks hanging out in the alley.

You'd go down a small set of cement steps and find yourself in a dingy network of rooms underneath the Pussycat Theater. It was a cross between a warehouse and a cinderblock bunker, like an underground garage with a really low ceiling and graffiti everywhere. It was a punk rock rite of passage to spray paint your band's name on the wall after you'd played a gig there.

The Masque wasn't really a club; it was a rehearsal space for bands during the day and a clubhouse at night. Sometimes people would meet up in the alley outside the Masque even when there wasn't a show. Make no mistake: the shows were amazing. I saw the Bags, the Controllers, the Dickies, the Eyes, Fear, the Germs, and the Weirdos at the Masque—the whole front line of the second wave of LA punk rock.

What I consider the first wave of LA punk rock includes bands like the Doors' "Break on Through to the Other Side," Love's "My Little Red Book," the Seeds' "Pushing Too Hard," and the Standells' "Good Guys Don't Wear White" and "Riot on Sunset Strip." That's *my* definition, but it probably isn't yours.

The great thing about seeing a band at the Masque was that there was no barrier between the performers and the audience. There was no stage. No backstage. No rock and roll bullshit. If you wanted to talk to Alice Bag, Darby Crash, or Dix Denney after they got through with their sets, there was nothing stopping you because everyone was on the same level.

I met so many people in the punk rock community at the Masque, from musicians to fans to thrill seekers who came to check out what was going on. I used to run into *Slash*'s Kickboy Face there, but he was everywhere. He shared my interest in livening up the evening's entertainment with a few bumps of blow.

"Hey, Keith, what's going on with you?" he'd ask me in his heavy French accent. "I've never been to Hermosa Beach. Tell me what it's like!"

I think he had this idea from listening to Black Flag that it was this dark, horrible place. It definitely wasn't a side of LA he saw very often.

The first time I met the guys from Fear was in the alley outside the Masque. I had this trick where I was able to stash a pack of tallboys under my shirt and down my pants. That's how I would sneak beer into the venues. So I offered Derf Scratch, the bass player, a beer. He opened it and, rather than drink it, emptied the can on my head.

This kind of thing would happen from time to time. One of the things about Black Flag is we had this reputation for being a bunch of thugs, like we were beach brawlers or something, which couldn't be further from the truth. Our music was loud, aggressive, and in your face, so they assumed the members of Black Flag would be that way too. When people would meet me for the first time and see this little guy with shaggy hair buzzing around, it didn't match up with their perception of Black Flag. It wasn't unusual for people to test me, just to see what I would do.

I never responded physically because that would have been suicidal. I weighed 115 pounds—I wasn't going to win any fights. I wanted to get to know these people, not get confrontational with anybody. After Derf got done pouring beer on my head, I pulled out my bindle and did a couple of bumps of blow. When I was done I offered some to Derf, and we became really good friends.

Having a club in such a strange and occasionally dangerous place attracted the attention of the authorities, and as a result, the Masque was always being shut down, sometimes temporarily and then permanently. Brendan had fundraisers for the Masque all over town and eventually opened up what was known as the Other Masque or the New Masque at Santa Monica and Vine in a place that's now occupied by a drive-through Japanese fast food joint.

There were plenty of great shows there too. I saw the Cramps play to a crowd of about three dozen people, and I saw a band from Philadelphia called Pure Hell that many consider to be the first all-black punk rock band. I also remember the Kinman brothers, more commonly known as the Dils, arguing with Brendan Mullen because he was charging an admission price that was a dollar more than what they'd agreed on. The whole thing struck me as funny because the cover charge was only three or four bucks, but I guess this went against their agenda. No one got rich at the Masque.

On the night of the Fear show one of their fans, a guy named Joe Blow (that was his punk rock name) got so excited that he did donuts in the dirt lot where everyone parked. It had been raining, and when he started ripping around he threw mud all over the cars. It was just a big fuck you with mud being the exclamation mark.

When Black Flag finally got an opportunity to play at the original Masque on Cherokee it was a bittersweet moment: our first show at the Masque was the last one they held there before they closed their doors for good. Even though the original Masque had been closed for some time, they reopened it for the final show. The Mau Maus were the headliners, and we were the opening act. Because it was the Masque's closing night, the place was packed. I don't know what the legal capacity of the place was—I don't know if it *had* a legal capacity because Brendan was constantly fending off the Los Angeles Fire Department. I think there were about four hundred people there, and because it was such a big event, everyone wanted to go.

After us it was the Black Hearts, the Smart Pills from Salt Lake City, and then UXA from San Francisco. The Mau Maus never got to play because the fire marshal broke up the party with LAPD as backup and shut down the show. It was a really big night for us as a band, but the show itself was kind of a bummer.

BRAIN FRY

Even after we started to get gigs in Hollywood, something always seemed to go wrong. Sometimes it was on us: I'd get hammered, someone wouldn't show up—the usual band fuck-ups. But sometimes it was totally out of our control.

One night we played a warehouse show on Melrose with X. I think UXA was on the bill too, and the Gears were supposed to play right after us. I say "supposed to" because some shit went down that night.

We were the opening band. The place held about five hundred people, and there were about three hundred people in attendance when we were getting ready to start the show, which was a great crowd for us. Everybody was in tune and plugged in. We were ready to do our thing, show these Hollywood weirdoes what we were all about. Greg started the song with a downstroke, hitting the strings as ferociously as possible, and suddenly everything went black. We'd knocked the power out! Not only in the warehouse, but the entire block went dark. Black Flag had shut down the whole grid. That note was so strong and powerful, it just said, "Fuck you, Hollywood!" and that was the end of the night.

A couple of the members of the Gears weren't happy about the situation. They acted like we'd done it on purpose to sabotage their show or that the blackout was a direct result of our negligence. I found the whole situation amusing. The thing I loved about punk rock in LA was how friendly and festive it was. And I didn't take that for granted. I can't speak for the other guys, but before joining the band, I'd never been a part of group of people who valued who I was or what I could do. I was always dreaming of a time when I got to be the hero. I finally got that chance with Black Flag. When I was onstage with the mic in my hand, it was *my* turn. As the vocalist for Black Flag, I was able to create a different reality—my reality—but it was also a big fuck you to all the people who'd picked on me and pushed me around and told me I wasn't good enough. I was finally able to do some damage.

When we were creating the stew that would become Black Flag, when we were stirring the pot and adding all of the ingredients to this thing we were making, there was a lot frustration. We were the guys who were laughed at and ignored. Frustration was part of the band's DNA. If we had other outlets like sports or had been popular kids with beautiful girlfriends, we wouldn't have brought so much aggression to what we were doing. Anger wasn't just a part of the mix; it was the main ingredient. But that didn't mean I went around with a chip on my shoulder, pissed off at the world—far from it. When the power went out that night in Hollywood my attitude was, *Who cares? We're all here. Let's have a good time and hope that the owner doesn't show up or the police don't come.*

I liked to have a good time as much as the next guy or, in some cases, more than the next guy, but I didn't take my friends for granted. You can say, "Oh, that's Keith. He's just happy to be here." Well, that's because I was. I was very happy to be a part of something so creative and cool. To me, it wasn't something that was worth getting upset about. Just because the building blew a fuse didn't mean we had to.

SOMETIMES WE AGREED TO SHOWS even though we knew the venue was totally wrong for us.

We had friends who lived in the Hollywest Building, which was on the corner of Hollywood Boulevard and Western. It was a big thick brick building that harkened back to Old Hollywood, but in the late seventies it was kind of a flophouse. A place to crash. A place to party. There were two or three spaces where people were living. The guys from the Cheifs, who had a self-titled seven-inch on Playgems Rec–ords, lived there. We'd grab a case of cheap beer and hang out with them from time to time. We'd run into guys from the Simpletones, guys from the Gears.

Down on Hollywood Boulevard, about four or five spots from the Hollywest Building, was a place the Cheifs rented out for rehearsals. We were having a hard time getting gigs, so we figured, "Why not have a show here?"

We rented one of the spaces and invited a bunch of people. The space wasn't very big. It was a sardine-can type of situation. You could maybe pack fifty people in the room. Two hundred showed up.

The guys who ran the building were a couple of hippies. They were standing around behind the front desk, and some of us were keeping an eye on them and listening to what they were saying to see if they were going to call the police, which was something that would nor-mally happen in scenarios like this. They looked like they were on the verge of freaking out. One of them turned to the other and said, "This is a total brain fry!"

Another memorable gig that seemed like a good idea at the time but was very nearly a disaster was a show we played at the Bla-Bla Café on Ventura Boulevard in Studio City.

We were supposed to play two Mondays in a row, like a mini resi-dency. We were very proud of this gig, as it was one of our first shows at an actual venue and not some theater or hall we'd booked on our own. We were stoked not to be playing in someone's basement or backyard, but we should have checked the place out first.

The Bla-Bla Café was a place for singer-songwriters and stand-up comedians in the Valley to try out new material in front of thirty or forty people, but it was clear right away that it was the wrong place for us. Somehow Chuck or Greg had convinced someone we were some-thing we were not, because anyone could see that we didn't belong there. Cozy is the word I would use to describe it. A nice place to go with some friends and nibble on some crackers while you sip your tea or your wine.

We arrived at the venue and started setting up. All the punk kids who'd been waiting for us came in. After a few minutes the place was packed from wall to wall, which the staff wasn't prepared to deal with. We started playing, and suddenly bodies were flying through the air. Wine glasses and wine bottles were being tossed around. Salt and pepper shakers went airborne. Punks were beating each other over the head with baguettes. I'm amazed no one threw a bottle through the plate-glass window that faced Ventura Boulevard. It was very chaotic and wildly exciting, but it was also pretty comical.

After the show the woman who owned the place was shaken up. "You can't come back next Monday night. . . . This isn't right. . . . This isn't supposed to happen here!"

We were a little bummed, but it ended up being a good thing because Black Flag got its first gig at the Hong Kong Café in Chinatown the following week thanks to our friend Joe Nolte of the Last. There were two places to play in Chinatown: Hong Kong Café, which was the punk club, or Madame Wong's, which was more pop and new wave. You didn't play both—it was either one or the other. Madame Wong didn't like punk, so if she heard you'd played at the Hong Kong Café, you were automatically banned from playing at Madame Wong's. That rigid mindset trickled down to the fans, and the general perception was that only poseurs played at Madame Wong's. If you wanted to see the Knack or the Naughty Sweeties, you'd find them at Madame Wong's.

Once we started getting gigs, we had a hard time turning them down, and that led to some bad situations. Because our set was only fifteen minutes long, we figured why not book more than one show a night? Why not book shows at all of the clubs?

We said yes to every gig or party we got invited to play and, at one point, ended up with a bunch of shows in one night. Like five or six. I don't remember how many were actually booked, but it was a marathon. We were the opening act at the first venue, the second act at the second venue, and so on. We were going to be playing with all of these different bands all over town, and it was going to be amazing. Well, it looked great on paper.

For the first show we were the opening band at the Hong Kong Café with Fear and the Germs. We showed up and played the gig. Immediately afterward we had to grab our gear, go down the stairs, and get it in the van because we had to get along to the next gig. We didn't get to hang out with all of our friends or talk to the people who wanted to talk to us. It was kind of a drag.

We went from Chinatown to the Roosevelt Hotel. The Mau Maus were the headlining band. We got there, and there were maybe forty people there, the show hadn't started, and the Mau Maus were nowhere to be found, none of which was very encouraging.

In all of my experiences with the Mau Maus there was always some kind of funky vibe. It didn't matter when they were scheduled to play, they would find a way to headline. Not because of some weird ego trip but because they were always late, and that ended up derailing the party train. Heroin will do that.

We never got out of the Hotel Roosevelt and missed all of the other gigs we had scheduled that night. Like a lot of things, we were gung ho to play, but it wasn't meant to be.

We played a show at the Hong Kong Café and only a handful of people showed up, and by handful, I mean a half dozen people, but three of those people were very interesting. Two were extremely large black dudes who looked like offensive linemen for the LA Rams, and sandwiched in between them was none other than the Thin White Duke, Ziggy Stardust himself.

David Bowie must have had a night off and decided to come see what all the fuss was about in Chinatown and check out some local music. It wasn't a particularly memorable show, and by the time we got our gear off the stage and loaded it in the van, Bowie was gone. It was one of those deals where once word got out that Bowie had been in Chinatown, everyone claimed to have been there.

FOR WHATEVER REASON, a band called Parsec, a Rush-wannabe prog metal band, asked us to play a show at Gazarri's. They knew who we were and asked if we wanted to play. We didn't sit around to discuss it—"Well, they're this kind of band, the crowd isn't going to like us, blah blah blah"—we never took any of that into consideration. We just went out and played.

Our options for promoting our shows were just as limited as our opportunities to play. We had the telephone and we had our flyers, and that was pretty much it. We'd stick some in the record stores and some in the head shops. If we were going to a party or an event, we'd bring flyers with us, but after that we had to get creative or else we'd end up with gigs like the one David Bowie attended.

The Buzzcocks were playing the Santa Monica Civic, so we flyered the hell out of the parking lot. When we'd passed out all of our flyers we went in to see the show, and as soon as the Buzzcocks stopped playing, we rushed over to Gazzarri's to play our show. We brought the same kind of intensity level of our performances as we did to the flyering: "Let's go out and do some damage!" It's all we ever wanted to do.

POLLIWOG PARK

Of all the shows I played with Black Flag, the most infamous was the free show at Polliwog Park in Manhattan Beach. There are a lot of rumors about this show, so let's get a few facts straight.

Polliwog Park is dominated by a manmade lake that has all of the charm of a drainage ditch. You can't fish in it, and you wouldn't want to. No swimming or boating either. Welcome to America: land of a million rules. One thing Polliwog Park has that was appealing to us was an amphitheater with a band shell that gave the concrete slab the appearance of a stage. There are picnic tables and trees. It's a nice place to take your family on a sunny summer afternoon.

Polliwog Park sponsored a series of Sunday shows that drew pretty decent-sized crowds. The article they wrote about us in the local paper after the show estimated there were a thousand people in attendance. Usually you could expect to find acts like the Air Force Marching Band or the Army Brass Band—we didn't belong there.

We had to swindle our way into the gig by concocting an incredible story. Greg told the organizers we were a light jazz band that played Fleetwood Mac covers, which was a little bit of a stretch.

There were maybe one or two other times when we had to lie about who we were and what we were about. One time we were able to get on a gig at Club 88 in West LA as the opening band by telling the booker we were a band from Bakersfield called the Vegetable Farmers.

Whoever was scheduled to play that day in Polliwog Park had gotten sick or something and had to cancel. Maybe their dog died or they got ahold of some rotten potato salad, I don't know. Somebody had to fill in for them, and who better than Black Flag covering a few of Fleetwood Mac's top forty hits along with some jazz standards?

It being a Sunday, I'd worshipped at the church of the living, breathing six-pack earlier that morning, and by the time the gig rolled around I was absolutely obliterated. I don't remember much about the opening acts Big Wow and the Tourists other than that they played. Jeff and Steve McDonald of the Tourists saw us play at the Moose Lodge and reached out to see if they could play a show with us. They said we were the loudest band they'd ever heard.

I wandered around the crowd, checking out all the people. There were cars parked all over the street and on the lawn. I found one to roll under and passed out. After a while someone found me.

"Keith! Wake up! You gotta play!"

I got up, chugged another beer, and was ready to go. We rehearsed so much that I had the songs down cold. I knew them inside out and backward. It didn't matter how much I'd had to drink—I was ready to do some damage. The alcohol just made me more obnoxious.

A lot of the squares left after the first two bands, but sensing that the worst was yet to come, there were still hundreds and hundreds of people on hand to witness the abomination that was about to unfold. Cute couples and new families and innocent children who were about to have their pleasant Sunday afternoon destroyed by Black Flag.

As soon as we hit the first note the heavens opened up and it started raining down beer cans and banana peels, half-eaten cantaloupes and watermelon rinds. KFC bones and soggy sandwiches. All sorts of stuff. Whatever the crowd could find they threw at us. They would have thrown the benches and picnic tables at us if they could have lifted them up. I wasn't too happy about the tossed fruit treatment, and I let the audience have it. At one point I yelled, "You can either be here with us or you can go home and watch Walt fucking Disney!"

The head of Parks and Recreation for Manhattan Beach then stopped the show, telling us, "You can't use that kind of language!"

I agreed to keep it clean, and they swept the stage of debris and let us continue. I had a can of Budweiser glued to my hand the whole time, and we managed to finish the show. Our set usually lasted only about twenty minutes, tops, but it took longer with all the stoppages.

People are under the impression that we were attacked by a suburban mob that was horrified by our presence. That's not entirely the case. Although it's true the show didn't go over well with the locals, we had lots of friends in the audience.

We had Jay Bentley, who would go on to play bass in Bad Religion, Jeffrey Lee Pierce was there on a date with Diane Chai, the bass player and one of the vocalists for the Alley Cats. Diane was a distant cousin of Steven and Jeff McDonald of the Tourists, who were one of the opening acts. Black Flag regulars Dez Cadena, Ron Reyes, and Raymond Pettibon were there, as were all three of the Nolte brothers from the Last. Spot took a great picture from behind the stage that shows Dez and Ron rolling around in the filth. Maybe they were wrestling to see who would be my replacement in Black Flag.

Word was starting to spread about Black Flag, and there were a few hundred freaks in the audience who wanted to check us out, which was a little strange. We weren't used to seeing so many people we didn't know at a show.

Afterward we told everybody, "Party at the Church!" Everyone who was down with what we were doing came over, and we ended up playing a second set at our rehearsal space. We weren't the only freaks in the beach cities. We had a group of people from the South Bay who liked to hang out with us at the Church, but more and more we started to see people from other parts of LA. There would be kids from Hollywood, kids from the Inland Empire. On any given night after rehearsal we'd have ten to twenty people hanging out.

If we had a party, people would travel from all over. The Simpletones would come out from the Pasadena area. The Gears would drive down from Hollywood and East LA. Friends from Long Beach and San Pedro would come up the 405. We had Greg Hetson and Jeff and Steve McDonald from Hawthorne. We had Jill Jordan, who lived up the street and was going to Mira Costa. We had Brian Grillo, who would become the lead vocalist in Lock Up with Tommy Morello, who would go on to Rage Against the Machine. Kara Ella Black would hang out pretty regularly. There were a couple of girls from Torrance who were active in the Hollywood scene and would go on to marry K. K. Barrett and Paul Roessler, who were both members of the Screamers. Ron Reyes and Dez Cadena were part of the crew, and they were always together.

Eventually Ron would rent out the basement. There's a photo that appeared in *Flipside* of a party down in Ron's little bachelor pad, which actually wasn't that little. You could cram a hundred people into that space.

That night, after the "riot" at Polliwog Park, the Tourists played at the Church. The show was in the big room, but it didn't last very long. A ride cymbal fell over and severed the microphone cord, and that was the end of that. We couldn't even have a show in our own space without something going sideways.

LAPD

After the fiasco at Polliwog Park got written up in the newspapers, things started to snowball for us, especially in Hermosa Beach. The cops followed us everywhere we went. They never bothered us at the Church, which was odd. You would think Hermosa Beach's finest would be itching for the chance to swoop into the Church and start cracking heads and cuffing kids. There was always plenty of underage drinking going on, but they mostly left us alone.

However, as soon as we got in the van to go to a party or play a gig somewhere, the cops would be right on our tail. It happened every single time. The second we pulled out of the driveway the cops would be on our ass, waiting for us to make a wrong turn or forget to use the turn signal—any excuse to pull us over. We couldn't go anywhere without the police hassling us.

The same thing happened at our gigs. The cops would break up the show, and their MO was always to bust heads first and ask questions later—except they never did get around to asking any questions. They acted as if they were above all that, and as punks we were made to feel as if we were beneath contempt, presumed guilty because of the way we looked. This got to be really frustrating.

On St. Patrick's Day I succeeded in convincing the guys in the band to end rehearsal early so we could go up to Hollywood. It turned into a massacre.

A bunch of people we knew were playing a gig at the Elks' Lodge over in MacArthur Park. The flyer advertised X, the Alley Cats, the Go-Go's, the Plugz, the Zeros, and "another band." That other band was the Wipers, but they didn't get to play.

The hall was in a big, beautiful building with a sweeping set of stairs that has been used in lots of movies. The fight scene in David Lynch's *Wild at Heart* where Nicolas Cage's character Sailor Ripley kills a guy with his bare hands was filmed there.

I went outside to get something out of the car. The show had already started, but there were fifty people on the stairs. The Go-Go's and the Zeros had already played, and the Plugz were midway through their set. I hit the street and turned left and saw dozens of cops lining up on the sidewalk. It looked like it went on for at least a block. They were strapping on their riot gear. The helmets were going on and the plastic shields were coming out. It didn't take a rocket scientist to figure out what was about to go down.

I ran back inside and told everyone I recognized that the cops were coming and they'd better get out of there. I was heading back down the stairs to leave when the cops starting coming through the door. I grabbed a couple of my friends—I think it was Skunkhead and Donny Rose, who was part of the Germs crew—and pulled them into the men's room.

"We gotta hide!"

I explained the situation, and after a while we made a break for it, but the cops were still swinging on whoever didn't get out of their way. They shut the place down. No one else got to play. They arrested eight people, and there were a lot of injuries. Some of the kids had to get stitches where the cops had beat them with their batons. The next issue of *Flipside* fanzine ran photos of people who'd been beaten by the police without provocation. It's known as the Elks' Lodge Riot, but the only people who were rioting were the police. It was a very mellow show until the cops showed up. It was the first time I experienced police brutality en masse.

BLACK FLAG TOOK A FIELD TRIP to the New Masque to hang out. We drove up from the beach in Greg's little Toyota station wagon. It was a comical scene. Greg and Raymond looked like they could be forwards on a basketball team, so they sat up front. Then you had Chuck and Robo in the middle seats, while I laid out in the back and drank beer.

I forget who was playing, but on this particular night I remember hanging out with Darby Crash before going inside. After a while the police showed up and were really aggressive. They were asking everybody, "Who are you?" and demanding, "Show us your ID" like it was Nazi Germany.

I don't know what happened. We weren't doing anything. We were just listening to music. The pigs started pushing people around, and it quickly escalated to where they were kicking and clubbing people. A real fascist scene.

I got really upset. Nobody had been belligerent. Nobody had done anything to deserve this type of treatment. There was nothing cool about any of it. So I went out to the parking lot to blow off some steam. I noticed a black-and-white parked in the middle of the parking lot, and they'd taken an actual parking space rather than pulling up to the front. How considerate of them!

The parking lot wasn't lit. I ducked down in the shadows, pulled out my Boy Scout knife, and, without giving it another second's thought, slashed one of the tires. I don't really know what was going through my mind at the time; I was so angry about the cops beating up my friends that I just lashed out.

I crept through the parked cars, and when I thought the coast was clear I stood up, and three or four cops immediately tackled me. I didn't realize the lot was full of unmarked cars, and while half the force was inside picking on all of the punkers, the other half was keeping a close watch on the lot. Oops.

I was cuffed and dragged face first across the dirty, dusty parking lot to the street. The cops propped me up against one of the unmarked cars. It was a pretty big operation. The cops were all rookies, fresh out of the academy. The punk rock show was on-the-job training for the riot squad. A little professional development. The commander gave the order to put me in a chokehold, one of the cops choked me out, and I went to sleep.

I wasn't resisting. I was already in cuffs, so I wasn't going anywhere. The only reason they put me in a chokehold was retribution for slashing a tire.

When the oxygen started flowing through my brain again, they lifted me up and propped me against the side of the car. I was surrounded by cops with their billy clubs hanging out. They'd cleared the majority of the people from the New Masque. Kids were coming out of the club, looking at me and shaking their head as if to say, "You are so fucked." They were right.

Once the scene was cleared the cops got to have their fun. They proceeded to do whatever they wanted to do to me. I got kicked in the face, stomped on the forehead, punched in the ribs. A couple of them poked me with their billy clubs, and some of them even tried to kick me in the Morris family jewels, but I was able to close my legs so I only got kicked in the knees and shins. There were about twenty of them in the gauntlet, and each one of them took their best shot. When they were done they all got in their cars and drove back to the pig farm or wherever they came from. Everyone except the commander. He put me in his car and we went for a drive.

"You're in a lot of trouble, son," he said, and for the first time I started to worry. People had been taking shots at me my whole life. You had to do something really messed up to get my attention. This was starting to qualify. "What you did was seriously fucked up," the cop said. "Here's what we're going to do. You like slashing tires? We're going to get up on the freeway and pull over and you're going to change my tires."

I had visions of the cop kicking the jack out and getting pinned by the squad car or being chucked off an overpass like a piece of trash. I didn't like this scenario one bit. When the commander took a break from his little sermon I tried to butter him up by apologizing—do the right thing and all of that wonderful shit. It didn't matter because the commander was messing with me the entire time. We pulled up in front of the county jail and they booked me.

It was a pretty dehumanizing experience. They didn't let me sleep. They moved me around from cell to cell to fuck with me. Oppression 101. The first cell they put me in held eight guys, and one of them was your typical wimpy crybaby Caucasian. The golf instructor who had too much to drink at the country club and got pulled over running a stoplight. He went on and on, "I'm not supposed to be here. Why don't you let me out?"

I finally got moved into a big cell, where it was like one big dormitory with lots of bunks. They place was packed. There was no way I was going to get a bunk. You had your African Americans on one side and your Latinos on the other, with a handful of pathetic white dudes in between. I didn't want to hang out with them, and they didn't want to hang out with me.

I ended up talking to this Mexican kid with a necklace of hickies. He told me he was having sex with his girlfriend in his car on the side of the road when the cops showed up. They told him to get out of the car and he told them to hold on—he wasn't finished yet. The LAPD didn't like that and they pummeled him. So we had that in common.

They came for me around seven in the morning. "Don't ever come back," they said and let me go. I had a massive hangover and was covered in bumps and bruises and hadn't gotten any sleep. Luckily my injuries weren't too serious, and the only permanent damage was a deep mistrust for anyone in a police uniform.

NOT HAVING FUN

The punk scene was changing and getting bigger by the day, but Black Flag was still having a difficult time finding places to play.

A new wave of punk bands was emerging, and they brought a younger, more athletic fan base to the scene. I don't know whether Black Flag helped spark this wave or if we were at the front of the swell, but all of a sudden you had all these surfers and skaters coming to the shows and starting bands, and it totally energized the scene.

In my mind skaters like Tony Alva and the Dogtown guys invented slam dancing and stage diving. The movement of someone in a circle pit looks a lot like someone grinding away on a skateboard. If you don't know what you're seeing, it can look brutal and crude, but it's actually graceful and athletic. And what's more Californian than diving into a pool? A stage dive is nothing more than leaping into a pool full of people. All of that fun shit started with the skaters. Slam dancing, circle pit, the hokey pokey—whatever you want to call it—it all started in Southern California. In the beginning all those these skaters were listening to bands like Aerosmith, Black Sabbath, and Ted Nugent. Then punk rock came along and made it more exciting, and it kicked things up a couple of notches.

It wasn't just the art school crowd anymore—the drug addicts and the degenerates, the scenesters and the zinesters and all the creative misfits who were part of the original Hollywood punk rock movement. In fact a lot of those people were put off by what was happening.

They didn't like it when we'd come up to Hollywood to play a show and our fans would go crazy, breaking bottles, smashing windows, ripping sinks off the wall, or smashing holes in the toilets. They didn't like that at all. "These outsiders are ruining the scene!"

I totally understood where they were coming from. I didn't like it either. I can't tell you how many times I tried to keep the peace and prevent someone's house from getting torn apart, but there were times when I contributed to the madness. Most of my bad behavior was of the self-destructive variety, but there were times when I'd smash a bottle for no reason or piss in the silverware drawer in someone's kitchen because all of the bathrooms were full. I'm not proud of that behavior. That's not how you're supposed to act, and I regret it. In those early days of hardcore there was this feeling that everything had to be burned to the ground. Destroy everything. It was hard not to get caught up in it, especially if I was wasted. Somebody would drop a bottle into the toilet or stop up the sinks and leave the faucet running. Mindless, stupid stuff. Some of it I participated in; some of it I could have stopped but didn't. It was really counterintuitive: "Hey, this is really fun. Let's destroy the place and make sure we never get to come back here again!" The problem with punk rock parties was you had people coming from all these different suburban scenes, and it was no skin off their ass if windows got broken and walls were spray painted.

It wasn't just club owners who didn't like this faster, louder, more aggressive style of music; a lot of the original Hollywood punks turned up their noses at hardcore. It was too much for them. At the same time, the crowds were expanding and the fan base was spreading to other parts of LA and the surrounding communities like a virus. The genie had been let out of the bottle, and there was no putting it back.

THE POLICE DIDN'T LIKE IT EITHER. Gone were the days when they'd bust up a show at the Masque and chase a bunch of art school dropouts, hustlers, and queers from the venue. This new crowd was younger, more athletic, and lot angrier. It was the end of the seventies.

The squeeze was on. When the cops tried to push these kids around, they pushed back.

For a lot of people Black Flag was the symbol of that. "Don't book Black Flag—they'll trash your place." Or, "Don't play with Black Flag or else the police will shut down the show." We were getting it from all sides—bands, club owners, and cops. We went from being unknowns to pariahs.

In spite of all that, even though we were having a hard time booking shows, we were still rehearsing five, six, seven nights a week, from anywhere from two to five hours a night. We were a well-oiled machine with no purpose or function. We could play our set in our sleep. We could get up in any condition and play the songs. Those were all good things.

But we were spending way too much time together. I was living in the Church at the time, so I couldn't get away from it. It was like living in your workplace or being in the military. I can't speak for the other guys, but I was starting to dislike Chuck because he was the one who was always cracking the whip. Practice, practice, practice.

We rehearsed for all of these hours but weren't playing many shows. The gigs in Hollywood were drying up, and we were going back to playing in living rooms and garages. This would eventually lead to bands getting in the van and going on the road, the whole touring route, but that wasn't an option for us. When I was in the band we never really talked about playing anywhere outside of Los Angeles except the occasional trip to San Francisco. We were stuck in a rut.

I loved playing our songs. Getting in the rehearsal space and making a bunch of noise was the highlight of my day. We'd let people hang out while we were practicing, so there would usually be a few girls who would show up, which was cool, but the rest of it was starting to feel like a job. Why be in a band if you're not having any fun? It was a question I would ask myself over and over again.

There wasn't any one incident I could point to where I was like, *Fuck this shit*, but there was a growing rift between Chuck and me. I was tired of constantly being told what to do. On occasion I'd skip out on rehearsal. I'd go up to Hollywood and see the Dickies at the Whisky or the Go-Go's at the Hong Kong Café. I wanted to have some fun. I thought that's what being in a punk rock band was all about.

The guys in the band didn't like that, and they were getting tired of all of my drunken antics. I wasn't easy to deal with. I was consuming whatever I could get my hands on. If you're not having fun, you've got to have a sense of purpose or else it becomes a grind. That's true of any job. I had the utmost respect for Chuck's work ethic, but we were basically playing for ourselves. Why were we rehearsing so much? What were we killing ourselves for?

I didn't know what the vision for Black Flag was. If there was a vision, either I was kept out of those discussions or I wasn't paying attention. Greg would point the finger at me for holding the band back. I was constantly being blamed for the band's failure to make any progress, and that didn't sit too well with me.

We had sixteen songs in our set, which we were expanding by adding another four or five. I had lyrics I was working on in my own half-assed way, but it had already turned into a whatever-Greg-says-goes situation. He was in a hurry for me to learn the new songs. My attitude was, "What's the big rush? We're not playing any shows anyway."

A few weeks after I left the band, Black Flag played their first gig at the Whisky. Did Greg book the show while I was still in the band and "forget" to tell me? Is that why he wanted to expand the set? You'd have to ask him, but I didn't know about the show. I don't blame them for wanting me to learn the new songs. When you're in a band, that's what you do—you learn some songs, you make a record, and then you go play those songs for the people. You want to keep progressing and moving forward. But the fact of the matter was we'd never been in a hurry before; Black Flag moved at its own pace. So I just kind of shrugged my shoulders at the whole thing.

Pretty soon, instead of one person pointing the finger at me, it was three. Whenever there was a group decision to make, it was three against one. Every. Single. Time. Everything became an argument or some kind of confrontation. I'm not really big on confrontations, and I was getting sick of losing all the arguments. Who wants to deal with that all the time?

Every day I'd go from my job at my dad's store to my second job playing in Black Flag, except the money was leaving my pocket instead of coming in because I was *paying* money to rehearse. If we had a show or a gig or plans to get back in the studio, I was always the last to find out about it. I was out of the loop. It was time for me to find something else to do.

No one forced me out. It was my own decision to leave the band. Nor did I leave on bad terms. There was no big fight. There was never any physicality or anything like that. I had no ill feelings toward the guys. I didn't hate them or hold a grudge. I was still living at the Church, after all. I went to see them play when Ron Reyes took over as vocalist. We were still bros—or so I thought.

Many years later Chuck told me that if I hadn't left, Greg would have found a way to hand me my walking papers and boot me out of the band. The difficult thing was I was the only other founding member left, so it was a tricky situation, but it wasn't that complicated for me. It wasn't fun anymore, so I left. That's really all there was to it.

I think everyone was relieved I'd decided to quit the band. I wasn't cut out for their militaristic approach to rehearsing. I'm not going to speak for Henry Rollins, Black Flag's *fourth* vocalist, especially as he's written so much about himself already, but I think that's one of the reasons he succeeded in that role. He always struck me as a rigid type of character. Here was this kid from a military family who'd gone to military school. He was used to following orders. He was working as a manager at Häagen Dazs in Washington, DC, when he got the opportunity to play with his musical heroes. Of course he's going to make the most of the situation. He thrived in the environment Chuck and Greg laid down, and he stuck with it until Greg broke up the band.

That wasn't me. I came from a very laid back environment. I wasn't used to following orders—not from my dad, not from Greg, not from

Chuck, not from anybody. I was going to do what I was going to do. It was time for me to do something different. It was the end of the seventies and the beginning of the eighties. Out with one era, in with another. I wasn't a kid anymore—far from it—but I was still a problem child. I had plenty of growing up to do. I was partying on a regular basis and keeping the coke dealers in business. I didn't care what my dad or Greg or anyone thought about me. As far as I was concerned, the party was just getting started.

WHAT'S NEXT?

My departure from Black Flag started a chain reaction in the punk rock community that can still be felt today. That's not me being grandiose; that's just the way it went down.

After I left the band Ron Reyes became the vocalist for Black Flag. It was an easy decision for Greg Ginn to make. Ron was living in the basement at the Church and already knew all the songs. He was constantly around the band, so he already had an idea of what was expected of him.

Ron had been playing drums with Red Cross (later renamed Redd Kross), and the band had been using his space at the Church to rehearse. Ron got into an argument with Jeff McDonald during a show and quit. That paved the way for Ron to slide into my spot in Black Flag, and now Red Cross had a vacancy to fill. I was still living at the Church and would hang out from time to time, and I heard through the grapevine that Jeff and Steven McDonald had auditioned a new drummer for Red Cross and that it had not gone well.

Greg Hetson, Red Cross's guitar player, had talked his bandmates into letting his friend Lucky Lehrer audition as the drummer. Red Cross was going for a rude, crude, we-can-barely-play-our-instruments kind of sound that was somewhere between the Germs and the New York Dolls. They were looking for a sloppy rock drummer who could hold down a beat and stay out of the way.

That wasn't Lucky. Lucky was a supremely talented drummer who learned to play by listening to American jazz legends like Louie Bellson and Buddy Rich. These are amazing drummers with incredible prowess, musicians with serious chops, guys the McDonald brothers wouldn't have known much about at the time. I love Jeff and Steve, so I don't mean any disrespect, but Lucky was too polished for what they were trying to do. Keep in mind that the McDonald brothers were really young, and Lucky was closer to my age. He had a fancy drum kit, which probably turned them off. They were still living with their parents in Hawthorne; in fact, the audition took place in Steven's bedroom.

The audition went down and apparently neither Jeff nor Steven was impressed. Greg, however, was blown away and wanted Lucky in the band, but the McDonald brothers weren't having it. They must have had a heated discussion, because they decided not to see any more drummers. I'm not really sure what went down: either Greg quit or Jeff and Steve decided to break up the band, but either way, now both Lucky and Greg were looking for something to do. Starting a new band was the furthest thing from my mind, but the flow of the universe made it very apparent what needed to happen next.

Not too long after the audition I was hanging out in front of the Whisky with Greg and Lucky. Here was Lucky, an amazing drummer, Greg, an amazing guitar player, and me. None of us were in a band. I'm not the smartest guy in the world but a light bulb clicked on above my head.

"You guys want to start a band?"

It was that simple. I knew Greg from back before the Tourists morphed into Red Cross, and Greg was tight with Lucky. All we needed was a bass player, and that situation presented itself shortly afterward outside another Hollywood establishment. I was sitting in front of the Anti Club down on Melrose, waiting for some friends to show up. This guy was leaning against the wall and brown-bagging a bottle of cheap beer. He was friendlier than most and asked if I wanted some beer. In those days the answer to that question was always yes. We started talking, and it turned out he'd recently spent some time playing bass with the Angry Samoans. I told him I was starting a band and was looking for a bass player. "You want to play bass with us?"

That's how Roger Rogerson, a perfect stranger, became the fourth member of the band. The only thing we needed was a name, some songs, and a clue.

WE CAN BLAME RAYMOND PETTIBON for the Circle Jerks. Just as he was instrumental in naming Black Flag, he had a hand in naming the Circle Jerks.

I had created a list of names I was considering. The Runs. The Bedwetters. The Plastic Hippies. We tried out all of those names at one point in time, but none of them really stuck.

One day Greg and I were in Raymond's workspace and going through his art. That was how Raymond worked: he didn't make art for flyers; bands used his art for their shows. That's how it was in the late seventies and early eighties, and that's how it is today.

We had already booked a gig and needed to put a flyer together— fast. You'd think we would have come up with a name *before* we started working on the flyer, but that's just how we did things. It was apparent that it was time to get serious about a name.

I was looking at a bookshelf filled with Raymond's books and pulled out a dictionary of American slang. I was flipping through the pages, and all of a sudden Greg was standing there next to me, and we were looking at the words on the page together and there it was: circle jerk.

I looked at Greg and said, "Circle Jerks," and Raymond started laughing. I don't know if Greg knew what it meant, but I have a feeling Raymond did. In any case, the definition was right there. If you don't know what it means, I can tell you it refers to a gathering of friends, but you should really go look it up for yourself.

INGLEGOOD

After I quit Black Flag I moved into the little pink house on Sims Avenue in Inglewood that my mom rented from one of my dad's friends—we just called it the Pink House. It was just a few houses down from my grandparents' house, where I had many childhood memories.

My mom's family moved to California from Texas during the Great Depression. They were factory workers and laborers, blue-collar people who worked with their hands. Her father worked in a wheat-grinding mill. When Texas turned into a dust bowl they headed west in search of a better life. While passing through New Mexico my mom, Maudena, and her twin sister, Laurena, were born. They eventually settled in Inglewood, where her dad found work as the transmission specialist at Felix Chevrolet near the Los Angeles Coliseum on Exposition Boulevard. When he got home from work at night he would grab a Schlitz beer and take a bath, where he would scrub himself with Lava soap. He was built like a little gorilla and looked like someone you wouldn't want to mess with, but he was a really nice guy.

My mother had four siblings. There's an interesting story about her youngest sister. Apparently when my mother was just barely a teenager, her mother, Eurena, took off for a year, and when she came back she had a little blonde-haired, blue-eyed baby in her arms that was obviously not my grandfather's. That was my Aunt Frances, who has always been a free spirit—she's the one who had the backyard gathering that turned into an LSD dance party—and is one of my favorite people.

My grandparents were kind, decent, church-going people, but for most of their lives they were racists. They had certain ideas about the world that they brought with them to California, and that was that. They say people don't change, but that wasn't necessarily the case with my grandparents.

The part of Inglewood where they lived was called Imperial Village, the westernmost tip of south central LA, and over the years they watched it go from a mostly white neighborhood to a mostly black one. They were just six blocks from Compton. In fact, Ice-T lived on the other side of Crenshaw Boulevard when he went to Crenshaw High.

Despite the changes, Imperial Village remained a middle-class neighborhood. You had police officers and county workers and people with civil service jobs. Everybody was working hard and going to church and raising families. Same morals. Same values. I don't know what exactly triggered their epiphany, but my grandparents realized that the only thing that had changed about the people who lived in their neighborhood was the color of their skin.

After they retired they opened their doors to the working families in the neighborhood who had kids who needed someplace to go after school. My grandparents gave them a place where they could do their homework, have a meal, and maybe watch some TV until their parents came home from work. It was kind of like an unregulated after-school program. The parents would make a donation that went toward the food and the utilities, and my grandparents looked after the kids. It worked out for everyone in the neighborhood and was a really cool thing they got to do.

MY GRANDPARENTS WERE REALLY MELLOW. Nothing rattled them. One of the things they enjoyed doing was driving out to the desert to collect rocks. They collected gems and polished stones. They took my sister and me on trips to Death Valley, Quartzsite, Hemet, Needles—just about every California desert town you can think of.

Their house was a rock museum with crystals on the bookshelves and amethyst on the coffee table next to the *TV Guide*. They had a fifty-gallon fish tank, and some of their precious stones would end up in there. It was something for the fish to look at.

One day my sister and I got in an argument. She was always telling on me and ratting me out. She got me all riled up about something, and I picked up one of these chunks of rocks and threw it at her. Of course, I missed, and the rock hit the fish tank and shattered the glass. There was a crack, a splash, and then no more fish tank. My grandfather was sitting underneath the tank in his recliner watching television when it happened. All things considered, he was pretty calm about it. He sent me to the old Chevy that sat in front of the house, which was how we were punished. Being banished to the Chevy was our time-out. In those days the car radio was connected to the battery, so I could just turn on the radio and jam on some tunes or listen to the ball game while I served my time.

Some of my happiest memories as a kid are of hanging out at my grandparents' house, reading comic books that my dad's friend Art the Fart Watson would bring over. He and my dad would hang out and smoke pot together, and he would always bring over a stack of comics for me to read. Jack Kirby and Steve Ditko were some of my earliest heroes because they created the Hulk, Thor, Spiderman, and the Fantastic Four. These were characters I grew up with. They were part of my world, stoking my imagination. When I read them I wasn't the kid who was always getting picked on but a superhero with the power to change the world.

YOU'D THINK THAT WITH MY DAD being such a rebel he would have encouraged me to do whatever I wanted, but by the time I was in high school he was a business owner and was actually pretty conservative in his views. He didn't want me doing my own thing; he wanted me to work. My younger sister wasn't very encouraging either. She had no trouble fitting in with other kids, the jocks, and the cheerleaders. She was always part of that scene. My biggest ally was my mom. She was *always* encouraging. She told me to do what I wanted to do and have fun and don't worry what anyone else says. It was great advice then, and it's great advice now.

My mom had quit her job at the *Los Angeles Times*, where she had been running the computer teletype system. She was getting ready to move to Hawaii, so I took over the lease at the Pink House. There were three bedrooms, and the rent was cheap. With my grandparents down the street, I was never far from a free meal. I had a little green Barracuda that was mostly broken down in the driveway, but for the first time I had my own place, my own wheels, and my own band.

I wasn't feeling any pressure to start another band after I left Black Flag. I wasn't trying to prove myself or show the world what I could do. If anything, I felt a sense of relief that I was no longer stuck in the undertow of conflict and paranoia that always seemed to surround Black Flag. To be perfectly honest, I didn't think about the guys all that much or dwell on what I'd left behind. I was glad to be gone and doing my own thing, and that wouldn't change until some time after Henry Rollins joined the band.

The whole idea behind the Circle Jerks was to have fun: No pressure. No rules. Let's party and have a good time. Tap the keg, turn up the volume, and break out the party supplies. We wanted to be the band who was playing the party, pumping the keg, and pouring drinks for everybody.

Things got hectic in a hurry. We'd booked a couple of shows before we were ready to go, and that created a situation where we really had to hustle. I was definitely feeling the pressure, which I didn't like.

The first thing I did was set up a rehearsal space in the garage at the Pink House. We nailed some carpet to the walls and had rehearsals there. Nobody ever complained. The only people who ever bothered us were the neighborhood kids. The adults didn't care what we did, which was kind of surprising when you consider all the activity going on in the garage, but the kids wanted to know what we were doing. Who were these guys and girls carrying instrument cases and cold beer? We'd also opened the rehearsal space to Lucky's younger brother

Chet and his band, Wasted Youth. We were happy to share the garage with them because we weren't going to follow the Black Flag schedule: rehearse every night for two years and never do anything. Between the Circle Jerks and Wasted Youth, the place was always rocking, but we never got any complaints from anyone in the neighborhood.

I needed roommates to help cover the rent to make sure I had money for beer and cocaine. Greg lived in Brentwood with his dad. Lucky lived in West Hollywood. Roger was living with his girlfriend, Laura, and I started dating her best friend, Karen, but everyone called her KJ. Usually the lead vocalist in the band is the guy all the girls gravitate to, but I was never that guy. I've never been a womanizer. Early on, a lot of girls who were interested in our music were either out of my league or I wasn't attracted to them. If there were pretty girls hanging out after the show, I didn't notice them because I was too busy trying to get directions to the party, locate the liquor store, call up the drug dealer, and find a couch to crash out on at the end of the night. Who wants to hook up with a drunken cokehead Tasmanian Devil?

KJ was from Pasadena, and she was my first girlfriend. We shared a lot of the same interests: drinking, partying, going to shows. We dated for about four years, but she never lived at the Pink House.

My first roommate was none other than Jeffrey Lee Pierce. He loved Black Flag and the Circle Jerks, and he would write things in *Slash* like, "They look like they're expending so much energy they're going to explode" or "It's like witnessing an exorcism!" He'd been in a band called the Creeping Ritual that he wasn't happy with because he was the only one who knew how to play. Everyone else in the band was learning as they went. One of them was Kid Congo, who would go on to play with the Cramps and the Bad Seeds, and another was Don Snowden, who would end up writing for the *Los Angeles Times* and coauthoring a number of books about punk rock and the blues.

The best gig Jeffrey could get was being the opening act on a Monday night, but Jeffrey was writing these amazing songs that would eventually become *The Fire of Love*. Not only was Jeffrey a fan of what we were doing; he was also heavily into the blues. He was very knowledgeable about the music that came out of the plantations, songs the slaves sang while they worked the fields. And all those influences came together in a way that made him a unique performer.

We'd see each other in the alley outside the Masque or in front of the Hong Kong Café in Chinatown, and eventually we struck up a friendship. "Hey, you got a light for my cigarette?" or "Do you have an extra beer?" "Why don't you take a huff of this?" We just hit it off.

Jeffrey knew about all the great venues in Inglewood. They were neighborhood bars that had amazing entertainment in the evening. Right around the corner from the Pink House was a place called the Five Torches, which was a joint where Ike and Tina Turner or Red Foxx would have performed. We'd go to these places and run into the guys from the Blasters or Los Lobos. In LA, punk rock was so much more than a bunch of guys and girls bashing on instruments they didn't know how to play; there was incredible variety and depth to our scene.

I DIDN'T WANT THE CIRCLE JERKS to be like Black Flag, where one guy called all the shots and everybody had to fall in line or get the fuck out. In the beginning of Black Flag I was so blown away by what Greg Ginn was doing, I didn't really need to participate in the band's creative development. All I had to do was interpret Greg's lyrics, add my personality, and scream the songs. As we moved forward I started writing lyrics. The further we got into it, the more I wrote. Granted, some of those lyrics were weak, but I was bringing *something* to the table. I wanted to contribute, but Greg wasn't interested. I made sure we did things differently in the Circle Jerks.

It was more of a free-for-all with everyone on equal footing. Each musician tossed his ideas into the pot. When we booked our first shows we were still writing new material. We only had, like, six songs. We were probably looking at a seven-minute set, if that. It wasn't nearly enough. It was getting close to panic time.

Our songwriting sessions went like this: we all piled into the garage and stared at each other. I'd say, "Does anybody have any music? Does anybody have any lyrics?"

Greg and Roger had some riffs they'd written in Red Cross and the Angry Samoans. I had some lyrics I'd written while I was in Black Flag. It wasn't much, but we cobbled together some songs that way. Virtually all of our songs were about a minute long.

I think our first show was at Kahuna's under the pier in Redondo Beach. A ton of people came out to see us. They wanted to get swept up in the energy and excitement of what we were doing, and we delivered. It was a really fun show, but not everyone had a good time.

The McDonald brothers were there, and I'm pretty sure Chuck and Greg were there too, and I can tell you they were not happy. After the show a rumor started going around that Greg Hetson and I had stolen songs from Red Cross and Black Flag. People were pretty pissed off about it, especially Greg Ginn.

All I'd done was take the songs I'd written and reworked them. When you write the lyrics to a song, you own half the song. As for Greg Hetson, he did the same thing with riffs he'd written. After Lucky's disastrous audition, the McDonalds decided to break up and gave Greg Hetson permission to use any of their songs, however he wanted.

We took the bits and pieces we'd contributed and created something new. But that's not how our ex-bandmates saw things, and it was a big mess. We stirred up all of these bad vibes, which wasn't our intention at all. I'd been out of Black Flag for less than a month, and I was still knee-deep in their drama. It wasn't the way I'd envisioned things, but the bottom line is we didn't steal anything. We did what musicians have been doing for years and years. Musicians get together and collaborate. Some of it makes it into a song, some of it doesn't, but sooner or later those scraps—a riff here, a line there—will get used in something else.

As opposed to Black Flag, where things moved at a glacial pace, we were moving at lightning speed. We weren't exactly overthinking things.

IT'S A SMALL WORLD
AFTER ALL

We started talking about doing an album right away, but we still needed a few more songs. My roommate, Jeffery Lee Pierce, was going through the same struggles we were. Jeffrey was starting a new band, but he needed a name.

"I've got a name for you," I told him.

"Let's hear it."

"How about the Gun Club?"

"I'll take it!" Jeffrey said.

"What are you going to give me in return?"

"I've been writing this song," he said. "How about I play it for you, and if you like it, you can have it."

We had ourselves a deal. He knew we were hard up for material, so he gave me a song and it eventually became "Group Sex," which is a pretty important song. It was the last song we wrote before we went into the studio, and it's the last song on the album, so we named the album after it. What else are you going to name a record by a band called the Circle Jerks?

But Jeffrey ended up having the last laugh because "Group Sex" sounds an awful lot like a swampy, souped-up version of "It's a Small World After All." If you were really wasted and cranked up on some good speed and falling down a flight of stairs while playing "It's a Small World After All," it might come out sounding like "Group Sex."

I got the lyrics out of the want ads section of a fine, upstanding men's publication. I think it was *Oui*. The ad was for a swinger's hot-line in the Hollywood Hills. I didn't change much. The ad was pretty self-explanatory. If you wanted to get your vagina fiesta on, that was the number to call. Lucky thought it would be funny if he used his phone number in the song instead of the number in the ad, so we did. For somebody as smart as Lucky, that was a pretty dumb thing to do, because he would get calls all night long. I think people are still calling that number! As Roger would say, "He ordered it."

In Black Flag everything was always so *serious*. Any sarcasm or humor in the lyrics just got buried under layers and layers of negativity. With the Circle Jerks we wanted to keep things light. That was the great thing about the LA scene: it was very festive. Everybody wanted to hang out and party. We never felt like we were competing with anybody.

That wasn't necessarily the case with Black Flag. I remember feeling like we were in competition with bands like the Cheifs and the Gears. They were really great guys who we would party with—we'd pass out on their floors and they'd pass out on ours—but Black Flag had a way of making things more intense than they needed to be. The Circle Jerks were the opposite of that.

OUR FIRST ALBUM WAS MADE with the help of a big bag of marijuana. Lucky had a friend who had a friend who worked at a studio on the Desilu lot in Culver City, which was owned by Lucille Ball and Desi Arnaz of *I Love Lucy*. So we can thank Desi and Lucille for introducing the world to *Group Sex*. With the help of a grocery bag full of weed of dubious quality, we were able to record there. Because Lucky's friend was the one who greased the skids and got us the studio, he was given credit as the producer on the record. Normally the producer is someone with musical know-how who shepherds the band through the recording process like a director guiding actors in a movie. That wasn't the case with this record.

There wasn't a schedule or a set time when we had the studio booked. They would bring us into the studio whenever they could fit us in. If they had a window of three or four hours when no one was in the studio, they'd give us a call and we'd come down. So basically it was a situation where we were sitting around waiting for the phone to ring, and then off we'd go to Culver City.

We did all of the recordings in a small voiceover studio. It wasn't a full-blown music studio with separate rooms for the various instruments. It was just a room where they did sound effects. We set up our gear in different corners of the room—drums over here, guitars over there—and went for it. We would knock out a couple of songs, and then it was time to pack up our gear again. I think it helped that our songs were so short. No guitar solos. No extended bridges or extra-long intros or outros. No dicking around whatsoever. Just get in and get out.

This went on for a couple of weeks. A couple of hours here, a few more there. We'd get an hour or two on Tuesday, then nothing on Wednesday, but maybe on Thursday we'd get a call to come in for a couple of hours. We recorded fifteen songs that way. It wasn't the best way to make a record, but we didn't know any better.

LISA FANCHER AT FRONTIER RECORDS released *Group Sex*. At that point she'd put out the Flyboys first EP, which was LA's answer to the Buzzcocks or the Jam and featured at least one future member of the Crowd. It was a modest deal, but the contract was very friendly for a bunch of guys playing in a band that never made more than $250 on a Friday night. It wasn't something we needed a lawyer to take a look at, and we still own the songs. Lisa had worked at Bomp!, so she probably knew about the Black Flag *Nervous Breakdown* fiasco and wasn't going to make that mistake.

The photo for the album was shot by Ed Colver down in a skate pool at Marina Del Rey where they held shows a couple of times a month. That particular show was with the Adolescents and featured a mock wedding between Rob Henley and Michelle Gerber Bell. I believe the photo was colorized by Diana Zincavage, who was a staff artist at Frontier Records.

The Circle Jerks type logo was created by a guy named Doug Drug who was a fan on the fringes of the scene. I don't remember how exactly it went down, but there wasn't a contract or anything like that. He gave us the logo, and we invited him to our shows, let him into our parties, and offered up our beer. That kind of deal. He was a part of our circle as much as he wanted to be.

As for the infamous image of the skanking punk kid with his fists clenched, flannel tied around his waist, and boots decked out with bandanas, that was drawn by Shawn Kerri, an illustrator and cartoonist from San Diego. She also did the famous Germs flyer with the mohawked skull tearing through the paper. Shawn had her own zine for a while and contributed to all kinds of magazines and publications. I believe Shawn has passed on, but there are rumors she's still alive somewhere. In either case, she left her mark on the Circle Jerks in a big way.

GROUP SEX **IS A STRANGE RECORD**—fifteen songs, sixteen minutes (if you bought the cassette you got the entire album on both sides)—but we felt pretty good about it. Our goal, if we even had one, was to provide the soundtrack to the celebration, punk rock for party people. Even though Frontier was a new outfit and didn't have national distribution, *Group Sex* flew off the shelves in Southern California. It brought in enough money for Frontier to be able to put out a couple of other records by bands like the Adolescents, TSOL, and Suicidal Tendencies. It felt like all these local bands were stepping up their games and making amazing music. All of the recordings from that time period are absolutely essential. If you are a fan of punk, no matter what scene you come from, you have to listen to these bands. They each had their own personality. Put on the Adolescents' blue album or the Suicidal Tendencies' self-titled first album, and you know right away what you're listening to. We hadn't reached the point where you couldn't tell the bands apart, which is the way it is now. No one was making a lot of money, so there wasn't a template to follow for fame and fortune.

In spite of the record's success, the band had a lot of the same problems I'd had in Black Flag in that we were completely unknown. We were brand new and no one knew about us, but the word was starting to get out.

Once a year *Slash* magazine ran a story about new bands you had to check out, and that year we were one of the bands. So that got us a little exposure. We weren't turning down any gigs. If there was an opportunity to play, we took it, which resulted in some pretty strange shows.

One memorable gig was at a Catholic school: Sister Mary's School for Wayward Girls or something to that effect. We played their prom, if you can believe it. The students got to vote for the band they wanted to play their year-end dance, and somehow we won. I thought it was a gag, like maybe the punks at the school had rigged the ballot box. I have no idea how we even ended up on the ballot, but we won and came to play. As soon as the show started, all the girls rushed to the front and starting spitting at each other. Those Catholic girls knew what was up, but it really offended the sisters, who didn't know this was what went down at punk shows. To them it was absolutely vulgar, which it was. Honestly it's the one thing about punk rock I hope never comes back. Who the fuck wants to stand on a stage and get spit on for half an hour?

At least the girls were polite enough to spit at each other and not us, but the nuns weren't too thrilled about it. About ten or fifteen minutes into our set, right after we played "Group Sex," the nuns shut down the show.

"We are not going to allow this to happen at our school!"

That's when the sheriffs showed up. There were actually a few helicopters flying over the school. It was basically Black Flag all over again.

ANOTHER WEIRD GIG WE GOT was a birthday party for a thirteen-year-old girl. We had Lucky to thank for that one.

Lucky's parents were living out in Malibu and decided to throw a birthday party for their daughter. For some reason Lucky talked them into letting us play, which wasn't so far-fetched, as Lucky's brother Chet was also in a punk rock band and his band, Wasted Youth, played too.

I was my usual inebriated self at the party. At certain points in our set I screamed, "Bong ludes!" at the top of my lungs in front of all of these kids. The parents stood off to the side, scratching their heads, wondering why they had agreed to let this happen. Whatever they'd imagined, this wasn't it. But the kids were jumping around and having a good time, so the madness continued. I think we might have even played a ramshackle version of the Beatles "You Say It's Your Birthday," interspersed with outbursts of "Bong ludes!"

We also played a garage show at a party down in Orange County with True Sounds of Liberty right before they became TSOL. It was well attended by scraggly surfer types from the beach cities. As you might expect, that one got pretty wild. They had a couple of kegs, the beer was flowing, and everybody was getting loose and flying around.

We even played a couple of shows at the Polish Auditorium on Crenshaw Boulevard just up the street from the Pink House. One of the shows was with the Adolescents, the Urinals, and No Crisis, and then another show was with Fear, the Mentors, and 45 Grave not too long afterward. The night we played with the Adolescents I was standing in the men's room, minding my own business and pissing in the trough when all of the windows above me shattered at once and all of these punks came pouring in right as I was taking a leak. I peed on tennis shoes, steel-toed boots, broken glass. There must have been, like, thirty people who got into the show for free.

We had a real scary situation go down at another club down on Crenshaw Boulevard. Roger usually drove us to the show because he was the man with the van. He'd park in front of the club and go about his business. Roger and his girlfriend, Laura, used the van as a rolling motel, and that's where we'd usually find him after we'd taken out all of the gear and loaded it into the venue.

I was standing across the street with a crowd of fifteen or twenty people when all of a sudden this car came racing down Crenshaw

Boulevard at full throttle. The car went right through the red light and sideswiped about seven cars parked in front of the club, and the last vehicle he hit was Roger's van. He must have hit the gas tank because the van exploded in flames. No exaggeration. Kaboom! Huge fucking fireball.

My first thought was, "Oh shit! Roger and his girlfriend are in there!"

Everyone started freaking out. There wasn't anything we could do because the van was completely engulfed in flames. No survivors.

All of a sudden I see Roger and Laura walking back from the liquor store. They must have gone to get more booze or smokes, but obviously they were fine. I have no idea how we made it back to the Pink House that night.

THE PINK HOUSE

The Pink House was located just off the intersection of Crenshaw Boulevard and Imperial Highway. To get to and from Hollywood, I would either get a ride from a friend or someone in the band or catch the bus that went up and down Crenshaw Boulevard. On one particular night I got on the last bus out of Hollywood and headed home. It was pretty empty except for some unsavory characters in the back of the bus. I don't remember what their affiliation was, but living in Imperial Village, I knew the difference between a rowdy teenager and a gang member, and these guys looked like gangbangers.

I was drunk, and the vibe was pretty hairball. I had a very strong feeling that it was only a matter of time before some violence went down. It would have only taken one or two of them to work me over. I didn't want to get stabbed and tossed off the back of the bus. At that time of night I probably would have laid there and bled to death. I felt like I needed to do something drastic, so I decided to give these guys an impromptu history lesson.

"Do you know where the word 'nigger' originated?" I asked as I lurched to the back of the bus and fell into an empty seat.

These guys couldn't believe what was coming out of my mouth. Not because they were offended or appalled but because they assumed there was no way a sane person would talk to them like that: *Wow, this white guy must be fucking out of his mind!* Rumor had it that the gang members in the neighborhood had a rule among themselves that you don't mess with the mentally insane. My rash decision to imitate an emotionally disturbed person probably saved me from a beat-down that night.

I USED TO HAVE PARTIES IN THE GARAGE, barbecues in the backyard. Jeffrey Lee Pierce dragged me to the big annual bash at Verbum Dei High School that always had really good music. The festival regularly received a nice write-up in *Los Angeles Times*. John Doe and Exene Cervenka from X, Chris Desjardins from the Flesh Eaters, the Alvin Brothers from the Blasters, people from *Back Door Man*, *Slash* magazine, and Ruby Records all went to see Clifton Chenier, the king of the Zydeco, and afterward we had a big party at my house.

Occasionally things would get out of hand. I had a summer barbecue where all of the guys in the Circle Jerks brought their girlfriends. We were hanging out in the back, grilling food and drinking beer. By one o'clock in the afternoon I was completely shitfaced. I ended up getting really upset about something, and instead of saying, "Hey, could you not do that?" I ended up kicking the barbecue over with all of the burning coals and scorched the grass in the backyard. Then I fell down on top of the coals and started rolling around. I don't know why I would be wearing a jean jacket in the summer, but thankfully I was and burned all kinds of holes in my jacket. Somebody stomped out all of the embers, and I started screaming and yelling. People were like, "We gotta get out of here!" Everybody split, including my girlfriend, KJ, who left with her best friend, Laura.

I was all by myself, completely wasted. My clothes were burnt, and my hands and face were covered in barbecue sauce and soot. I wanted a beer, but it was all gone. I decided to go to the store to get some more, but I couldn't even walk. That's how bad off I was. A normal person would have taken that as a sign that it was time to shut it down. But not me. I *crawled* to the liquor store. With my face streaked in soot and ash, I looked like a commando crawling behind enemy lines. I made it all the way to the village liquor store two blocks up the street and managed to purchase some adult beverages.

My night didn't end there, though. Somehow I managed to drive myself to Chinatown to catch a show at the Hong Kong Café. I have no idea who was playing, but my friends were all shocked to see me.

"You're not supposed to be here!"

"You didn't drive here, did you?"

"What the hell happened to you?!"

I looked like the barbecue blew up in my face—a complete mess.

Jeffrey didn't stay at the Pink House for too much longer after that. He'd fallen in love with Texacala Jones, and they would eventually start a band together called Tex and the Horseheads. Jeffrey was their first guitar player. He wanted to move up to Hollywood to be closer to all of the action. He was still writing for *Slash* and had to check in at their building on Beverly and Martel a couple of times a week.

After he left, I was on my own for a couple of months, and then I got another roommate, a guy named Jim who worked three days a week at Recycled Records on Pacific Coast Highway in Hermosa Beach. He was a big, tall, redheaded guy who looked like a basketball player, but he was very mellow like Jim Carroll, the poet who wrote *The Basketball Diaries*. Really cool guy. His sister went out with Gore Verbinsky, who played in a band called the Little Kings. Gore would go on to work in Hollywood and directed the *Pirates of the Caribbean* movies, so he's done pretty well for himself.

The only trouble I had living in Inglewood besides the commute to Hollywood was the time when KJ and I woke up at the Pink House to discover that the Chevy she'd just bought had been stolen. When it was time to contact the police and go through all of the rigmarole of reporting it stolen, I was like, "I'm not doing this! You handle it." I was too hungover, too coked out, or too whatever to deal with it. I didn't want anything to do with it. I left it up to her to sort it out. Zero moral support and a whole lot of attitude.

I've done some pretty fucked up things, but that sticks out because it was such a shitty thing to do. We didn't stay together for too much longer after that. There wasn't a fight or altercation or anything—we just fizzled out. She went her way, and I went mine.

GIN LING WAY

If Black Flag came along at the tail end of the second wave of LA punk, then the Circle Jerks were at the front of the next wave of hard-core bands from LA and Orange County. I was free to do as I pleased, and I made good on my promise to have fun. When we weren't partying in Inglewood I'd head up to Hollywood or Chinatown.

Lucky's apartment was right across the street from the Whisky, so that was our go-to spot in Hollywood. There were plenty of nights when all we'd do was grab a couple of six-packs, stand in front of the Whisky, and hang out with whoever was there. It didn't matter who was playing—punk rockers, new wavers, hair bands, whatever. It wasn't one of these, "You're this, and we're that, so we can't hang out" kind of deals. We were all a bunch of freaks.

We might end up drinking beer with the guys from Mötley Crüe, who lived right up the hill behind the Whisky and were really cool. At that time they were puffing up their hair and wearing makeup like the New York Dolls, only they'd kicked it up a couple of notches by wearing high heels. Not platform boots—they wore actual high heels, like something a fashion model would wear. It was totally outrageous.

One night Jeffery Lee Pierce and I found a dumpster on wheels behind the southwest corner of Sunset and San Vicente. We thought if we pushed it really fast and really hard, it would roll all the way down the hill to the sheriff's station on Santa Monica Boulevard four blocks away. Just to make sure the cars speeding through the intersections saw the dumpster coming, we decided to light its contents on fire. We lit the trash inside the dumpster and pushed it down the hill. We didn't stick around to see how far it went or if the dumpster made it all the way to the cop shop. We got the hell out of there. That was how we did things: we'd roll a flaming dumpster down a hill into traffic without a second thought about the consequences. We could be real assholes.

I also spent a lot of time partying in Chinatown. I'd go hang out in the pedestrian plaza in Gin Ling Way and smoke cigarettes and drink beers. Every once in a while Madame Wong would let someone play who'd played at the Hong Kong Café, but it usually ended in disaster. I think the Germs played Madame Wong's a couple of times, but they were the exception. The Go-Go's may have played there once, as did the Avengers from San Francisco and DOA from Vancouver. I think it was easier for punk bands to get a gig there if they were from out of town. The night the Bags played at Madame Wong's I remember watching Nickey Beat, the drummer for the Bags and the Weirdos, getting thrown down the stairs for some reason.

I never really got caught up in the rivalry between the two clubs. I'm a fan of music. I saw some great bands at Madame Wong's, like Los Lobos and the Plimsouls. A great band is a great band, no matter what labels are attached to it, but I'll admit there were plenty of nights when I had nothing better to do than hang out in the square and make fun of the poseurs going into Madame Wong's.

One night I bumped into Todd Haizman, the bass player for the Angry Samoans, in the alley behind the Hong Kong Café. He outweighed me by about seventy-five pounds, and he wanted to bash my skull in. I tried to find out what I'd done to make him so upset, and he accused the Circle Jerks of stealing an Angry Samoans' song. I told him I loved the Angry Samoans and had no idea what he was talking about. He calmed down a bit and we discussed it like adults over a couple of chilled beverages, and eventually we figured out what had happened.

Apparently, during our bass player's time as a member of the Angry Samoans, Roger had swiped a couple of riffs they had worked on and volunteered them to the Circle Jerks as his own. This was back when we were scrambling to come up with enough material to put a set together. After going through a similar deal with Black Flag and Red Cross, I understood why Todd was upset. I apologized to Todd and told him I had no idea that Roger had done what he'd done. Eventually we became really good friends.

On another occasion I was with Mike Ness, the front man for Social Distortion, and we were hanging out on Gin Ling Way outside the Hong Kong Café. It was a weeknight, a Tuesday or Wednesday, and we were drinking. We were sitting on the curb under a streetlight. A guy came walking up and started giving Mike an earful of shit. Back in those days Mike had a reputation as a brawler, and this kind of thing would happen from time to time. It was obvious the situation was going to escalate. I just stayed where I was, perfectly happy to not get involved, but Mike had heard enough.

Mike stood up to shut this guy up, and the guy clocked him. Mike's head snapped back and hit the lamppost with a hollow thud, and he crumpled to the ground. Out cold. The guy must have felt really good about himself because he stood over Mike and taunted him. When he got tired of spewing his macho bullshit he turned and walked away. I checked on Mike to see if he was still alive, and he started to come out of it. It didn't take long—it's not like he was seeing stars and hearing birds. All of a sudden Mike sprang to life. It was like something out a movie, where a switch is flipped and the dead come back to life. Mike jumped up and darted after the guy who'd sucker-punched him. He chased him through Chinatown and when he finally caught the guy, he just destroyed him.

You never knew who you would bump into or what you would see in Chinatown. Gin Ling Way was our home base, the place we'd go to find out where the party was and catch up with our friends. Who's got a record coming out? Who's going on tour? What bands are coming to LA, and where will they be playing?

I was partying in Venice Beach on the Fourth of July with Darby Crash, John Doe, and Chris Desjardins when we decided to go to

Chinatown. We got in the car and were driving along, and I wasn't feeling very good about the world and my place in it. I was completely inebriated, and the only thing keeping me upright was the copious amounts of white powder I'd snorted. I was barely coherent. For whatever ridiculous reason I thought it would be a good idea to jump out of the car and donate all of my organs to the Santa Monica Freeway. I opened the door and everyone panicked because we were flying down the freeway, but as I got ready to leap out, Darby reached over, grabbed my belt loop, and pulled me back inside the car. People thought of Darby as this effeminate David Bowie type of guy, but he was strong enough to haul my skinny ass back to safety. No question about it, Darby saved my life.

But I wasn't done yet. We made it to Chinatown and hung out in the square in Gin Ling Way. After a couple of hours we went into the Hong Kong Café. They let me in, but I was so wasted, they refused to serve me. I was running all over the place, yelling and screaming and calling the employees "gooks." That wasn't cool, and it wasn't right. Normally I'd never disrespect someone like that. Normally I wouldn't try to jump out of a moving vehicle. But it wasn't a normal night. I was babbling like an idiot, but my actions would catch up with me in a hurry.

I was running down the stairs to Gin Ling Way when I saw a bunch of cops coming up the stairs. It was one of those nights when they decided to put on their own fireworks display. The riot squad rolled up, and they were ready to crack some skulls and beat some ass.

I'm not getting involved in this, I thought.

I turned around and ran back through the club to go down the backstairs. As I opened the door, congratulating myself for being so clever, I saw the police were already lined up and waiting for me. Talk about instant karma!

The cops put me in the paddy wagon, and it was actually a pretty funny situation because there were about ten of us in the back of the wagon and nowhere to sit besides the wheel wells. So every time the driver hit the brakes or took a turn, all of the drunks would fall over each other. There was one guy who had a bottle of booze shoved down his pants that he wouldn't share, and every time there was a pileup on the floor of the wagon he'd get groped for the bottle. But I wasn't about to put my hand down some guy's pants for a bottle of booze. I was thirsty but not that thirsty.

The cops took us downtown to county jail. They put me in the drunk tank, which was a holding cell with padded walls and a rubber mat on the floor. They didn't want anybody keeling over and cracking his head open. I found a quiet corner, and then it was blackout time.

TDOWC

Not too long after I left Black Flag and got the Circle Jerks going, Penelope Spheeris got in touch with me about a project she was working on. I'd gotten to know her from hanging out at *Slash* headquarters. At the time Penelope was married to Bob Biggs, who'd bought out the original owner of *Slash* magazine and Slash Records. We weren't friends at the time, but we knew all of the same people.

"I'm making a movie," she said, "and I want to film Black Flag with you as the vocalist."

I scratched my head and told her that probably wasn't going to happen. They had a new vocalist, and I had a new band. Besides, the vibe from Black Flag wasn't very good. They *really* disliked me. Penelope was persistent. She insisted that it had to go down that way for Black Flag to be in her movie. Penelope persuaded me into going to see Greg Ginn and Chuck Dukowski and running the scenario by them. Reluctantly, I did what she asked me to do. If we hadn't been through all the things we'd been through in Black Flag, the two of them probably would have gotten together and beaten me to a pulp. As it was, they laughed me out of the room.

I went back to Penelope and told her the news: "If you want Black Flag, you have to film them with Ron Reyes."

I think she might have had a problem with Ron, but I don't know what the situation was. I just know that if she was going to put Black Flag in her movie, it was going to be without me.

That movie, of course, was *The Decline of Western Civilization*. I was in the audience when Black Flag played in a tiny little practice space across the street from where the Masque used to be. But I wasn't there to see Black Flag. I was there to see the Germs. Darby Crash and I had become pretty good friends—in addition to saving my life, he'd given me my Germs burn—and I had a feeling he would put on a pretty wild show for the cameras. He didn't disappoint. The show was pure chaos. Everything you'd expect from a Germs show and exactly the way you'd want it.

Penelope told me, "Keith, I want you to be in the movie too. I want to film the Circle Jerks."

I asked her who else she wanted and helped her put a bill together. It was the Alice Bag Band, Fear, the Gears, the Gun Club, the Urinals, and the Circle Jerks at the Fleetwood in Redondo Beach down in King Harbor. I think it was four or five bucks to get in. Not everybody on the bill made it into the movie. I think Penelope had a pretty good idea of who she wanted in *Decline* before the show even started, but I can't speak for her. I've heard rumors she'd filmed part of the Gun Club's performance. I know the Gears were extremely upset they weren't in the film.

To this day there are people who want to know why bands like the Plugz, the Screamers, and the Weirdos weren't involved in Penelope's project, but it was never supposed to be representative of the entire LA scene; it was just one person's vision. Thanks to *Slash*, Penelope had access to a great roster of bands, and I was honored to be a part of it, especially as the Circle Jerks were so new.

The performances in *Decline* filmed at the Fleetwood have a totally different South Bay vibe to them. It's definitely not a Hollywood show, although a lot of Hollywood punks came down to be in the movie— the allure of being immortalized on film was too great to resist.

Each band played a set. There weren't multiple takes or anything like that. Everyone was allotted the same amount of time. The Circle Jerks were able to squeeze more songs into our set because our songs were so short. Most bands played three songs. We played five or six.

The kids in the audience knew they were being filmed. Each band read a disclaimer before their set, and the audience was told that their likenesses could be used. If you don't like it, go hang out in the men's room. Consequently the energy of the crowd was really intense. People were jumping around, getting up on stage, and diving into the crowd. You had all these people doing wacky stuff they might not ordinarily do, which created problems for the bouncers. They weren't used to punk shows, and it was confusing for them to have to sort through what was cool and what was uncool. They were tossing people out left and right. At one point during our performance Greg Hetson chased down one of the bouncers on his side of the stage and tried to kick him, which I don't condone. He's lucky he didn't get pulled off the stage. It was a great show but kind of a hectic scene. Nothing we weren't used to.

ON DECEMBER 7, 1980, in between the filming of *TDOWC* and its release, Darby Crash overdosed and died. It was a strange situation because the poster for the movie had already been released, and it featured Darby lying prone on the stage in a kind of crucifixion pose: Darby was barely in the ground and he was already being made into a martyr. I'd been at the show and had seen him thrashing around on the stage—just Darby being Darby—but it was still really sad to see.

The Circle Jerks had a gig at the Starwood a couple of days after he'd passed away, and it was a really heavy show. Normally our shows were celebratory and fun. Not that night.

The Germs had broken up not long after the *Decline* shows, and Darby went to London for a while. When he came back he had experienced Ant Music from Adam and the Ants and had changed up his look, like a snake shedding his skin. And there was something sad about that too. The thing that had made the Germs amazing was that they were so unpredictable—Darby had really bad stage fright and had to get wasted to perform—but he was becoming more cliché by the day. There were times when I thought the Germs didn't really exist as a band but as a kind of performance art, an engine for generating chaos. I'd go see them, and maybe they'd get through a song and start up another one, but they seldom made it through the next one.

When Darby came back from London he started up the Darby Crash Band. Lucky actually played drums with him for a gig at the Starwood, but it didn't make the impact Darby was looking for and never really amounted to anything. Maybe he felt he'd been passed by. He was very literary and intelligent, but not on a street level. His passion was from the head, not the gut. Darby wasn't going to get in a van and go out on the road for two months. He didn't have the constitution to go out and play night after night. Maybe he realized that and decided to pull the plug.

Darby's overdose was intentional. He'd carefully orchestrated his death, but he was upstaged when John Lennon was shot and killed in New York the next day.

I think Darby had a built-in self-destruct mechanism. He was a big fan of David Bowie. Maybe the song "Five Years," the opening track on *The Rise and Fall of Ziggy Stardust and the Spiders from Mars*, instilled this idea in Darby that we only have so much time. Darby had his rise, but things changed after London. I think he knew his fall was coming. His heroin use was a sign that he was looking for a way out.

DARBY'S DEATH SEEMED TO SIGNAL a shift—if not in the scene itself, then at least in the way it was portrayed in the media. The music was getting faster and louder, and the people who came out to see us were more physical and aggressive. They brought a level of athleticism to the shows, and even though that sometimes resulted in violence, it was never about hurting people. But when that started to change, the media pounced.

The problem was that people from the outside looking in didn't understand what was going on. The parents and the teachers and the squares didn't know what they were looking at. When punk made the news all they talked about was the violence. Suddenly punk was this violent, dangerous thing that was ruining teenagers' lives. There were newspaper articles and news stories and even prime time TV shows, many of which were written and produced in LA, that associated punk with violence. There was no mention of the lyrics or the music or the message. The stories were all about how brutal the scene was and how punk rockers were Neanderthals who only went to shows to beat the crap out of each other.

Here's the thing: it *was* getting more violent. All the attention the media gave to punk rock for the wrong reasons attracted the wrong kind of people to the scene. Jocks, meatheads, and military guys who didn't understand the concept of slam dancing would come to the shows and throw themselves into the circle pit, looking to hurt people. These people would come to *our* shows and call *us* names. They'd call us "Devos," like *we* were the ones who didn't belong there. It made no sense.

First came the jocks, and then came the gangs. You had people from the beaches, people from the Valley, people from up in Oxnard, people from East LA. All of a sudden, when the LAPD came to thump heads at the punk show, they were encountering a totally different crowd: faster, stronger, and a hell of a lot meaner—and some of these guys fought back. Of course that meant more cops and more violence.

We played a show at the Stardust Ballroom on Sunset Boulevard, and the bill was Black Flag, Fear, the Circle Jerks, China White, and the Minutemen. Toward the end of the night, after Black Flag had played, my friend Derf Scratch, the bass player for Fear, got jumped by three knuckleheads. He ended up with two black eyes, a concussion, and fluid on the brain. The doctors had to poke a hole in his skull to get the swelling down so he wouldn't end up with permanent brain damage. There wasn't a confrontation or any kind of motive whatsoever—it was as random as it was senseless.

This went counter to what the Circle Jerks were all about. Our MO was, "Let's party." If you're gonna do what you're gonna do, take it out in the parking lot. We're not here to play the background music for your gang war.

NEW YORK CALLING

In spite of Darby's death, *Decline* painted a picture of LA as a thriving punk rock scene, but in reality the situation wasn't particularly good. The LAPD were romping and stomping and kicking ass. A lot of the venues were getting shut down, and those that stayed open got tired of the hassle and banned punk bands from playing. The writing was on the wall: if you wanted to have any kind of chance at making a go at being in a punk band, you had to hit the road. For whatever reason this was something the majority of bands in our scene didn't know how to do.

When Penelope presented us with the opportunity to be in *The Decline of Western Civilization* we thought it would be a cool thing to represent our scene in LA. We had no idea it would lead to opportunities outside of it.

Decline was our business card and demo tape sent out to all of these other places around the country. For the first time, people who'd only read about the punk scene in LA or heard somebody talk about it were able to see and hear what was going down. This is what a punk show looks like. This is what it sounds like. This is how you dress. This is how you dance.

It seems bizarre that people took a movie about punk rock so seriously, but they did. We're a lot savvier now. Most people have wised up to the fakery of reality TV and news as entertainment, but this was pre-MTV, pre-*Real World*, pre-Internet. *Decline* opened doors for us we would have never been able to open on our own. When *Group Sex* came out, we didn't really have a tour to speak of—just a few gigs here and there. Our idea of touring was getting in the van and driving down to San Diego or out to Riverside or up to the Valley. I think we may have done a few shows in San Francisco. But *The Decline of Western Civilization* introduced a lot of the bands who had never traveled outside their zip code to the rest of the world and allowed them to tour from city to city and town to town.

After *Decline*, one promoter wanted to fly us out to New York for a handful of shows. This was something that happened to rock stars, not to bands like the Circle Jerks. Of course we wanted to go, but we almost didn't make it. Less than a week before we were supposed to leave, Lucky's girlfriend's car was stolen while it was parked outside his place in West Hollywood. Lucky was able to track down the guy who stole it. He went into his house, got in a fight with the thief, and broke all the knuckles on one of his hands while doing it.

I don't care how much of a badass you are, you can't play drums with a busted hand. I'd seen Arthur Killer Kane play bass with a cast on. It didn't really slow him down. You can get away with that if you're a bass player, but for a drummer, it just doesn't work. So here we were, with our first big break, and it looked like we were going to have to cancel the trip. The three of us—Greg, Roger, and myself—agreed that the opportunity was too important. We had to find a way to make it happen. I asked my friend Charlie Quintana from the Plugz if he would fill in, and he agreed. We rehearsed once and flew out the next day.

We played at Irving Plaza with the Stimulators and the Necros. That was the first time I met Harley Flanagan, who bashed drums in the Stimulators and would eventually become the bass player in the Cro Mags. At that time he was probably about twelve years old.

John Belushi was there too, and he really enjoyed the show. He hung out with us afterward in the little dressing room. He wanted to know if we had any 45s so he could put our music in the jukebox in the bar Dan Aykroyd owned. John Belushi told me, "I love what you guys are doing, and I want you to be on *Saturday Night Live*."

That was a pretty big deal because at that particular time the actors on *Saturday Night Live* were able to pick the bands they wanted on the show. That famously fell apart after Fear played and their performance turned into a riot. All of these kids had bussed up from Washington, DC, and ran amok in the studio. They started knocking things over, acting like a bunch of wild hoodlums, and, consequently, fucking things up for other punk bands.

Next we played the 9:30 Club in Washington, DC, with Minor Threat. I think it was one of their first half-dozen shows. Ian MacKaye had laryngitis, so he'd taped a piece of paper to the front of his shirt that said, "I can't talk so don't ask me any questions." Something like that. I remember him shaking hands with everybody and nodding his head. When they played they were fantastic, even with Ian's voice as wrecked as it was. You didn't need a pretty singing voice for what we were doing. In fact, you needed the exact opposite.

Our next show was back in New York at a place called the Mudd Club. It was a little bit ritzier than Irving Plaza, but nobody showed up except the employees and Cheetah Chrome. Cheetah Chrome happens to be one of my favorite guitar players. That first Dead Boys album is untouchable. We started playing, and there was absolutely nothing going on in the club except Cheetah running around, gathering up all of the tables and chairs, and piling them in front of the stage like he was building a bonfire. He had this wild look on his face like he was a nine-year-old kid getting ready to torch the place. He kept jumping up on stage. He'd run over to the guitar amps and turn the knobs all the way to the right to one less than eleven.

We'd stop in between songs to drink some beer and adjust our amps, and when we started up again Cheetah would be back onstage cranking the knobs. Of course, no one told him to cut it out. I wasn't going to tell Cheetah Chrome to stop what he was doing. You don't tell a guy of that stature what he can or can't do. Plus, he looked like a maniac crazed on methamphetamine. He added some excitement to what would have been a really boring show. He was entertaining the entertainers.

YOU'RE PROBABLY THINKING THAT my relationship with Black Flag was pretty toxic at this point, but that wasn't the case. We'd shared the stage a couple of times, and on more than one occasion they asked me to fill in for Ron Reyes, their second vocalist, when he had quit the band. They'd booked a show at the Fleetwood with the Subhumans from Vancouver. I don't remember who else was on the bill, but I filled in for Ron. Shortly after that, we got in the van and drove up to San Francisco to play on a bill with Geza X and the Mommymen at the Mabuhay Gardens. My old friend Brendan Mullen was playing drums.

We pulled up to the club and unloaded our gear. After the bands finished their sound checks everybody was chitchatting and bullshitting and shooting the breeze. Chuck wanted to go do something. I guess Brendan had had his fill of the guys in his band on the drive up to San Francisco because he decided to hang out with Black Flag instead.

For as long as I'd known Brendan I didn't know him as a person all that well. We'd never really hung out as peers before. As we drove around San Francisco we got to talking and he told me that although he was highly skeptical of me at first, Black Flag was his favorite band from the Los Angeles punk scene. We would eventually become good friends. In fact, Brendan was the one who convinced me that I needed to write this insanely bitchin' book that you're reading.

I had no regrets about my time in Black Flag, nor did I regret leaving. If I had to do it all over again, I don't think I'd change a thing. I did what I wanted to do, and when I didn't want to do it anymore I got out. What's wrong with that?

That doesn't mean I don't sometimes wonder what it might have been like if I'd remained with the band when they achieved their full potential. I don't even know if they knew what their full potential was. I could have done some of the things Black Flag went on to do. I wasn't afraid to get in the van. I could get by on five dollars a day. I just didn't want to hang out with those guys anymore. They were no longer my friends. But that doesn't mean I have a vendetta against the band.

I was friends with Ron Reyes and Dez Cadena before they became the second and third vocalists for Black Flag. I never saw Dez when he was the vocalist, so I can't speak to his performance, but a lot of fans feel he was the best, and I respect the opinions of those who feel that way. Ron was only in the band for six months. During Ron's time in Black Flag they did a full-blown recording session. Someone close to the band told me they wanted to release a full-length album but they didn't have enough quality material. So they took the five best songs and put that out as the *Jealous Again* EP. This wasn't an ideal situation for the band because their first two records were EPs with two different vocalists, neither of whom was with the band anymore. It's hard to break out and build a following that way.

I love Ron like a younger brother. I have the utmost respect for everyone who was in the band with me and all the members who came after. When Henry Rollins joined the band, things slowly started to change for Black Flag. It took a little time; it didn't happen overnight. I went to see Black Flag with Henry at the helm at the Olympic Auditorium, and I left before they finished their set. I walked out the door, shaking my head.

"That was fucking horrible. I can't believe I used to be a part of that."

I might sound like an arrogant asshole at times, but I put in my time. I dodged the beer bottles, dealt with the threats, and put up with my share of drama—just like everybody else. As one of the founding members, I get to have an opinion.

That changed after I saw Black Flag play at the Cathay de Grande at Argyle and Selma in Hollywood. It was an early Sunday evening show when there couldn't have been more than twenty people in the room, and they fucking destroyed the place. Black Flag played with the power and energy of an atomic bomb. If you harnessed that energy, you could have blown up all of Hollywood and leveled the entire town. That's how great they were. I was yelling and screaming and jumping around like a monkey with an M80 shoved up its ass. They were beyond amazing, and when it was over I was jealous. I wasn't jealous like, *That should be me up there.* I was jealous because not only did Henry get to be part of Black Flag when they achieved the promise I always knew they'd had but because he was instrumental in bringing it out. It was also strangely validating, like I could be proud of my time in the band again. Of course, that was just one peak in my roller-coaster ride with Black Flag, and what goes up usually comes down . . .

WILD IN THE STREETS

The Circle Jerks were an unusual band in that we didn't have a leader. After my experiences with Black Flag, I wasn't interested in going on another ego trip, nor did I want to be the guy doing the ego tripping. It was a one-for-all and all-for-one kind of deal. No one had any more say than anyone else in the band. A punk rock democracy without an executive branch. But that didn't mean we didn't have our share of drama.

All bands have guys who are go-getters and guys who are the opposite of that. Lucky was our go-getter. Even though he was the only one who'd never been in a band before joining the Circle Jerks, he was a highly motivated individual who had plans to enroll in law school. He was the only one who had any kind of vision beyond what we were doing. As for the opposite, that would be Roger. There was always some kind of outside drama with him. Why are you late to rehearsal again? Why do you have three strings on your bass guitar when you're supposed to have four? What do you mean your car ran out of gas again?

At this point in time we were all going as fast as we could, running hard and partying harder. Our mentality was to go for it, whatever "it" might be. Like dropping in on a wave or hitting the half-pipe on a skateboard. Maybe something amazing will happen. Maybe you'll splatter all over the place. You won't find out sitting on the sidelines, and no one can say you didn't try. So go for it. Do some damage. This mentality put me in a nonleadership role. We were all along for the ride together, and we were equally committed to taking it as far as we could.

In our own half-assed way we started writing material for a new album, hacking away here and there. We didn't have a plan for what it would sound like or how it would be different from *Group Sex*. There was no thought process, no artistic vision beyond, "Let's make a rec– ord." We didn't sit around and say, "This record's gonna be darker" or "This record's gonna be poppier" or "This record's gonna have horns and a synth player and string section." There was none of that. Let's just write the songs, and then we'll take it from there.

We were approached by John Gueneri, who was the A&R guy for Faulty Products, which was a division of I.R.S. Records. How he heard about us is a pretty convoluted story. After *The Decline of Western Civilization* came out, we hired Gary Hirstius to manage us. Gary was a sound guy in Hollywood who worked with bands like X, the Plugz, and the Flesh Eaters in places like the Starwood and the Masque. He did the sound for many of the *Decline* shows and recorded the soundtrack for the movie. He's listed as a coproducer on the soundtrack. In fact, he has a brief cameo. He's in the scene where he meets with all of the security guys, explaining the difference between acceptable violence and unacceptable violence. The bouncers would see all these punk rockers rolling around in what looked like a mas- sive gang fight and feel like they needed to step in and punch some- body's light outs. Gary was the one who gave them a crash course on punk rock behavior. Of course, you still had a few overzealous types, guys with daddy issues who got kicked off the football team or flunked out of the police academy and needed to take their frustrations out on somebody.

Gary had developed a relationship with David Anderle at A&M Records, and Gary invited David to come see us play at the Starwood. It was a pretty wild, no-holds-barred show. Afterward David pulled me aside and said, "I need to record you before you kill yourself!" I think he intended that as a compliment. He compared me to Jim

Morrison, which is something these record company executives like to do to make you feel like you're special. I don't know why he picked Jim Morrison, maybe he could see that I was on the same destructive path as the Lizard King or maybe I was channeling Iggy Pop, who I loved and was most certainly influenced by Mr. Morrison.

I don't think David thought we were A&M material, so he probably went to I.R.S., whose releases were distributed by A&M, and I.R.S. hooked us up with Faulty Products, which was kind of like their farm league, if that. Nevertheless, it seemed like a good fit for us. The Circle Jerks were picking up steam, and although it didn't make sense for us to be on a major label, there were things that A&M and I.R.S. could do for us. At least that's what we hoped for at the time. But we caught a lot of flak through the punk rock grapevine for "selling out." It's not like we had a huge payday and were suddenly buying houses and filling up our garages with new cars—far from it. I think people were expecting a slick, overproduced record, which ended up not being the case.

While we were getting ready to go into the studio, Faulty Products hooked us up with a rehearsal space on the old S.I.R. lot on Sunset Boulevard. We were in one of the smaller rooms, and there weren't any other bands in the space. After several weeks of working our asses off and rehearsing every day for five hours, the studio manager came in and said, "Pack up your stuff. You have to leave. We can't have you in here anymore."

What had happened was the night before, one of the people at S.I.R.—either Jan or Dean from Jan and Dean—got drunk, let himself into one of the rooms that had a grand piano in it, and just started bashing away, detuning and damaging the piano in the process. The people at S.I.R. figured it had to be the punk rock guys, because that's what punk rockers do. Of course, we had nothing to do with it. We knew better than to mess around with equipment that didn't belong to us. We were grateful to be able to rehearse in a place where we could actually hear what we were doing, but we were guilty by reputation.

David Anderle's role in the situation was to get us recording time at A&M studios. We were in a room that was the size of a sixteen-car garage—and that was one of the smaller ones. David was involved in the production of the record, but he didn't turn any of the knobs and didn't offer up any suggestions or recommendations. He didn't bring anything creative to the table. He just nodded his head a lot. Our manager, Gary Hirstius, did the recording. He was the guy who sat at the board.

We basically recorded *Wild in the Streets* live. Gary had never worked on a record before. He was a live sound engineer. His approach to recording an album was to treat it like a gig: load in, set up, play the show, pack up, go home. That's what he knew, and that's why the record turned out the way it did.

Wild in the Streets took less than a day to make. The entire album was recorded and mixed in twenty-one hours. We may have recorded the album in a major label studio, but it sure didn't sound like it. That said, I don't know if we needed to be in the studio for much longer than that because the weeks of practice leading up to it were so grueling. We played those songs over and over and over again in rehearsal until they were burned into our brains. When we got to A&M Studios we weren't standing around looking at each other, trying to figure out what to do. We were ready.

People ask me what my favorite song is on this album or that album. I don't really pay attention to that. I don't have a lot of ego when it comes to songs and records. When you listen to your own stuff you're always second-guessing yourself. Why did we record it that way? Why didn't we bend the note here? Why was my vocal approach this way as opposed to that way? Why did we push this part down and bring that part up? Why am I even in a band?

It's that way with every record. I go back and listen to it, and rather than enjoy the music, I'm thinking about what I could have done differently: *I could have done this. I should have done that.* I'm never completely satisfied. I try to treat each recording like a time capsule, a statement about a particular moment in time. That's all it is. I can't change the past, and I have no interest in living in it, so I don't spend a lot of time listening to my own stuff. A record is a representation of time, nothing less and nothing more.

That's especially true of the cover photo for *Wild in the Streets*, which was taken in San Francisco. The night before the shoot, we announced from the stage at On Broadway, which was a little club above Mabuhay Gardens, that we were going to do a photo shoot for our new album and anyone who wanted to be in it was welcome to come. As it turned out, there was a big parade going on with the National Guard and the Army Marching Band and military guys in full regalia with their shiny helmets and fancy decorative rifles.

To get the shot we wanted, we ended up crashing the parade and marching along behind the band. It looks like we're on a deserted street but actually there were people everywhere. Punks were darting around, banging on the soldier's helmets. I was yelling, "People, you're not supposed to be doing that!" The soldiers showed a lot more restraint than we did.

The photo features a mix of San Francisco, LA, and Orange County punks. The guys in the Circle Jerks are in black and white and everyone else is in color. One of the most prominent is Mike Ness, whose band Social Distortion had played with us the night before. A couple of our roadies are in the shot, and the rest are San Francisco punkers.

When *Wild in the Streets* came out we were actually starting to get in the van and go out and play every bar or nightclub that would have us. We hit all the major cities and had some pretty memorable shows. Occasionally we'd play a VFW hall here or a Moose Lodge there. I remember playing a show in the Deep South where some of our fans actually broke into the glass display cases and pulled out the muskets and swords and started "fighting" in the reception area. All sorts of knuckleheaded goofiness.

But we were in the van, out there doing it, working our asses off. Our "tour" was really just a series of one-offs with long gaps in between. We weren't picky. We'd play anywhere. I remember driving sixteen hours to play a bar out by an airport in Memphis. It was in the middle of a deserted parking lot next to a FedEx terminal. There was sand in the parking lot, and the interior had been redone to look like a beach scene because the Ventures had played the night before and the place had been jam-packed with people.

When we played, it cost $3 to get in and six people were in attendance. It was disappointing, but mostly we were excited to have these opportunities to play. If the bar was twenty-one and over, and most of them were, we'd convince them to open a couple of hours early and not serve any booze so the kids could come in. Of course, that meant playing two shows a night, which could get pretty grueling, but we didn't care. We were doing what we wanted to do.

WORLD UP MY ASS

We had our first line-up change when things started to go sideways with Faulty Products. I.R.S. was owned by Miles Copeland. His brother Ian owned a booking agency called F.B.I., and his other brother Stewart was the drummer for the Police, and I don't mean the LAPD. Their dad, at one time, was the head of the CIA. So you had the I.R.S., the F.B.I., the Police, and the CIA. Looking back, it was kind of an omen, a sign that we were about to get screwed. Miles Copeland came to us and said, "We want you to record in England!"

The International Record Syndicate had a recording studio in London, and they had a two-story flat with a recording studio on the bottom floor and a living area upstairs. The plan was that while we were making our next record, we would live in London and a have a jolly good time.

This presented a problem. Lucky couldn't go. He'd reached a point in his pursuit of a law degree where he couldn't leave the country indefinitely. So we had to make a decision, and we decided to move forward without Lucky. It was a mutual agreement. Lucky didn't want to hold us back, and we couldn't wait on him to finish law school. We were trying to pay our bills by playing in a band and barely scraping by. At this point Roger was living in my garage, Greg and Lucky were temping at a law office in Beverly Hills, and occasionally Roger and I would get a law firm job. Of course, I was still working for my dad.

There's nothing like working in the bait business to keep you hungry and humble.

My dad didn't really get what I was trying to do with music, which I kind of understand. I didn't get it either, but at least he was starting to accept that maybe it wasn't a complete waste of time. His friends kept him informed about what I was up to and what I was doing. My dad always had friends in high places, people who were at the top of their field. They would call him up or swing by the shop and tell my dad that he needed to pay attention to what I was doing, that the Circle Jerks were doing interesting things and moving up in the ranks. They would recite lyrics to him and not in a derogatory way.

One of my dad's friends, John Napoli, was like an older brother to me. John lived with my dad while he was in law school. He took up space on the couch and would eat all the food in the refrigerator. He was also responsible for a Circle Jerks song. We were driving to go pick up some sandwiches in the neighborhood. He was always under a lot of stress, a lot of pressure, and he drove like it. He was tearing out of the parking lot and almost hit another car.

"Hey," I said to him. "You need to calm down before you get us killed!"

I'll never forget what he said to me, and I'm guessing you won't be able to either, as his response was the inspiration for one of our songs.

"I can't," he said.

"Why not?"

"Because I've got the world up my ass!"

ROGER TOOK IT UPON HIMSELF TO CHOOSE our next drummer, a friend of his from Kansas City, a twenty-two-year-old kid named John Ingram. He was a good drummer, but he was no Lucky Lehrer, which wasn't his fault, but that's the way it was. He was brought into a situation he really had no business being a part of. If I had been paying more attention, I probably wouldn't have picked John to play with us, but we were dealing with the Miles Copeland situation, and the next thing we knew, John showed up from Kansas City ready to play. So he was in.

We had another meeting with Miles Copeland and a guy named Gene October, who was the lead singer of a band called Chelsea. I wasn't really a fan of their music and even less so of Mr. October, especially when he started to tell me that the Circle Jerks were going to open up for Chelsea on their first American tour. I wasn't too thrilled about that. We'd been hitting the road for three solid years and had been all over the country. Yeah, we'd played some shitholes with a dozen people in the audience, but in the major cities we could get two to three hundred people, and in New York and Los Angeles those numbers swelled to four to five hundred. All of a sudden this bloke from England with his mediocre band no one had really heard of was telling us we're going to open for *him*?

I told Mr. October and Miles Copeland we weren't interested, and that was the end of our relationship with Faulty Products. Just like that, we were out of a record deal.

There were a lot of changes in the air. When our manager, Gary Hirstius, got busy with other gigs, we replaced him with a woman named Amber who was living with Don Kirk, the guitarist of the Flesh Eaters. Her claim to fame was her relationship with Darby Crash. She was the one who financed Darby's trip to London. Whenever we'd go see her she'd answer the door in a wheelchair. Her boyfriend would wheel her around the apartment like some freak scene straight out of a David Lynch or Andy Warhol movie. She wasn't disabled, but she was about four feet tall and built like a bowling ball with black hair, giving her the appearance of a member of the Munsters or the Addams Family. She helped us get gigs, but we still did most of the work. We were getting the majority of our shows on our own, so we thought, *Why give up a chunk of the earnings?*

Around this time I was spending a lot of time with Charlie Quintana, who'd filled in on drums during our first tour, if you can call it that. The Plugz were morphing into the Cruzados and getting ready to sign a major label deal. They were being handled by Far Out

Management, who had their own record label called LAX, which was owned by Jerry Goldstein. Goldstein had been a member of the Strangeloves and helped write, "My Boyfriend's Back." He also wrote "I Want Candy," which Bow Wow Wow made famous. They also put out all of WAR's albums, and they had the gold records lining the hallways to prove it.

In Southern California there wasn't a bigger band than WAR. Every time they put out a record, there would be three or four hits off of it. Granted, it wasn't a nationwide thing, but with the low-rider population in Southern California, they were the soundtrack to car culture. They were untouchable.

Far Out had one of Charlie Chaplin's old soundstages next to the Guitar Center in West Hollywood. The Cruzados would rehearse there on this amazing sound system, and there was always plenty of blow. Naturally, that got my attention.

It was a very appealing set-up. I saw how well my friends were being treated, and I started thinking, *This is where* we *need to be.* So I asked Charlie if I could approach Jerry Goldstein about signing with Far Out Management, and he said, "Go for it!"

I talked to Jerry, and he was interested. After telling him what the Circle Jerks were all about, we had a record deal. When I wasn't down in Inglewood, I was couch surfing around Hollywood. Far Out set me up in a seminotorious house in the Hollywood Hills. It was a tacky two-story faux pagoda with white shag carpet in every room, an elevator that took you from the garage up to the living room, and an indoor/outdoor pool. Its previous owner was a dentist who hosted wild orgies. All of the rooms in the house were equipped with cameras, and he'd perv out in his bedroom and monitor what was going on in the various rooms in his fuck palace. He ended up getting shot and killed during an argument over a parking space outside of a drug store.

The person I dealt with on a daily basis was this big boisterous guy. He was very much a party animal with a seemingly never-ending supply of cocaine. In other words, he was my kind of guy. Somehow I'd stumbled into a record deal, a place to stay, and a coke connection. It all seemed too good to be true.

As a management team, Far Out should have been in cahoots with a booking agent and setting up places for us to play. That wasn't happening. They told us they only dealt with bands capable of getting their own shows. Instead of getting us gigs, they encouraged us to finish writing the material for our new album. But creatively I was having trouble. The songs weren't coming, and I was lacking inspiration. While some of our contemporaries like the Minutemen and Hüsker Dü were writing two and three albums a year, we were on a much slower schedule. I was partying a lot and caught up in my own thing. Songwriting simply wasn't a priority.

Here we were with this great opportunity, with gold records on the wall and a hit-maker in the studio, and I wasn't able to get things going. I was surrounded by all the trappings of financial success in the music industry, things that should have inspired me, and instead it had the opposite effect. I was starstruck and struggling.

Eventually our handler took me to a workshop inside the soundstage where they brought all of their cocaine and stepped on it with Mannite, a substance used in an Italian baby laxative. Sometimes they would send me to the head shop to buy snow princess or arctic queen or whatever else they were going to cut the coke with. At night he'd go and sell it to the drunks at the Cat and Fiddle up in Laurel Canyon and make stops at various parties in the Hollywood Hills. Occasionally I'd go on these excursions with him. We never went any earlier than 1:30 a.m. to make sure the people were completely wasted when they were buying our shitty product. I never did any of the selling, but he made me part of the pitch: "We're managing Keith and his band. Have you ever heard of the Circle Jerks? They're amazing!"

He'd give me a bip and a bap here and there to keep my attention. I have no idea if Far Out knew about these late-night excursions, but I never stopped and asked myself, *If this guy is such hot-shit, why does he need to sell drugs?* I was so strung out that it never occurred to me to ask.

At this point I was a full-blown cokehead. I'd always used cocaine to get my party going, but during this period of my life I was whited out for three-quarters of the day. I wasn't just flirting with Tinker Bell; I was a full-on fiend. I'd start the day by walking down the hill with maybe six or seven bucks in my pocket. I'd go to the soundstage. Maybe somebody would buy me a cheeseburger next door at the Sunset Grill, the same place the Eagles sang about in that shitty song. Maybe I'd work on some lyrics or rehearse for a while. Maybe I'd hitch a ride back to Inglewood with John Ingram, who was renting one of the rooms in the Pink House. Maybe I'd crash at the fuck palace. After our handler chopped up the blow in the kitchen and headed up to the Cat and Fiddle, I'd scrape the counter for whatever residue was left over. If someone had been careless with their bag, I'd get down on my hands and knees and sift through the shag carpet, this long white wannabe yak fur, looking for specks and pebbles and shiny particles— anything that might be cocaine. I'd add it to the pile on the kitchen counter, and it would all go up my nose. There was always a couple of six-packs in the fridge, so I'd drink until I passed out, catch a few hours of sleep, and get up to do it all over again.

GOLDEN SHOWER
OF HITS

I had an idea for a song. What if we took a bunch of popular tunes, the sappiest, most unpunk songs we could find, and strung them together in a way so that they told a much darker story?

A medley. No punk rock band had ever done a medley before.

We started cobbling bits and pieces of songs together, the cheesier the better. We started with "Along Comes Mary" by the Association, followed by "(They Long to Be) Close to You" by the Carpenters and "Afternoon Delight" by the Starland Vocal Band to tell the story of two people falling in love. Then shit got real with "(You're) Having My Baby" by Paul Anka, "Love Will Keep Us Together" by the Captain & Tennille, and "D-I-V-O-R-C-E" by Tammy Wynette. It was the perfect story of boy meets girl, girl gets pregnant, boy and girl split up. The quintessential American drama. We called it "Golden Shower of Hits."

I also came up with the concept for the album cover, which features a bunch of gold records in a urinal. In case you didn't get the double meaning from the song, that picture sealed the deal. Just to make sure nobody missed the joke, we took it another step further by having Roger piss on the records in an actual urinal in the bathroom at Far Out Management headquarters. For the record, those are actual gold records in the pisser. We took a bunch of WAR's records off the wall and out of their frames, jammed them in the urinal, and Roger hosed them down.

The songs were starting to come together, and we slowly got them recorded in the built-in studio at the soundstage. It was a lengthy process, the opposite of our previous record. Far Out brought in an engineer whose big claim to fame was he'd worked on a couple of Grateful Dead albums. That should have sent us running for the hills. He was a tinkerer. He had a special technique for this and an unorthodox method for that. I really couldn't have cared less; I just wanted to get the album done, but the recording dragged on and on and on.

Around this time the Plugz pulled the plug on their relationship with Far Out Management. They complained that they weren't progressing as a band and that Far Out was holding them back. There were other red flags. I'd heard that Far Out Productions had been cheating WAR out of their royalties for years, and we might be next in line.

The smart thing to do would have been to follow the Plugz out the door, but we didn't. The cocaine helped sustain the illusion that we were on the verge of something amazing. I knew the fancy soundstage and the gold records on the wall were props, but I kept walking around in a stupor, wondering when the party was going to get rolling, waiting for our own shower of hits to fall out of the sky.

ONCE WE FINISHED RECORDING THE ALBUM it was pretty obvious that John Ingram was not the guy we wanted to be playing in the band. Roger had lured him out with a Hollywood fantasy of Playboy bunnies and Hustler honeys. But it didn't turn out that way. John had bought Greg's little yellow truck, was dating one of the secretaries who worked at Far Out Management, and was living with me. Everything was intertwined. He probably came to the realization that he wasn't going to elevate himself out of his position. If anything, I was a role model for someone going in the opposite direction, a poster boy for the downward spiral. John was with the band for the year or so it took us to write and record *Golden Shower of Hits*, and then I asked him to leave, which must have been as awkward for him as it was for me because I was also his landlord.

This situation probably would have caused more of a stir if Roger hadn't had his own substance abuse issues. He overdosed and was rushed to the hospital. He ended up in the red blanket room at USC, which is where they put people who are on suicide watch. Thankfully he pulled through, and we went to see him in the hospital. We were in there chatting with him, asking how he was doing, and the whole time there was some guy in the next bed crying at the top of his lungs. He'd tried to commit suicide by drinking Drano, and it had burned through his organs. The surgeons had to cut a hole in his side and insert a vacuum pump. Judging from the way this guy was carrying on, I'm guessing he felt as horrible as he sounded. Moral of the story: don't drink Drano.

I'm not sure I ever heard what Roger overdosed on. It was a probably a combo of heroin and cocaine, whiskey and beer, maybe throw in some pills. I really don't know. I didn't mess around with needles, and Roger knew not to involve me in that. We were struggling to keep our heads above water, so if there were warning signs that Roger was on the verge of going under, I missed them.

Roger was never the same after he ODed. He wasn't able to get his bearings. The experience took something out of him, changed him somehow. He was really fragile and would trip and fall over a matchbook on the sidewalk. It was painfully obvious that Roger wasn't going to be able to play bass again. He just didn't have the oomph to hammer down on the bass. He was, however, capable of playing guitar, and we suggested he come back in that capacity, but we were going to need a new bass player.

First I had to find a new drummer. I recruited Chuck Biscuits, who had also done a brief stint with Black Flag. Chuck established himself as the drummer for DOA and many consider him to be one of the best punk rock drummers to ever sit behind a kit. Period. He would go on to play long stints with Danzig and Social Distortion.

Chuck was the complete opposite of Lucky, who could sit down with any jazz or swing band and hold his own. Chuck was more in the John Bonham or Keith Moon mold. He drummed like he was trying to hammer his way to China. The thing Chuck did that made him so special was he reversed the roles of the kick drum and the snare. He looked like a madman back there. At the time he was dating punk rock princess Michelle Gerber Bell, and he moved into Far Out's fake fuck palace with me.

For the bass I turned to a guy from the South Bay. Earl Liberty's real name is Mark Vidal, and his father was a famous Cuban percussionist. Earl was from Redondo Beach, and his dad and my dad were old friends who'd hang out at the Lighthouse from time to time. I didn't know Earl that well, but being from the South Bay, we kept tabs on each other, and I knew he had just left the SST band Saccharine Trust. He was floating around, looking for another opportunity when I asked him to join the band.

The infusion of new blood was invigorating, and we were excited to hit the road as a five-piece—a first for the Circle Jerks. We played a few gigs together and were finally ready to go on tour to support *Golden Shower of Hits*, but Far Out Management was nowhere to be found. They didn't disappear, but they didn't offer up much in the way of support. We were virtually on our own.

A lot of the bands that came up with us in the LA scene didn't go out on the road like we did. The celebrity of bands like Black Flag, which put out all of their own albums without major label support, can be attributed to their widespread touring. Touring had become part of our DNA, but a lot of bands were hometown heroes who didn't have the vision or wherewithal to take their show on the road. They didn't take Henry Rollins's advice and get in the van. Some of the bands we looked up to when we were starting out never made it out of Southern California.

We set up a short tour while we figured out what to do. It was immediately apparent that Roger had changed and not for the better. The first thing he did was fly his girlfriend out to join us, so now there were six of us in the van. Between the gear and the merch and a half dozen people, it was a sardine can. That would have been fine, except Roger had this new attitude that everybody was supposed to stay the fuck out of his way, and his girlfriend wasn't much better. He seemed to think that he should be the one calling the shots. He was basically acting like a completely different person, and he was unbearable to be around.

It was a toxic situation. There were no rock stars in the Circle Jerks; everybody pulled his own weight and everybody got an equal share. So one morning we gathered at the van without Roger and drove off. We just left him at the motel and continued the tour without him. He and his girlfriend flew home.

A week later he somehow got ahold of one of the band members on the telephone and said, "I'm coming back! Pick me up at the airport!" Whoever was talking to him said, "No, we're not doing that. There's no reason for you to fly out here. You'd be better off just staying where you are."

At first Roger seemed to take it pretty well. At the end of the tour he met up with us at the house in the hills and crashed with us for a few nights. It was a fairly loose situation, with party people coming and going. However, he was still holding a grudge, and when the opportunity presented itself, he drove off in the van. It wasn't even his van anymore—we'd bought it from his dad before the tour. He took it and drove off into the sunset, and we never saw that van again.

I CAN'T BELIEVE
I USED TO LIKE THESE GUYS

When Alex Cox offered the Circle Jerks a role in his movie *Repo Man* we didn't even think about saying no. There was no pay involved—just food and beer—but that wasn't a consideration.

Alex asked us to participate because he was a fan of our music. He knew what we were about. He knew we were an us-against-the-world kind of band, and that fit with his vision for the movie. All of the musicians on the soundtrack were bands he had in his record collection, bands he'd seen perform live. Some of the acts may not have been familiar to the rest of the world, but they were familiar to us. It was a very LA soundtrack.

We had a whole new rhythm section, with Chuck Biscuits on drums and Earl Liberty playing bass, and we were eager to play—anywhere, anytime. We have two songs on the soundtrack, both from the new record: "Coup D'état" and "When the Shit Hits the Fan." Alex wanted an acoustic version of "When the Shit Hits the Fan," so we recorded one for the movie. They blocked out time in a recording studio down in West LA, and we went in and recorded it. I did the vocals, and Greg, Earl, and Chuck all played acoustic guitar along to a taped drum track. It was our first—and last—recording session with that lineup. The irony is that it's the only recording of Chuck Biscuits's time in the Circle Jerks, one of the best rock drummers in the world, and he's playing acoustic guitar accompanied by a drum machine.

Our scene in *Repo Man* was filmed at a tiny little bar with a stage in the back on Sunset Boulevard in Silver Lake. It was the middle of summer, and we had to be there at ten in the morning to be fitted for the tuxedos we wore in our scene. We were told we couldn't remove the tuxedos because they used straight needles for the custom fitting. They stuck us in a trailer and told us to wait. The air conditioning wasn't working, and it was like a hot box in there. All of us were hung over because we'd all partied the night before, and it was close to 110 degrees.

It was torture. The deal was there would be beer and free food, but the beer supply was very limited. We were told we could have a beer or two but not an entire six-pack and definitely not a case. "We need to be able to film you. You have to be able to shoot your scene." Obviously that was a smart move on their part.

While we were in hurry-up-and-wait mode, Zander Schloss, who plays Kevin, Otto's coworker at the grocery store who sings the "Feeling 7-Up" song in the movie, showed up and introduced himself. Zander was in the band Juicy Bananas, which was also on the *Repo Man* soundtrack. I don't know if it was because we were hungover or dying of thirst or broiling in the sun, but many years later Zander would tell me that, for whatever reason, we were total assholes to him that day. In any case, everyone on the set was really nice to us—not that anyone knew who we were—even though they wouldn't give us any beer.

Naturally, we didn't shoot our scene until one in the morning. After waiting around all day, they had us get up on stage and go through the motions of playing the lounge version of "When the Shit Hits the Fan." In the movie we're the house band for this club where Otto, the young punker dunker, has an important meeting. You can't really make out any of the song itself because it's in the instrumental section.

When we were recording the song I improvised some "scatting" in between verses. Scatting is spontaneous lyrical nonsense that follows the flow of the music. I think it goes, "Shooby do doo wop! Say what? Yeah!" It was totally unplanned, completely ad libbed. It was my Dean

Martin, Frank Sinatra, and Jerry Lewis moment, something I came up with during the break, but Alex liked it, and that's the part he wanted to use, so that's what I had to lip sync, over and over until he got the take he wanted.

When all was said and done we were only in the movie for a few seconds, but it's an important scene for a couple of reasons. Our performance prompts Otto to say, "I can't believe I used to listen to these guys."

It's a brilliant quote. One of many great lines in the movie, but it's also a real sharp take on the idea that everything that came before punk rock was uncool and should be destroyed. You were no longer allowed to like what you used to like. It was almost like an initiation. You weren't really punk until you threw away your Led Zeppelin records. That was the point of the fashion and the clothes: to break with the old and show your allegiance to the new.

Obviously I didn't subscribe to that point of view, and a lot of the people I associated with didn't either. We just loved making music, plain and simple. Those who got into the scene to make some noise had their moment, said their piece, and went on to other things. Those who had a real love of music, a genuine passion, are the ones who are still playing today.

There were plenty of punks in LA who agreed with Otto's worldview, people who thought being a punk rocker meant you had to tear everything down that went before you. I think in his portrayal of Otto, Alex was taking a piss out of punks who were constantly taking the temperature of the scene, deciding what was cool and what wasn't, and seeing where they fit in. There's another name for people who are obsessed with appearances, style over substance: poseurs.

THE FUNNY THING ABOUT *Repo Man* is that, up until a few years ago, I'd never seen the move in its entirety. I didn't own a TV or have a copy of the movie. I'd only seen bits and pieces here and there, so I wasn't all that familiar with the story line. My mom couldn't believe it.

"Oh, Keith, you've got to see the whole thing! It's one of my all-time favorite movies!"

That was a head scratcher. "Mom, why would *Repo Man* be one of your favorite movies? I'm only in it for like five seconds."

"That's not it," she said. "It's a very spiritual movie. When they leave at the end, they're going to heaven."

She kept encouraging me to see it until I finally did, and I was surprised by how much I liked it. I think the fact that Alex is English was a great advantage. He had a sharper vision of what America was all about at the time, and it's reflected in the movie. It's not really a punk movie—it's not supposed to be; it's more of a coming-of-age film about rejecting the values that are put on you and finding your own way—or else.

Ultimately *Repo Man* was another opportunity to get our music in front of a bunch of people who had no idea who we were. When people who did know our music saw the movie they had one of two reactions: to roll on the ground in hysterics or call us sell-outs.

There are always going to be people with that mentality. When you're a band and you do a certain thing, if you step outside of that or do something different, something you wouldn't normally do, people will get offended. They're used to you being a certain way, and then all of a sudden you're doing something different. They freak out. They can't help themselves. We got a lot of that after *Repo Man* came out.

I'm proud to be in the movie. It's part of the Criterion Collection. It's a cult classic, which means everybody knows the movie but nobody got rich. It's been called one of the best soundtracks of all time. It was one of the last movies with a soundtrack that came out on vinyl and one of the first movies released on VHS. Both factors contribute to its enduring popularity. I'm glad the Circle Jerks played a small role in the story.

WHILE WE'RE ON THE SUBJECT OF Alex Cox, a few years down the road we would work with him again on *Sid and Nancy*. We did a version of "Love Kills" for the soundtrack, and Alex brought us in to do some sound effects. When the police and firemen run up the stairs after Nancy overdoses, those are the Circle Jerks' feet you hear. There's also a scene that involves a box of kittens, and we dubbed the sound of the cats meowing. I did such a great job as a cat impersonator that I was offered a role in the movie: I was going to be Sid Vicious's drug dealer, which is hilarious for a billion different reasons.

Unfortunately the logistics didn't work in my favor. They were shooting in the middle of a Circle Jerks tour. Alex only needed me for a few days, so I was going to fly out from wherever we were to where they were filming in New York. The weather at that particular time of year was bad, and they didn't want to risk me getting snowed in or having my flight delayed and disrupting their shooting schedule. So Mother Nature took away my big Hollywood break.

YOU DON'T
BELONG HERE

I've always been a lone wolf on the road. I don't mix or mingle much. I don't want to be the guy who's always saying, "I don't wanna do this" or "I can't do that." So I just do my own thing.

I don't really need to be around the guys all the time. When we travel we're constantly breathing down each other's necks. I need some space and some head time to collect my thoughts. We all do.

After we pull into town and check in at the venue and do our sound check, I usually take a walk around the neighborhood. Scope things out. See what's happening in the environment. Check out the people and the stores. I look to see if there's a record store, a place to eat, a bookstore, or a public library with computers.

One day I went for a little walk after our sound check. I think we were in Florida. We were somewhere near the middle of our six-month Golden Shower of Hits tour. The sun was shining and the birds were chirping. A great day to be in a punk rock band. After getting my fill of the local scene, I was headed back to the club when I saw our van in a grocery store parking lot with the windows rolled down and the engine running.

Normally when you arrive at a venue you leave your vehicle out front where there's primo parking and you can keep an eye on it. You don't give up your spot to run an errand to the grocery store because when you come back you might not have a place to park.

I went to check things out and see who had driven the van away from the venue. I peeked in the passenger side window, and there was nobody in the van. I couldn't believe it. Either our van had been stolen or someone was being really irresponsible. I say the van was "ours," but we didn't own it. Far Out had leased the van for us, and they were super anal about it. I jumped in the van, threw it in reverse and drove back to the venue, which wasn't that far away. I parked, rolled up the windows, and went inside with the keys.

About ten minutes later Earl came running in, huffing and puffing like he wanted to blow the whole place down. I could feel the anger coming off him—he was breathing fire with smoke coming out of his nostrils and laser beams shooting out of his eyes. He demanded to know if I'd moved the van.

The answer was pretty obvious: I was the only one from the band in the bar. I said, "You left that van in the parking lot with the keys in the ignition and the engine running. Of course I moved it. What were you thinking?"

Earl came at me with his arm raised and his fist cocked like he was going to rearrange my handsome facial features. I wasn't going to let him hit me. Fuck that. I decided I needed to protect myself with the bar stool sitting next to me. I tried to pick it up like I was in a Burt Reynolds movie, but nothing happened. The stool weighed like 175 pounds, and I could only get it a couple of inches off the ground. It was pretty comical.

Luckily Greg and Chuck showed up and got in between us so that Earl and I didn't come to blows, but I don't think he ever really got over it. Later Earl told me that when he came out of the grocery store and saw that the van was gone, he had a panic attack and ran back to the venue as quickly as possible so he could call the police. He said when he came back and saw the van at the curb and me at the bar, he lost it.

Earl was getting tired of all the antics, the hassles of being on the road, the drudgery of being in a band. A long tour will do that to you, and these experiences shook him up.

We played a show in Pittsburgh at a place called the Electric Banana. At the end of the night the owner of the club decided he wasn't going to pay us our $250 guarantee. It wasn't like he had a bad night—the place was packed and the show had sold out. He just didn't want to pay us the money we were owed.

After we loaded up all of our gear and were ready to go, Earl went inside to collect the dough. The owner thought he was a real tough guy. He'd had a laryngectomy and spoke through a battery-operated electro-larynx that he held up to the hole in his throat.

"You don't come in here and fuck with me! I know a bunch of gangsters who will fuck you up!"

The owner pulled out a gun and shot three holes in the ceiling. Earl didn't stick around to argue with him after that. It wasn't worth dying over $250 dollars.

WE HAD A LOT OF WEIRD THINGS HAPPEN on that tour, but one of the strangest was the time Chuck Biscuits decided to take the van for a joyride.

We had played in Kentucky but stayed across the river at a shitty motel in Ohio. It was cold and there was snow on the ground. Chuck carried all of his stuff in a big military duffel bag. He never folded anything. There was no order or separation between the clean clothes and the dirty underwear. He just tossed everything inside and let it all mix together.

It was late, and we were all crammed into a single motel room because that's all we could afford. We'd had a long day of traveling and were trying to get to sleep. Sometimes one of us would get lucky and crash at someone's house or maybe someone would decide they needed some privacy and sleep in the van, but on this particular night it was too cold to crash in the van, and we were all crammed into a single room.

Chuck was up and making a lot of noise. He was looking for something in his duffel bag but wasn't able to find it. He took everything out of his bag, went through his belongings, and then put them all back in the bag. Then he did it again: everything out, everything in. This went on for hours.

Either he finally found what he was looking for or he decided to look for it in the van, but he grabbed his bag and the keys and left. We were all so relieved he was gone that we didn't bother to wonder what he was up to. One of our hardcore, unbreakable rules was that Chuck didn't drive the van. Like, don't even think about it. He didn't have a driver's license and was completely unpredictable. I love the guy and I loved that part of his personality, but you never knew what he would do or what he would be like from day to day, hour to hour, minute to minute. He was always chain-smoking, and if he wasn't smoking, he was drinking, and if he wasn't drinking, he was doing something else. Giving Chuck the keys to the van would be like lending your motorcycle to Evel Knievel. You were probably never going to see your bike again, and if you did, who knows what condition it would be in.

We woke up the next morning, and Chuck was nowhere to be found. We grabbed our stuff and got ready to go. It had snowed through the night and covered everything as far as the eye could see— except in the motel parking lot, where our van was turning circles, and there was Chuck, behind the wheel, going around and around and around.

We could tell by the tracks in the snow that he'd been driving in circles in the parking lot for hours. Maybe the snow confused him and he couldn't find the exit. Maybe he thought he was out on the open road. Maybe he couldn't sleep and this was his way of keeping warm. Maybe he'd finally gone off the deep end. Whatever the reason, it was the kind of thing only Chuck Biscuits would do.

IF I WERE A SUPERSTITIOUS PERSON, I'd say that all of the incidents with the van were a sign that something terrible was going to happen. We were lucky that Earl hadn't gotten the van stolen or that Chuck didn't wreck it during his midnight ramble in the snow. Somehow we made it through the entire six months of the Golden Shower of Hits tour in one piece, but on the way back home our luck finally ran out.

It was a couple of days before Christmas, and we were hauling ass through Texas. Our final show of the tour had been in Houston and had been a pretty good show on what amounted to a pretty good tour. We'd been away from home for six months and were eager to get home. We'd decided we weren't going to stop and spend the night anywhere. We were going to drive straight through.

I was chosen to be the first driver because I'd gone four or five days without drinking or doing any drugs. (I don't remember how or why, but every once in a while I'd shut it down and walk the straight and narrow for a bit.) I was going down the highway in the middle of Nowheresville, Texas, where the roads are straight and every now and again you go up or down some sad excuse for a hill that stretches for miles.

It was cold, but the sky was clear and the roads were in decent shape. I was hauling ass when a highway patrolman came cruising up alongside me. He didn't pull me over or signal for me to slow down. He just looked me over and zoomed away, so I kept my foot on the floor and continued on our way.

We crested a rise and were coming down the hill when I saw a road crew on the side of the highway. No sign. No cones. Just a bunch of guys standing on the side of the road. I looked over, and some of them were pointing and laughing at us, like they were saying to each other, "Hey, guys! Watch what happens to this van. This is going to be hilarious!" I couldn't figure out what they were pointing and laughing at. I was like, *What the fuck is their deal?*

Black ice.

I hit the ice, and all hell broke loose. When you're driving across black ice, there's not much you can do. You can't even *walk* on black ice, and we were going seventy miles per hour. It was like the entire road was pulled out from under the van, and now we started going sideways. I had no control of the van whatsoever.

Being the responsible driver I was, I alerted my bandmates to the situation: "Oh, we're fucking dead. We're dead meat. Dead fucking meat."

I thought it was curtains for Keith and the rest of the Circle Jerks.

The van pitched over on its side and started rolling. Gear was flying everywhere. Guitar cases, amps, drums, bags of clothing—everything. We rolled right off the road and down the grade. Somewhere during the course of the tumble I remember being aware of that fact that I was wearing my seatbelt, which I was immediately grateful for. If I hadn't been wearing it, I would have gone right through the windshield.

We came to a stop. The van was upside down. I fumbled with the door and tumbled out of the van. The engine was smoking and the wheels were spinning. What tripped me out was that the van was compressed to about half its original size. It didn't even look like a vehicle anymore. One by one, the rest of the guys emerged from the crushed vehicle that used to be our van and climbed up to the side of the highway.

All of our stuff was strewn across the field. Everything had been ejected from the van. There was a guitar over here, an amp over there, speakers and pieces of the drum kit. Circle Jerks T-shirts, stickers, and buttons littered the scene. It looked like a bomb had gone off. There wasn't a single piece of equipment, merchandise, or gear left in the van.

I don't know how we managed to survive. None of us had any significant injuries. A couple of bruises, a separated shoulder, and a sprained ankle. I had pieces of the windshield embedded in my scalp, but nothing major.

The guys made it up the hill to an emergency vehicle that seemed like it had been there the entire time. The van stopped, and there it was. It was really weird, like something out of a sci-fi movie.

I couldn't take my eyes off the van. Standing there by the side of the road in my London Fog trench coat, it was hard to believe that just a few minutes ago we were speeding along in that thing. There was no way we should have walked away from that accident. Maybe it was a Christmas miracle.

The emergency vehicle took the guys to the hospital in Pecos, and from there they flew home. Greg wasn't traveling with the band. He was in rock superstar training and was flying from city to city. He was already back in LA, worrying about what Christmas parties he was going to attend.

When the adrenaline wore off it was up to me to figure out how to get the van and all of our gear back to LA. Our management company wasn't going to be happy to hear we'd totaled their precious van.

I gathered up all of our stuff and figured out a way to put it back in the van. A big diesel tow rig dragged the van up the grade and hauled it up onto a flatbed. The driver gave me a ride to Balmorhea, which was the closest town. It had a gas station on each end of town and a truck stop that had a restaurant and a convenience store in the middle. That was Balmorhea. If you were on the highway and you blinked, you'd drive right by it.

I called Far Out and told them what happened. When they got done cursing me out, they said, "Put the van on a flatbed and bring it back to LA. We'll salvage it."

The mechanic at the auto shop thought that was a terrible idea. "You're wasting your time. You might get $500 bucks scrap metal if you're lucky. It will cost a lot more to haul it out there."

I was inclined to agree. The real priority was our stuff. The mechanic suggested I go down to the truck stop and see if I could find somebody with enough room in his rig to get me, the gear, and what was left of our merch back to LA.

Easier said than done. At the truck stop I dejectedly wandered around in my trench coat. Every time I tried to explain my situation to someone I got the brush-off. I wasn't looking for a handout: I was willing to pay to get our gear to LA. But no one would talk to me. I hung around for a couple of hours and was starting to get depressed. It was getting late and would be dark soon. Christmas was coming, and I had no vehicle, no place to stay, and was hundreds of miles from home.

"You look like you've got a problem you're trying to sort out."

I was so lost in thought I didn't notice the truck driver's approach. He introduced himself as Shorty from Dallas and wanted to hear my story. I told him how I'd rolled the van and needed to get to LA.

"I've got your solution," he said, jerking a thumb at his rig. "I'm going to San Francisco, but I've got to go through Los Angeles first. I'll take you and your gear to LA for $200."

"You've got a deal."

"Well, let's get going," he said. "I need to be back in Dallas in two days."

That seemed insane to me. He wanted to spend Christmas with his kids but had to get up to San Francisco first. I was in no position to argue. Shorty pulled his rig up to the garage, and all the mechanics helped me take the Circle Jerks gear out of the flattened van and put it into the truck. They were waving and hollering, "Merry Christmas!" as we sped away. You meet some sketchy people on the road, but those folks in Texas were lifesavers.

Shorty told me that we were going to take an unorthodox route to LA to avoid traffic. We traveled down roads I'd never been on before or since—I think we even hit a couple of dirt roads—but we cruised through without stopping at any weigh stations. We made a few pit stops to piss and fill up on coffee. Shorty popped a couple of cross tops here and there and hit on an industrial-sized thermos to stay awake.

Shorty was a redneck through and through, but he was a music fan, and as he drove we talked about the Grateful Dead and the Allman Brothers Band and other bands he liked. I told him about some of the shows I'd seen at the Hollywood Bowl and some of my adventures on the road. Not surprisingly, we'd passed through a lot of the same places. In spite of how he looked, he was actually a really cool guy. He was probably thinking the same thing about me.

We got to LA the next day at about three in the afternoon. Shorty pulled the rig right up to the management building on Sunset Boulevard and set the parking brake. He didn't even turn the engine off.

"Get your guys, Keith. I'm out of here in ten minutes!"

BUD CLUB

Every New Year Jeffrey Lee Pierce and I would partake in the annual burning of one of Club Lingerie's Christmas trees. After the New Masque shut down, Brendan Mullen became the talent booker at Club Lingerie, an eclectic rock and roll club. One night you could check out the Butthole Surfers or the Flaming Lips, and the next night you might see Big Jay McNeely or Screaming Jay Hawkins. Brendan would occasionally book punk rock bands from the old scene.

For the holiday season Club Lingerie would purchase these giant flocked Christmas trees. They'd buy the biggest ones they could find and stick these thirty-foot-tall trees in a corner of the stage, where they'd stay until about a week after New Year's, when someone would drag them out into the alley. That's when Jeffrey and I would make our move.

At around three or four in the morning we'd drag the trees into the middle of the intersection of Sunset and Wilcox. There was never any traffic at that hour, but we still had to be careful because there was a police station a block away. We'd set the trees upright in the middle of the street, and one of us would act as a spotter while the other set them ablaze.

Club Lingerie never watered the trees, so they were always completely dead and as dry as a bone. They might has well have had a sign on them that read, SET ME ON FIRE! So that's what we did. Because the trees were so dry, they'd catch fire instantaneously. And they were so big and tall, they lit up the entire intersection like it was daytime. It was pretty spectacular.

It was a brash and bold maneuver on our part, not to mention stupid, but we did it every year and never got caught. It was our way of saying, "Fuck you!" to the Hollywood cops, whom we lived in fear of.

In those days, because I wasn't doing enough drinking on my own, I was a member of a drinking association called the Bud Club. It started when I attended a gathering of another drinking club called the Royal Loyal Order of the Water Buffalo. All of the members were guys in bands who used it as an excuse to get together and drink. There were guys from Fishbone, Tex and the Horseheads, and the Vandals. I went to one of their meetings and made a suggestion they didn't like: we set up an emergency fund in case somebody gets in an auto accident after a meeting. Everybody was getting so blitzed that it was only a matter of time before someone was hospitalized, or worse. Let's take care of each other, I said.

They laughed me out of the room, so I took it upon myself to help start another drinking organization called the Bud Club. Our members included Greg Hetson, Jeffrey Lee Pierce, John Doe of X, Lee Ving and Derf Scratch of Fear, Chris Desjardins of the Flesh Eaters, Bob Forrest and Pete Weiss of Thelonious Monster, B. Otis Link, who was one of the artists for Goldenvoice, Flea and Anthony from the Red Hot Chili Peppers, and myself. We were spending a lot of time with the Chili Peppers because Michael Balzary, aka Flea, was filling in on bass for the Circle Jerks.

Not too long after we got back from the Golden Shower of Hits tour, Earl Liberty quit the band and became a born-again Christian. He saw the light, heeded the call, and we wished him well on his journey.

Flea played with not only the Red Hot Chili Peppers but also Fear. He wanted to play with Black Flag, but something happened. Punk rockers love to hate on Flea, but one of the greatest shows the Circle Jerks ever played featured Greg Hetson on guitar, Chuck Biscuits on drums, and Flea playing bass. The gig was in West LA at the Music Machine.

I don't know who came up with the lineup, but it went down like this: the opening band was Spinal Tap. Every once in a while they would put on their gear and play an actual show. This was one of those nights. They were followed by Slayer, a speed metal band that dialed it up to eleven every night, and they were amazing. Then we warmed up the stage for one of my favorite bands, the Blasters. From metal to thrash to hardcore to roots rock and roll. I think it cost $3 to get in.

It was one of those nights when we found our groove, got in the zone, and stayed there. You could fire howitzers and shoot bazookas and launch missiles at us, and they would just bounce right off our chests. Nothing could touch us. When we hit the stage the people in the front were blown ten feet back by our animalistic fury. We were invincible.

After we got through playing and went backstage to towel off and have a beer, John Doe and Jeffrey Lee Pierce cornered me and told me they'd never witnessed anything like what they saw. Dave Alvin of the Blasters came up next and said to me, "Keith, that was totally fucked! How are we supposed to go out there and play after that?"

The Blasters did just fine. They played with the same kind of attitude and energy and aggressiveness as the other bands. They were just as much a part of the movement as anyone else you could name in the punk rock scene.

IF YOU WERE A MEMBER OF THE BUD CLUB, you would get a call out of the blue, and the rule was you had to show up with a couple of six-packs or a case of beer. We held our meetings on the roof of the office building where Anthony Kiedis was living. Tomata duPlenty of the Screamers also lived there, but he wasn't a member. When the beer was gone we'd move on to Club Lingerie or wherever there might be bands playing, and sometimes things would get ugly, like the time John Doe brought his girlfriend, Gigi, to a show. I don't know what happened, but someone said or did something inappropriate to Gigi, and the vibe got really messy. The Circle Jerks played a short set, and it ended up being our last show with Chuck Biscuits.

I don't remember why, but Chuck and Greg got into a fight. It wasn't your typical heated argument between friends; it was more like something out of a comedy movie where the punches go through the air in slow motion. There was a lot of huffing and puffing and ducking and missing. The fight moved out of the club and down into the parking structure, where Greg hauled off and kicked Chuck between the legs like he was trying to punt a football. He kicked him so hard that he actually lifted Chuck off the ground. That was the end of the fight and the end of Chuck Biscuits being a member of the Circle Jerks.

ULTRA MEGADEATH

We replaced Chuck with a guy named Aaron Glasscock who was the drummer in a band called Mad Society, but he didn't last very long. We played a punk rock festival in Oakland called the Eastern Front. The highlight of the festival was when a big Budweiser truck pulled into the middle of the field. Free beer! There were ten taps on each side of the truck. All you had to do was walk up and fill your cup with free Budweiser. When it came time for us to play we were royally shit-hammered, as Pete Weiss of Thelonious Monster would say. No one was paying attention to what they were doing. We were terrible. Aaron was in the band long enough for us to realize we needed another drummer.

A few weeks later I went to see Megadeath—not Dave Mustaine's band that we've grown to love and hate, but a metal parody band that was popular at the time. All of the band members were musicians I knew who played in other bands I liked or had played with. They were just ridiculously over the top and wore chains and black eye makeup and leather and spandex. Their songs were great too. They wrote hilarious send-ups of heavy metal songs with titles like "Make the Bitch Pay" and "Killing for Jesus," which the Circle Jerks would eventually cover.

Megadeath would play once or twice a month or whenever the schedule for the other bands they were members of allowed it. The drummer, Keith Clark, really stood out to me. He had played in a really amazing pop band called 20/20, so he could do a lot of different things.

One night I was in Megadeath's dressing room at the Music Machine just hanging out, drinking their beer, and Keith was sitting there in his get-up. I sat down next to him and asked him if he would play drums in the Circle Jerks. He said he'd get back to me. Undeterred, I asked him again a week or two later, and he said, "I'll do it."

Keith was a really interesting guy. He was an accountant who prepared taxes for people in the music business because he understood all the unorthodox ways musicians get paid. He had a strong business mind, and when he joined the band our fortunes changed for the better. Thanks to Keith, instead of playing gigs where we would get a guarantee of $250 to $500, our guarantee jumped up to $1,000 to $2,500, depending on the size of the venue.

We had Flea, up until he had to go work on a Chili Peppers album. After he bowed out of the band we had a few others play with us while we organized an audition for a bass player. Jay Bentley of Bad Religion fame filled in, as did Tim Gallego of Wasted Youth.

I put the word out that the Circle Jerks were looking for a new bassist, and when I got about ten responses I booked a studio out in the Valley where we'd been rehearsing.

I'd never organized an audition before, and about seven or eight so-called bass players showed up. It was like a scene out of *Spinal Tap*. I gave each participant a list of six songs and told them to bring their bass. They had a week to learn the songs. My mistake was I didn't ask enough questions during the phone interviews before the audition, including the most basic questions like, "How long have you been playing bass?" or "What kind of bass do you play?" or even "Have you ever been in a band before?"

These would have been good things to know. I should have grilled them. I should have put them in a tiny room and shined a light in their faces. "What bands did you listen to while growing up? Who are some of your favorite bands right now?" If I'd been smart I would have really put the screws to them by asking, "Are you an alcoholic? Do you have a drug problem? What do you look like?"

Instead, the conversation leading up to the audition was more like, "How's it going? What's your name? Can you be here Thursday at noon?" I have no one but myself to blame for how things turned out.

On the day of the audition the other members of the Circle Jerks met at the studio. We had a rig set up that belonged to our friend Mark Walton, who was in the Dream Syndicate. As soon as the first guy walked in the door I knew we were in for a long afternoon. He showed up wearing his coveralls from work and was covered in grease and oil. He had a bass in each hand, and they looked like he'd bought them at a garage sale.

"How's it going?" I asked.

"I'm cool. I'm fine. This is really great!"

As he started fumbling around with one of his bass guitars he said, "I just wanted to come over here and meet you guys. I really like what you're doing. I'm not really a bass player, but I'm willing to learn."

The guys in the band wanted to kill me. They looked at me like they were going to take me out back behind the building, tie me to each of their vehicles, and pull me apart.

MOST OF THE GUYS WHO SHOWED UP that day were beginners who were still learning how to play bass. They liked the idea of being in the Circle Jerks but had no practical experience of being in a band. "I can get better as we go along!" That sort of thing. Some of these "musicians" looked like contestants from *The Gong Show*. They had no reason to be there. They weren't in the ballpark of what we were looking for.

Out of everyone who auditioned that day we had two real bass players turn up. The best one was a guy from Italy who'd played in a ska punk band that was heavily influenced by the Clash. The guy knew what he was doing. He played the songs really well, but I'm not a big fan of ska. It's never been my thing. And the guys were losing their patience with the process.

Our last bassist of the day was Zander Schloss. I didn't recognize him right away because physically he'd filled out some since the last time we'd met, but it was none other than the actor who'd played Kevin in *Repo Man*. He auditioned for us, and we didn't need to go any further. He got the job by default.

NOT SO WÖNDERFUL

We started working on our next album right away. Keith and Zander are both talented songwriters who play multiple instruments. Neither Greg nor I were on a mission to write a bunch of new material. If there's ever a full-blown historical box set of the Circle Jerks, there aren't going to be a lot of extra tracks because they don't exist—we never wrote more than what we needed to record.

Keith wrote some songs, and Zander wrote some songs, and pretty soon we had enough for an album. Plus, we wanted to cover a couple of Megadeath's songs, namely "Making the Bombs" and "Killing for Jesus," which they were happy about, as Megadeath didn't have a record deal.

Megadeath may have been a joke band, but Keith was all business. He took on the role of band manager and became the de facto leader of the Circle Jerks, making most of the business decisions. He had a lot of connections in the music industry through his tax service business—not just guys who played in bands but also the people who worked at record labels and recording studios. That's how he got our deal for our fourth album. He had a contact and was able to make the right connections. It wasn't arranged through A&R people; it was a who-do-you-know kind of deal.

Wönderful was put out by Combat Records, which was the heavy metal wing of Relativity Records. The album was recorded in Hollywood across the street from where the New Masque was located at

Santa Monica and Vine. Crystal Sound was built by a guy who'd recorded a bunch of jazz legends. The studio owner was kind of an eccen-
tric and had a console that was built from parts that he claimed he'd
purchased from NASA. He'd recorded some ultra-mega-superstars in
that room, and he was proud of it. Stevie Wonder, Sly and the Family
Stone, Earth Wind and Fire, and everybody's favorite, Fleetwood Mac.

One night when everybody was eating dinner he took me into one
of the storage rooms and showed me all of the racks of tapes he had
recorded. Normally the studio doesn't hold on to the tapes—the rec–
ord label gets the tapes for safekeeping—but he had these amazing
recordings. He played some of them for me. "Just pay attention to this.
Listen to how you can hear the brushes on the ride cymbal." It was
beautiful. A clear, pristine sound. It was exactly what you would want
for a jazz album. But for a punk record?

Not so much.

During one of our sessions we were listening to a playback in the
studio. and I sensed someone was in the room with us. I turned
around, and there was Sly Stone. He was cradling a giant boom box
wrapped in a baby blanket, nodding his head to the noise. The producer asked him what he thought of the playback. Sly had a big smile
on his face. He said, "This is pretty far out, man. This is pretty wild."

We did the photo shoot for the album on either Santa Monica or
Venice Beach. Our big expense for the shoot was the custom-fitted
tuxedos we wore. It was the first time we'd actually spent money on a
photo shoot. I think it was Keith Clark's idea. The various dogs and
cats and ferrets and what have you that we're holding in our hands
were pets that belonged to some of our friends. I don't know why, nor
do I have answer for why we all have mullets. I wish someone would
have slapped us and told us how ridiculous we looked. A simple "What
the fuck are you guys thinking?" would have been sufficient.

Today I can't answer those questions. To be honest, this period of
my life is really hard to see clearly. It's my dark period, my pathetic
period, my black plague days that were devoted to getting my hands
on something I could I snort up my nose or pour down my throat.

TECHNICALLY SPEAKING, I WASN'T homeless, but I was always a gig away from being penniless. I was mainly staying on a couch at our old manager Gary Hirstius's place off of Las Palmas over by the Hollywood Bowl. The building had about ten apartments; two were rented by senior citizens, people who had actually lived there all of their lives, and the rest all had musicians in them. There was a porno actress who lived with her punk rock boyfriend on the roof of the building. During the summer they lived on the roof; during the winter they lived in the stairwell.

Whatever money I made I spent on drugs and alcohol. I wasn't in a good place, and if you weren't careful, I'd take you down with me. Just ask Paul Westerberg of the Replacements.

Bob Forrest, who would graduate from Thelonious Monster to the TV show *Celebrity Rehab*, and I went to the liquor store to get some adult beverages when who should we see at the deli counter but Paul Westerberg ordering a corned beef sandwich with mayonnaise on white bread. I was pretty shocked. I mean, who puts mayonnaise on corned beef?

Bob was a big fan of the Replacements. Maybe it's more accurate to say that he worshipped the ground they walked on. Bob was quivering with excitement. Little beads of sweat were forming on his forehead. I didn't look down to see if he had an erection, but I bet it was there. As for me, I'm a fan—they're a good band, and Paul has written some good songs—but the adulation Paul receives from music critics has always struck me as a little over the top.

We talked Paul into coming back to our place to finish off the half gram of cocaine we had, and this led to purchasing more coke and making more trips to the liquor store until we decided we were going to charge hard all the way up until Paul's show that evening at the Palace. It's not called the Palace anymore, but it has a long history: Frank Sinatra and Dean Martin used to film their TV show in that room.

Eventually we walked over to the hotel where the Replacements were staying to raid the minibar. I think the Replacements had a suite where each guy had his own little room to hang out in. We were standing in the middle of the suite when my favorite member of the Replacements, Bob Stinson, made an appearance. He was slathered in Bengay and wore a shower cap. Maybe it was part of his routine, but it was a weird scene, so we went back to my place for more drinking, drugging, and carrying on.

Paul had to split for the sound check. Bob and I managed to talk our good friend John Doe into giving us a ride. Also along for the ride was my bastard dad Chris Morris, a talented writer and music critic who was also my Hollywood father. Things started to get ugly on the way over. I had recently broken up with my girlfriend, Alexandra, and was convinced that everybody in the car wanted to hear me bitch and moan about it. I went on and on until John Doe, who'd just broken up with Exene, let me have it. He told me to shut the fuck up, and for a little while I did.

Goldenvoice was doing the show. Goldenvoice started with Gary Tovar asking Greg Hetson, "How do you put on a concert?" Greg would say, "Well, you gotta rent a PA, get some bands, find the hall . . . " Because of that, we had prime standing with those people. For a while the Circle Jerks were the Goldenvoice house band.

We got backstage passes, and that meant free booze. I continued to rip my brain to shreds with alcohol. Somehow I managed to piss off Chris, who is one of the nicest guys in the world. When he had enough of my bullshit, he grabbed me by the shirt and threw me up against the wall.

Finally the Replacements started playing, and Paul Westerberg was not exactly in top form. The Replacements had just signed a deal with Warner Brothers, and their A&R guy had talked all of the big wigs at the label into coming to the show. The marketing people, the PR people, all of their assistants, all the people that matter and some that don't—they were all there.

When you sign with a record label, the deal is nothing more than a symbol of their commitment to you. The more they spend, the more likely they'll get behind your band and put you in front of as many people as they can. But it's no guarantee. That's why these showcases are important. The A&R guy gets to show off his shiny new toy and convince everybody else in the company he's just signed a star who will make everybody a shitload of money. In other words, it was one of the biggest nights of the 'Mats' professional career.

The problem with the Replacements was one night they could tear the place apart, and the next night they would be fumbling and stumbling around the stage, barely making it through their songs. Thanks to Bob and me, this was one of the ugly nights—one of the nights their A&R guy sure as hell didn't want the rest of the company to see. It was a "You signed these guys?" night, a "I can't believe I used to like these guys" night.

I remember at one point in the show I was crowd surfing. In the thousands of shows I've played in my life, I can probably count on two hands the number of times I've stage dived or crowd surfed. I was never into it. If you want to do it, fine, but I'm not going to follow you.

I was crowd surfing and got pushed up onto the stage. I made a beeline for the bottle of Jack Daniels sitting on top of Paul's guitar amp. I started chugging and glugging and glorphing and galumphing. When I had my fill I set the bottle down and jumped back into the crowd.

As for Paul Westerberg and the Replacements, the label wasn't too happy about their performance, and they never really got behind the band. Consequently the rumor started going around that it was my fault, that I was the one responsible for ruining their wonderful career. Despite my negative influence, the Replacements have done just fine, and a lot of bands would love to have the career they've had.

IT'S THE MONSTER . . .

Thelonious Monster was the house band at Raji's, and Bob Forrest and Pete Weiss were—and still are—good friends of mine. Their mantra was, "It's the monster. It's a party." They were a very popular band who never made any money because everything they earned went into supporting their lifestyle. They played shows just to pay off their drug dealers, played with a lot of amazing bands, and carried on as if they owned Hollywood. They went on tour with the Chili Peppers and Fishbone. Bob was one of those guys who had a knack for being in the right place at the right time.

I liked hanging out with the Monster because wherever they went, some kind of mischief was sure to follow. Someone always had a six-pack of beer or a bindle of blow or a place to go where there was more booze and more drugs. We'd go to Bob Forrest's place at the corner of Fountain and Gardener, where, according to local legend, Cary Grant had sexual intercourse with Marilyn Monroe in one of the bungalows. Or we'd end up at Flea's crash pad behind the Florentine Gardens on Hollywood Boulevard where guys from the Chili Peppers and Fear would gather before going to do whatever we were going to do that night.

One of my adventures had me hanging out with Flea before a show at the Olympic Auditorium. The RHCP were playing with the Minutemen, Suicidal Tendencies, and SSD from Boston. I was backstage, drinking their beer, and the rest of the band was freaking out because

Anthony was a no-show. Everyone in their crew was running around asking, "Where's Anthony?" like if they repeated this enough times, he would appear.

I thought I had a pretty good idea where he was. One afternoon I was riding with Anthony to score a measly $100 gram of cocaine, but to Anthony it was a matter of life or death. It was rush hour, and Anthony was driving like Mario Andretti or one of those NASCAR racers. He'd drive on the opposite side of the street toward oncoming traffic and then dart back into the lane we were supposed to be driving in. *This isn't right*, I kept thinking. *He's going to get somebody killed. Namely us!* It was like a car chase out of the *French Connection* or *Bullitt*, but without the hills and the hot rods. I thought for sure that if we didn't get involved in a pileup, we would get pulled over. I honestly didn't think we were going to make it.

Somehow we arrived at the coke dealer's place in one piece. Anthony said, "Give me the money. I'll go get it."

I gave him the money. He left, and a half hour later he came back out, and the gram had been whittled down to practically nothing. I'd risked my life and spent a hundred bucks on what amounted to a quarter of a gram of coke.

Drugs are fun, but they make you do stupid things.

AS IT TURNED OUT I WAS WRONG about Anthony. He'd been stopped by the police for jaywalking and was arrested because he had outstanding warrants. That's the way we rolled in those days: warrants, wasted, loaded on drugs, and looking for more. Skip out on your court date and hope they don't bust you for something else.

As soon as Anthony told them he wasn't going to make it to the Olympic Auditorium, I knew what was going to happen. Before I could slip out of the dressing room Flea said, "Morty, you gotta fill in for Anthony!"

I didn't know any of the songs. I didn't know the lyrics. But I also didn't know how to say no. They were my friends and I paid attention to their music, but I wasn't some chisel-dick who knew every word to every song. To make matters worse, I was blazing hard. On that particular night I'd bumped into a friend in the parking lot who happened to work for X. She had some coke, and I ended up buying a gram from her and doing it all in the parking lot before I even set foot inside the Olympic.

We—that is, the Chili Peppers—were the opening act. I grabbed a microphone, but I wouldn't call what came out of my mouth singing. I screamed and yelled at the top of my lungs. My lyrical theme for the night was "What you see is what you get." I think Flea ended up covering most of the vocals. They weren't superstars yet—they were still on the rise—so I don't think anybody really noticed. The funniest thing about that show was they paid me for performing with them, so let's just say that the white-out continued and the snow came down in the dressing room and parking lot all night long.

FOR A WHILE BOB AND I WERE ROOMMATES at his place on Fountain. The front door was always open, and people were constantly coming and going. If you were in a band from out of town and needed a floor to crash on and a fridge to stash some beer in, you were welcome at Bob's, but we were completely broke.

One of Bob's ex-girlfriends worked for a company that did advertising for large chain restaurants. Sizzler was running a special with a coupon: free salad bar with the purchase of a beverage. She gave him a bunch of these coupons, and we ate all of our meals at the Sizzler salad bar for a month.

I used to walk up to Ralph's on Sunset Boulevard and buy the bargain-basement-bonus-special-extra-sale-price-blue-stripe box of generic red wine. $2.99 a gallon. I'd bring it home, sit in the kitchen, and listen to tapes on the eight-track player that Bob had on the kitchen counter. Bob would get fixated on a band and listen to it over and over again. He'd go on these long rants about the greatness of Culture Club that were inspired but incredibly lame.

He was one of my best friends, but there are only so many times you can listen to "Karma Chameleon." He would make a point of listening to it for hours at a time. I got so pissed off, I took all of his cassettes, put them in a plastic Ziploc bag, emptied a container of chocolate milk into the bag, and stashed it in the freezer.

Another hero of his at the time was Sammy Hagar. A Sammy Hagar song here and there isn't the end of the world, but he had *Red* on the turntable for a week. When I couldn't handle it anymore I took the record and threw it like a Frisbee out the back door and over the cinder block wall into the construction site behind the house.

I was proud of myself and happy to have done him a favor by removing Sammy Hagar from Bob's collection, but he was pissed.

"You're going to have to buy me another one!"

That won't be hard, I thought. I could get it for 99 cents in the get-these-records-the-fuck-out-of-here bin at any record store.

ONE NIGHT WE WERE UP PARTYING at an underground club catty-corner from Capitol Records. When the sun came up we decided to go check out the Street Scene, a big outdoor music festival in downtown LA. I'd polished off a bottle of Johnny Walker Red that night so, naturally, I managed to get my hands on a bottle of Johnny Walker Black and drank it on the bus. In between bottles I'd gotten a nice-sized bindle of blow to help straighten me out. I was pretty obnoxious and nearly got into a confrontation with our fellow passengers a couple of times, but Bob steered me out of trouble.

I'm a bit confused about the chain of events, but I'm sure we had plans to check out various bands. There were probably about seventy thousand people there, and as soon as we got off the bus Bob and I got separated in the confusion. The beer sponsor was Stroh's fire-brewed skunk urine. After a couple of cans of golden chipmunk whiz, I found myself up on stage, dancing with the LA Raiders cheerleaders. It's one thing to jump on stage when a band is playing, but you don't disrupt the Raiderettes. You just don't do that and not expect to get harassed. Every gang member in Southern California and from the Bay Area had the Raiderettes calendar hanging on his wall—that's sacred ground.

I was yanked off stage and tossed to the ground. A couple of cops reprimanded me, demanding to see my ID. When they loosened their grip, being the scrawny little weasel I was, I slipped through the crowd and managed to lose them. So long, coppers!

I made my way onto another stage. After spending so much time on stages, I felt like it was my right to be there. I was standing on the edge of the stage, watching some band do a horrible Santana imitation. I was running my mouth nonstop throughout the set until finally the guy next to me elbowed me, and I went flying. The stage was set up in this nice grassy area except for this one spot where there was a rock sticking up out of the lawn. And that's where I landed, right on my back. The pain was so bad I blacked out. When I came to, I tried to get up, but I couldn't move. Someone called the paramedics. They strapped me to a gurney, put me in the back of their ambulance, and took me to County General. That's all I remember.

AFTER ANOTHER LOSS OF CONSCIOUSNESS, I came to in the red blanket room. Doctors and nurses were looking me over, asking me lots of questions that I was having difficulty answering because I was in so much pain. I suppose that was a good thing. When it comes to spinal injuries, pain is better than no pain, but I was feeling a level of pain I would only wish on corrupt politicians. To make matters worse, they started poking the bottoms of my feet with needles.

"Does that hurt?"

"Owwwww!"

"Can you feel this?"

"Gaaaaah!"

"How about that?"

"Fuck, yes, stop, stop!"

At least I wasn't paralyzed. Diagnosis: crushed lower lumbar vertebrae. They told me I could expect to be laid up in the hospital for eight weeks, which put a serious crimp on my social life.

In the hospital I had a lot of time to think about things—the way I was living my life, my reckless pursuit of a good time. As much pain as I was in, I was lucky I hadn't done some serious damage to myself. As bad as things were, it could have been a lot worse. I told myself that

I was never going to allow that to happen again. *I'm not going to drink anymore. I'm going to stop doing drugs. I'll go to the party, but I'm going to be straight . . .*

At the hospital I was surrounded by people much worse off than I was. The guy in the bed next to me had run his hand through a printing press. They probably would have been better off amputating it, but they put his hand back together with metal pins, and he was constantly moaning and groaning how he'd never have full use of his hand again. The guy directly across the room from me was an old black dude who'd gotten in a fight with his best friend over who would get the last few sips of the bottle of cheap crushed fermented grapes they were sharing when his friend pulled out a shotgun and shot him. They gave him morphine every hour, which he was really happy about. Next to these guys, I considered myself pretty lucky.

I must have looked like a scumbag drug addict, because the strongest thing they would give me was Motrin, which was what women took for menstrual cramps, and that wasn't cutting it. After a while I told them to keep it and save it for somebody else. Don't even bother pulling it out. The most painful part of the ordeal was when they would come in and lift me out of bed to change the sheets and pillowcases.

While I was laid up Bob, Pete, Flea, and Anthony would come check on me and cheer me up. I remember Pete sneaking into my room at six in the morning on the day they were going on tour. My mom would bring pizza when she came to visit, which was a treat because the food at the hospital was horrible. Dave Alvin and Bill Bateman of the Blasters came to see me. In fact, Bill was there the morning they wheeled me out of the hospital in a wheelchair.

I was released from County General after six weeks. They let me go early because I healed faster and better than they'd anticipated. They were planning on opening me up and running some pins through my spine, but that wasn't necessary. They fitted me with a custom-built body brace with Velcro on the sides so I could take it off to shower and bathe. I had to wear that for a while, but otherwise I made a complete recovery.

My only souvenir is a bone on my back that sticks out about three-quarters of an inch farther than the rest of my spine. When it acts up, that tells me it's time to slow down and get some rest.

Not too long after I got out of the hospital the Circle Jerks played a show at the Olympic Auditorium with the Vandals, Youth Brigade, Stretch Marks, and Detox in front of about four thousand people. I did the show in my body brace, but it wasn't armor. It wouldn't protect me if I fell. The guys were worried someone might jump up on stage, take out my legs, and knock me over. Even worse, someone might try to tackle me. I wasn't that worried about it. The gig had to go on because that's show biz, right?

Maybe, but the party train was about to go off the rails . . .

LAST STRAW

I didn't keep my promise to stop partying when I got out of the hospital. In fact, I was back to my old ways my first night out. If anything,
things were about to get more out of control.

I was running around every night. Hollywood being Hollywood,
you never knew who you were going to bump into. One morning I
partied with David Lee Roth of Van Halen. In fact, we smoked crack
cocaine together.

David Lee Roth used to hang out at 01 Gallery, which must have
had a half dozen locations over the years. The 01 Gallery was his not-
so-secret hideaway where he'd go when he didn't want to hang out
with his band or record company people. In those days 01 was a boot-
leg club that was run like a speakeasy. There was always art on the
wall, but every night, after the shows were over and the bars had closed
and there was nowhere else to buy booze, you might find David Lee
Roth at the gallery with a bunch of Hollywood lowlifes and scumbags.
It was where he went to lose his ego and be a seminormal person who
liked to have a good time. It was his oasis, his little island away from it
all. People would recognize him, but the kind of people who hung out
at 01 at four o'clock in the morning couldn't care less about Van Halen. You'd find people from Cathay de Grande and Raji's. Hollywood
vampires who didn't want the sun to come up.

Early one morning I was in the back room with the gallery's favorite bartender, Top Jimmy, who fronted the Rhythm Pigs when David

Lee Roth showed up. Top Jimmy was a workingman's Tom Waits or Chester Burnett and our go-to coke dealer. Van Halen wrote a song about him. He also makes an appearance in *The Decline of Western Civilization* when John Doe gives him a terrible homemade tattoo.

I've never been a fan of Van Halen, but when Mr. Roth asked me if I wanted to hit the pipe with him, I didn't say no. Michelle Meyers, the booking agent at the Starwood, had once called me the punk rock David Lee Roth, so I told him the story. He got a chuckle out of that and then we blazed up. The goofy part of this story is that the only time I witnessed VH was at the Starwood way before they signed a record deal.

Another morning I came stumbling out of the 01 Gallery—different location, same gallery—at around 8 a.m. and met Billy Idol. He knew who I was and I, of course, knew who he was. I didn't care for his solo stuff, but I was a huge fan of Generation X. We shot the shit and smoked coke-tipped cigarettes, hoping the cops wouldn't make a special guest appearance.

For a little while Bob Forrest ran a club out of a storefront on Melrose called After Everything Else. He figured he could have small shows that would bring in about three to four hundred people and make some quick cash. One night we played there with a band called Electric Hippie, and the place was packed. Afterward Bob took all the money, bought $500 worth of coke, and ran off to a house around the corner from Club Lingerie. If we wanted to get "paid," that's where we had to go. (Bob probably figured I would just spend our cut on booze and cocaine anyway.) We went up to the party, and the guy from Electric Hippie showed up and was pissed. "You owe us $250!" I think Nickey Beat, the drummer of the Weirdos, ratted us out.

We played another gig there with the Bangles opening, and of course I was extremely thirsty and ended up polishing off a minikeg by myself. Bob told me I wasn't getting paid that night because I drank up all of his profits. This happened about a half hour *before* he opened the doors.

At this point I was crashing on the couch of my friend Michael Kelly, who was also my coke dealer. After all, I was blowing all of my money on booze and cocaine, so why not go straight to the source?

Every morning, before I woke up, Michael would make sure there was a little ten-dollar pile of cocaine on the table. I'd wake up, find a cigarette, empty all of the tobacco out of the tip, load up the cocaine, and smoke it. That was always the best high of the day, and I'd spend the rest of the day chasing it. Michael was happy to kick down $10 worth of coke because he knew I was going to spend hundreds of dollars more. In the business world that would be known as a "loss leader."

ALL THE PARTYING, ALL THE LUNACY, all the bad times disguised as good times came to a screeching halt at a Thelonious Monster bash in Beverly Hills.

Our friends from Sin 34 threw a party at their parents' house. His dad owned a huge mega-mansion, and it was your typical the-rats-will-play-while-the-cats-are-away situation. Totally ridiculous. We were all in our thirties and getting way too old to be carrying on this way. I was trying to fly with Peter Pan and had no plans to leave Neverland.

Thelonious Monster played on the wooden deck next to the swimming pool so people could watch the band while they splashed around in the water. All it would have taken was one cord to come unplugged for everyone to get the shock of their lives. But nobody cared because it was the Monster. I got into the usual mischief and mayhem and blacked out. I came to in the swimming pool, completely naked, floating on an inflatable raft. It was around nine or ten in the morning, and people were still trying to keep the party going. I went in and found my girlfriend, Alexandra, and laid down next to her. I was in the mood for love, but she wasn't having it. I should have just closed my eyes and passed out, but we got into an argument that turned into a confrontation that became physical. She pushed me away and I pushed her back. We screamed and yelled at each other as the fight moved from the bedroom to the kitchen. All the party people left over from the night before drifted into the kitchen to see what the hell was going on right as I started throwing punches.

My friends jumped in and pulled me away. Some people grabbed my arms and others grabbed my legs, and they hauled me out of the house, kicking and screaming like a lunatic. They took me outside, threw me in the back of a van, and got me the hell out of there. It turned out that one of the guys who'd tossed me in the van was Michael Kelly, and we headed to his house. He made it clear that he wouldn't be selling me any more cocaine and that I needed to do something about my problem. It was the straw that broke that drug dealer's back. I considered Michael a friend, but what does it say about you when your coke dealer cuts you off?

Mercifully, I passed out for a few hours, but when I came to, the enormity of what I'd done started to sink in. You don't hit women. I knew that. That's something you just don't do under any circumstances. The fact that I wasn't big enough to be going around punching *anyone* was no excuse. I'd crossed a line. My girlfriend knew it, my friends knew it, and, most importantly, I knew it. The party was over. The party wagon had hit the brakes and screeched to a stop. It was time to get out and start walking before all the wheels fell off.

The first thing I did was call my dad. It wasn't really much of a conversation because I was in tears. "Dad, I'm in trouble. . . . I don't know what to do. . . . I've never been in a place like this before . . ."

My dad drove up from Redondo Beach and picked me up. He had opened a second store, Jerry's Tackle Box on Aviation Boulevard in Redondo Beach, and that's where we went. We sat in his office and talked. He was worried about me. He'd never seen me in such bad shape. We didn't have a heart-to-heart or anything like that, but once I calmed down he took me to stay with my sister, Trudy, in Lawndale. She worked for an ear, nose, and throat specialist and got me in to see him the following Monday. He gave me an examination. My sinuses were inflamed from all the cocaine I'd been doing, but I hadn't done any long-term damage. He warned me that I was lucky I hadn't deviated my septum or anything like that, but I was headed in that direction if I kept using.

I looked into going to rehab. I checked out a few facilities, from expensive luxury mansions on the cliffs of Malibu to shitholes in the Valley I never knew existed. I was talking with the nurse at one of the brainwashing clinics down in West LA, and he told me there was no need for me to go that route. He said that by admitting I had a problem and seeking help on my own, I'd cleared the first hurdle.

One of the things rehab does is takes you away from the bad influences and separates you from your friends. I didn't have to worry about that. *I* was the bad influence.

"Here's what you need to do," he said. "I want you to go to a meeting a day for the next ninety days. Your first meeting will be an Alcoholics Anonymous meeting. Your second meeting will be a Narcotics Anonymous meeting. Because you're an alcoholic and a cocaine addict, you'll switch it up."

That sounded reasonable. I started going to meetings. One of the first meetings I attended was at a place right next to where I went to junior high. I began my journey in sobriety steps away from where I first started to get high. By the third day I was going to a couple of meetings a day. On the fourth day a guy volunteered to take me around to all the meetings he attended and introduce me to his friends. It turned out he had dated a girl who had been a classmate of mine at Mira Costa. One of the interesting things about him was that before he got sober, things had gotten so bad that he tried to commit suicide by hang gliding into a power station.

I apologized to everyone who had ever been close to me. Alexandra broke up with me, so I didn't get to apologize to her right away, but I did eventually. She'd been telling me to get clean for a while, and I never would have taken the necessary steps without her. I just wish the circumstances had been different. I apologized to a couple of ex-girlfriends for being such a cruddy, miserable, horrible boyfriend. But the biggest hurdle was my dad.

I was thirty-one years old and had been drinking and doing drugs for over half of my life. I didn't know for many of those years I was an alcoholic and an addict, but through it all I'd worked at my dad's store and had been dipping into the till to pay for my party supplies. I'd sell some stuff and not ring it up, and when the other employees weren't looking I'd put the money in my pocket. When that wasn't cutting it, I'd take money from the safe. I estimate that when all was said and done I embezzled something like $60,000 dollars from the store, and I felt terrible about it.

Some of my relatives on my dad's side were having their fiftieth wedding anniversary at the Sportsman's Lodge in the San Fernando Valley. My dad was there with his new wife-to-be, and everybody was having a good time.

I waited for a break in the action and asked, "Dad, can you step outside? We need to talk."

He knew right way it was something serious. Our relationship was never conversational. We didn't recommend movies to each other or talk about interesting books we'd read. Our differences about music were so severe that it wiped out any kind of cultural exchange from happening. But it went deeper than that. He seldom opened up about his past or asked me who I was dating, and we never talked about him divorcing my mom—all that normal father-son chit-chat. Everything was always on a negative vibe. A me-versus-you kind of thing: I don't want to be like you and you don't like the things I do and that's just the way it is.

He was my dad, but he was also my boss. When we talked, it was always the prison warden wanting to see what the yardbird was up to. I didn't work for him because I had dreams of becoming a fishing tackle tycoon; I worked for him because it was easy work for me and when it wasn't enough, I took what I needed.

We sat on a wooden bench built around the trunk of a tree that was lit up with twinkling lights arranged to make them look like little fireflies. It was a beautiful summertime evening.

"Dad, I've got to apologize to you."

"Are you keeping your nose clean?"

"Yeah, Dad. I've been sober for a few months. I need to apologize to you for all of the money I took out of the cash register and from the safe."

Then I told him how much.

"No, no, no," he said. "You were part of the business. You don't apologize to me."

I thought that maybe he didn't understand what I was telling him, but then it got really heavy.

"If I had been a real dad," he said, "if we had been a true father and son, that wouldn't have happened. You don't have to apologize to me. I knew what was going on. I knew what you were up to. I'm the one who has to apologize to you."

That fucking blew my mind. I'd been carrying around the weight of my guilt for half of my life, and with a few words it was lifted away. It was a mind-bogglingly huge moment. I felt like I was up in the clouds. I've never forgotten the power of that moment. It opened up a new chapter in my relationship with my father that I otherwise never would have had, and it made possible a fresh start for the rest of my life.

You can get into a mindset where you're going over all of your fuckups and flaws and you start to think, *I've got to apologize to this person and that person.* All of the sudden your list is like three hundred people long. You might as well rent a big hall, invite them all in, and get up on the podium and say, "Okay, everybody: I'm a royal flaming fuckup and I'm sorry!"

But that's not how it works. On the night I tried to apologize to my dad, a switch flipped in my understanding. What I needed to do was stop talking about being a bad person and start being a good one. Set an example by showing up, living my life, and doing what I was meant to do.

V

While I was getting my act together, the Circle Jerks kept chugging along. We were really fortunate to have a player/coach like Keith Clark calling the shots. I wouldn't go so far as to say he was the Michael Jordan of the Circle Jerks, but we'd never really had a manager of that caliber. We weren't the kind of band that could go on autopilot, but under Keith's management we kind of did, even if I didn't always appreciate it.

Keith had a great relationship with our booking agent Andy Somers. Normally the people on the management side of things don't want to deal with individual members of the band because it can turn into a never-ending series of requests for favors, money, and so forth. Keith was such a pro that we never had any trouble and were able to take advantage of some great opportunities.

As soon as we finished *Wönderful* Keith started laying the groundwork for our fifth album, our second with Relativity Records. Keith wanted to call it *VI*.

"Let's toss everybody a curve," he said. "Let's pull one over on our fans and see who is paying attention." The whole idea was that when we put out *VI* we'd have all of our fans running around trying to find the album before it.

The album cover was Keith's idea too. I wanted the kid to be jackhammering a VI into the sidewalk with a bunch of people looking on, like something out of a comic book. Instead, we went with the kid with the hammer and chisel, carving out the Roman numerals VI.

There's a thing that happens after you've been in the music business for a while and you've put out a few records and been on a bunch of tours: you start to develop a know-it-all attitude. Even if your past experience hasn't been all that great, you develop a sense of how things ought to go: "This is how it works, so this is how it's going to be." It makes you stubborn, hard-headed, and less receptive to other people's ideas. It doesn't happen all at once, but it slowly creeps on you. My problem with Keith was he knew what he was doing and I didn't want to cop to it.

We'd started making money. Under Keith's management the Circle Jerks had some great years when we'd each made anywhere from $25,000 to $40,000 year. On average we were playing for five hundred to a thousand people a night. There were plenty of nights when we'd get a $1,500 guarantee and sell $3,000 to $4,000 in merch. That might not seem like a lot, but for a punk band of our stature, that was a pretty good run.

There were some dud shows. We played a show in Vegas at a place next to the Gold Nugget that was very badly attended because the promoter decided he didn't need to promote the show. Some bands will tell you it doesn't matter how many people show up as long as you get your guarantee, but that's bullshit. When a hundred people turn out for a gig in a venue that holds eight hundred, it matters. It's discouraging. It's the kind of thing that makes you reevaluate what you're doing.

I was slowly starting to realize that if something is working and you're progressing and moving forward, you go with it. You don't hit the brakes. You don't pour sugar in the gas tank. You let go and see where it takes you. In a way Keith taught me to be more open-minded, but it's a lesson I'm constantly having to learn again and again and again: go with the flow.

Keith didn't always make it easy. As much as I respected him, I was also becoming bitter toward him. You can take only so much of being told what to do.

One of the things Keith liked to do was give everybody associated with us a nickname. His nickname for me was Johnny, which was a reprise of Johnny Bob Goldstein. Greg Hetson became Gingles, like an elf in a Saturday morning cartoon. Zander's nickname was Snake because he had a way of entering a room like, "Here I am, everybody. Stop what you're doing and check me out." He had this weird arrogance about him that was funny and charming at the same time. Of course, our nickname for Keith was Adolph because he was the dictator of our operation.

We got a decent advance for *VI*. We didn't break the bank, but it was enough to pay some bills and put some money away before we hit the road. It's not our most popular album, but I love "Beat Me Senseless" and "Casualty Vampire." Greg and I wrote "Tell Me Why," which was an oddity for me in that I usually wasn't the one who came up with entire songs. I'd come up with a riff or a musical idea in my head and would have to rely on someone else to play them. *VI* came out at a time when punk rock and heavy metal were starting to influence each other in interesting ways. You had punk bands crossing over to a heavier sound and metal bands crossing over to a faster attack. You can hear a lot of our early rock influences in this album. It wasn't something we put a lot of thought into; it's just what we wanted to do at the time.

The *VI* tour was my first tour as a sober person, and it was interesting. To be honest, my approach didn't change that much. I was always the guy who would get on the high dive and leap off without worrying if there was a hundred feet or twelve inches of water at the bottom. I just went for it. What else was I going to do?

In the early days I would always get wasted before a show in order to deal with the nervousness and the anxiety I was feeling. Then it just became a habit, a part of the ritual, an essential part of my preshow routine. "I got a show tonight—I need to get my brain in the right place."

I don't want to sugarcoat the fact that I was an alcoholic and an addict. That's what we do. It wouldn't have mattered if I were playing in a punk band or working for my dad—I'd be getting my party on no matter what. I was never thinking, *What am I doing three hours from now?* It was more like, *Hey, I've got this window of time and I know exactly what I want to do with it.*

So I wasn't that nervous about playing sober. I only had about thirty days, but I was pretty gung ho about it: *Let's do this. Let's see how this goes. Let's put my sobriety to the test and see where it takes me.*

I was extremely lucky to have Keith Clark managing the band and playing drums because he was a great influence. He was the guy who would drink a beer after the show and then flip the page. He'd eat something, get some rest, and then it was on to the next show. He had a very good head on his shoulders, which is very rare in our line of work.

The music industry attracts extreme personalities. I think that's why so many musicians end up with drug and alcohol issues. But if you're lucky and live through your dark days and deal with those issues, you get to meet all the people who have been through what you've been through and have found a way to do what they love while clean and sober. And there are a lot of us.

Keith, however, was a rarity: a levelheaded guy who put what was best for the band above his own immediate gratification. He kept the rest of us in line. When he had to, he would pick us up by the scruff of the neck and make sure we were taking care of what we needed to take care of.

I knew there would be challenges. There was always going to be somebody chopping up a line and putting the coke spoon under my nose. It was going to take a while for word to get out that it wasn't my thing anymore. For instance, I went to see the Butthole Surfers. Before the show I stopped off backstage to say hello to everyone. Gibby Haynes was alone in the dressing room. Everyone had left. He was cutting up three-foot long rails. I'd never seen anyone chop out lines like that. Each one was easily four or five grams of coke. He held up a straw and said, "Morty, go for one."

The two-and-a-half-year-old cowboy outside the yellow house in Inglewood, California, in 1958.

My four-year-old sister, Trudy, with me as a studly six-year-old in Cathedral City, California, in 1961. I was almost a skinhead before you. (Jerry Morris)

Three-quarters of the Morris clan in Hermosa
Beach, California. Me, my mom, and Trudy
on our way to a Thanksgiving pow-wow.
(Jerry Morris)

My dad with two salmon, one of
which weighed 57 pounds and was the
California state record for 1965. (Bob)

Mom, Trudy, and me, loading the VW
van for a trip to Mexico, at 10th and
Monterey, Hermosa Beach, California,
in 1968. (Art "The Fart" Watson)

Wigging out at the Moose Lodge, along the Pacific Coast Highway, in Redondo Beach, California, January 1979.

BLACK FLAG
AT POLLIWOG PARK
(IN MANHATTEN BEACH)

(Imagine real nice orchestra music)
"It was such a lovely Sunday afternoon. Mom & dads brought along the kiddies, there was plenty of potato chips and baseball and lemonade. There was a playground and ducks and love and niceness and kisses all over until, (horrible music creeps in)
"Somebody let Black Flag into the park . . .
. . . ."

At about 7 o'clock, Pollowig Park's entertainment program burst into chaos like an alien jumping out of somebody's chest. The Park's first ever rock & roll show, exploded into a messy collage of punk noise, foul language, beer drinking, beer throwing, and monsoons of flying garbage. Vicious little Keith dug in, claimed his ground and wouldn't leave until he'd insulted, angered, and threatened everyone in the park.

A bunch of idiot surfers showered him with trash, (probably thinking they were gonna see Cheap Trick or something) parents screamed complaints about Keith's foul words, (In fact, enough to stop the show twice) but Black Flag's onslaught ran its course. And amazingly, nobody left. Maybe they were fascinated or horrified, but they stayed for it all.

One thing is for sure, Black Flag are soon to accompany the Germs, Damned, and Iggy in the Party-Wrecking Hall of Fame ... So "Tear It Up" as Johnny Burnette would say ...

Ranking Senor Lea

(*Top*) The first three vocalists of the first four years of Black Flag: Ron Reyes, Dez Cadena, and yours truly. (Spot)

(*Bottom*) Review written by Jeffrey Lee Pierce for *Slash* magazine.

A few refreshments for my first road trip with Black Flag
to San Francisco. (Spot)

X at Club 88

Due to a variety of flimsy reasons, I almost didn't go. Bad thoughts about the L.A. scene in general had me in a reclusive mood. At the last possible minute I jumped in my car and raced from Hollywood to the 88. X was in the middle of their first song as I squirmed through the door. From the back of the bar the PA was a transistor radio at low volume with the bass all the way up. After wading through the melee to the front of the stage, I heard a different story. It was an earthquake finally avalanching on thousands in this vale of beers; the desecration of the Holy of Holies by lovers who just couldn't wait for sex until they got home,'cause they got no home; it was the dynamiting of a shrine. X played this instrument called an audience and it shrieked, wailed, moaned and went up in flames (gratefully). Even if you just stood there, the nerd-like zombie that you are, you still ended up drenched from head-to-toe, you still felt like laughing and crying at the same time, you still wanted to live the rest of your life in the next five minutes. When the Mexican gang kids hoisted Exene into the air and rode her on their shoulders everything went over the top. And suddenly it didn't matter if they ever got signed to a major record company, it didn't matter if you have or ever will see them again...because they're the best fucking band in the whole world.

HALF COCKED

BLACK FLAG at the BlaBla June 11

Ventura Blvd. is a bleak and desolate stretch of road just after midnight on a Monday morning. No bull-necked jocks playing chicken with their custom vans; no sedate suburban shoppers browsing in the endless chain of small-time retail businesses. Hardly anyone was inside the BlaBla; not that it wouldhold that many swooning fans to begin with. We'd thankfully missed the Relievers. Still, a long wait was in store before Black Flag got their chance to detonate the microscopic stage. First, a few BlaBla house roadies sluggishly shuffled equipment while Rikki Lee Jones popped her oh-so lame, oh-so bogus be-bop fingers over the sound system. Keith wandered out on stage sheepishly sucking on a beer and acting as if he'd like nothing better than to just settle down with slippers and an evening paper. All at once it was showtime. The rest of the band positioned themselves. Keith made a few shy comments then, without *warning, the accelerator got pushed to the floor.* For the fifteen song twenty minute set nothing stood in Black Flag's way. They aroused in the audience of 10, one epileptic seizure (a dance), flying salt shakers and several mangled tables and chairs. A truly impressive debut; volatile, angry and not one full moment. They rival only the Germs in their potential for snowballing a room of sedate people into a mangled tumult of chaos. See them before they get banned from too many clubs. (The Hong Kong has already nixed future shows by them because of a recent debacle there.) They're going...to....EXPLODE!

V/D

Ginn, myself, and Chuck "The Duke" Dukowski at the Hong Kong Café in L.A.'s Chinatown, California. (Chris D.)

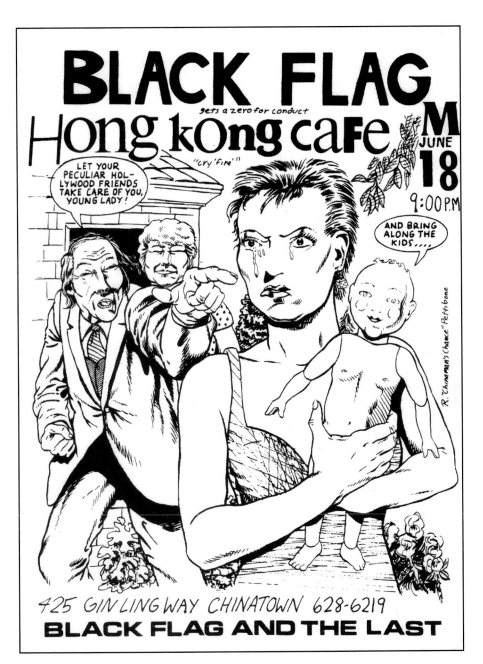

My all-time favorite Raymond Pettibon flyer. Reminds me of Jack Kirby and Steve Ditko. (Art by Raymond Pettibon)

Group Sex album cover photo shoot, with the Adolescents, at Marina del Rey Skate Park. (Ed Colver)

This was taken at the Errol Flynn estate for NO MAG in 1981
by our manager, Gary Hirstius's, girlfriend. (Rooh Stief)

Roger Rogerson and me, along with a chilled adult beverage and a freshly hocked loogie. (Brian Tucker FER YOUz)

REVENGE
I DON'T CARE
WHITE MINORITY
GIVE US A BREAK
MACHINE
I'VE HAD IT
NERVOUS BREAKDOWN
PARENTS AND RELATIVES
DEPRESSION
JEALOUS AGAIN
FIX ME   CLOCKED IN
WASTED   LEAVE ME ALONE
RED TAPE   NEW COOL
POLICE STORY
GIMME, GIMME, GIMME
NO VALUES

This is the set list from my last show with Black Flag. (Keith Morris)

Obviously I'm feeling a Bud buzz on stage at the Starwood with Greg Hetson. (Gary Leonard)

Lesson learned: never headline over the Bad Brains because they mopped the floor with everybody. (Art by Shawn Kerri)

I look like I should have been carded, even though I'm twenty-five years old. (Gary Leonard)

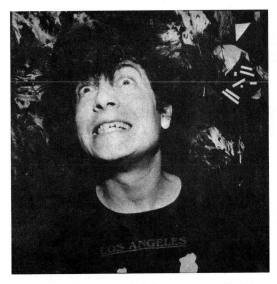

Not enough chilled adult beverages and white powder supplied by a South American cartel. (Bruce Kalberg NO MAG 1983)

Greg Hetson and me, pointing at Earl Liberty's missing teeth, and Chuck Biscuits at about one o'clock. (Glen E. Friedman)

Bugged out at CBGB's. (BJ Papas)

GREG HETSON   KEITH MORRIS   ZANDER SCHLOSS   KEITH CLARK

PHOTO CREDIT: WILLIE GARCIA

Hetson, me, Zander "The Snake" Schloss, and Keith "Adolf T. Bore" Clark down in Venice Beach. (Willy Garcia)

Dan Root, Bill with the Devil's Mask, a shrunken Carlo "Nuke" Nuccio, and myself with Bruce Duff in the field of weeds behind Hully Gully rehearsal studios, in Atwater Village, California, 1991. (Greg Allen)

Dimitri Coats, Steven McDonald, Mario "Speedwagon" Rubalcaba, and myself during a two-night stand at Alex's Bar in Long Beach, California. (Joby Ford)

Cousin It's second cousin. (Cathy Rundell)

Catching some air with Dimitri and Mario in Curitiba, Brazil.
(Rodrigo Melleiro)

"Gibby," I said, "that's extremely kind of you, but although I appreciate the offer, I'm going to have to pass."

Gibby looked up at me. He couldn't believe what he was hearing: Keith Morris saying no to blow? That was a first. He shook his head and went back to work.

HANGMEN

After touring for three months the Circle Jerks were ready for a break. As soon as we got back to LA each member ran off to his own corner of the world. This was especially true for Greg, who was also a full-time member of Bad Religion, and he'd let it be known that he wasn't going to be available for a while. As for me, coming back to LA used to mean it was party time because I had fewer responsibilities at home than I did on the road. I wasn't partying anymore, so I had to find something else to do, some other way to occupy my time.

In some respects Hollywood was brand new to me as a sober person. All of my friends and acquaintances were guys and gals like me: damaged souls doing whatever it took to get by. I basically did what I always do when I'm in a new place: I went to check out some new music. I had a flyer for a Sunday afternoon barbecue over by the warehouses in the arts district downtown. I didn't know any of the bands playing, but it was something to do, a way to kill some time. I thought maybe I'd run into some of my friends. If not, I'd go home.

There weren't a lot of people there when the Hangmen started making noise—maybe a couple of dozen people at most. I was really impressed. They were a really good rock and roll band with a way-happening sound. You could tell they were figuring some things out as a band. They reminded me of the Ramones playing Rolling Stones covers or vice versa.

I made a point to talk to the band after the show to see what they had going on, where they were from, what they were up to. The frontman was a guy from Montana named Bryan Small. He was the main personality in the band and cowrote all of the songs. Bryan told me the band had been playing in LA for a few months and were slowly building a following, but I don't think he needed me to tell him that playing to empty warehouses in the middle of the day wasn't the way to do it. I guess they were going after any gig they could get.

After I introduced myself I bombarded him with questions: Do you have a record deal? What are you aspiring to do? What are your goals? As I was talking to Bryan, I was thinking, *These guys are great, but they're totally lost. They could really use some direction and a manager.* As soon as it occurred to me, a second thought popped into my head: Why not me?

I was in a situation where I had a lot of free time on my hands. Greg was spending more time with Bad Religion than he was with the Circle Jerks. That will always be my biggest beef with Greg: he basically decided that whatever Bad Religion was doing was more important than what the Circle Jerks were doing. I tried to be cool about it, because I had no control over the situation—Greg was going to do whatever Greg wanted to do—but every time he went off to play with Bad Religion a big chunk of my livelihood was taken away, and there was nothing cool about that.

I was looking for a project to get involved with when I stumbled onto the Hangmen. Bryan told me they'd recorded a couple of tracks, but nothing they felt really good about. That's when the lightbulb went off: these guys needed to make a demo, and I knew how to get one made. Here was a golden opportunity to get on the ground floor of something exciting and new.

After that first show we met a few times and talked about the different things I could do for them as a manager. When we agreed to work together, we didn't have a formal arrangement; there wasn't a contract other than what we scribbled down on a cocktail napkin. The deal was I'd do what a manager does with an unsigned band: book shows, spread the word, do whatever it takes to get them signed. When they signed with a label, I'd get a percentage of the deal. That was as far as our agreement went. Most importantly, I believed in the Hangmen as a band and thought I could help.

The first thing I did was pick up the phone and call Brett Gurewitz, my friend at Epitaph, and told him what I was up to. He said we could come down and record at his studio, West Beach, in Culver City. It was a tiny little office space he'd stumbled across. It was extremely intimate, but he had a lot of great equipment. I knew Brett from his involvement in Bad Religion, and "Starbolt" gave me the bro deal.

I was willing to spend money out of my own pocket because I believed in Bryan and the rest of his guys. Granted, it wasn't a lot of money because I didn't have much at the time, but it was something. I was discovering how easy it is to save money when you're not giving it away to the bartender and the coke dealer every night.

I brought the Hangmen down to West Beach. Brett was intrigued, and we worked on the demo together. We recorded the Hangmen's best songs and were both really pleased with how it sounded. In fact, Brett was so moved by the band and the songs we recorded that he wanted to sign them to his label. Now I had to practice some tact and diplomacy and let him know that to sign the first deal that was presented to the band without knowing what other offers were out there would be unfair.

Next step: book some shows. When it comes to bands, my theory is simple: Why do you do what you do? If the answer is "play music," then that's what you go out and do. If the answer is something else, you're in the wrong business and need to find something else to do. It's important to rawk out as a live band because that's how you make your money and pay your bills. You might be offered a big record deal and you might make some money off the advance, but the only way you're going to have a career is by playing shows, selling merch, moving up the ranks, and letting everyone know that you exist as a band.

There was never a strategy where I'd try to book a particular venue in the hopes of attracting a specific audience. It was never like that.

You play every chance you get, and if you catch a break and a hot band asks you to play with them in front of a thousand people, you reach out to the people at the labels, send them a demo, and let them know about the show. But until you're presented with that opportunity, you have to work. And when that opportunity does come, you have to be ready. You can't dial up some buzz right out of the gates and hope things turn out for the best; you have to *earn* the right to play for those people.

The Hangmen were already on their way. They had a good amount of time under their belts and had written some great tuneage. It was time to take it up a couple of notches. Guns N' Roses were blowing up the charts, and all the labels were looking for the next big rock band.

Being a manager was a lot of work, a lot of hustle, but it was gratifying. There were always headaches and hiccups. Things rarely went as planned, and my job was to fix it. If it wasn't the promoter, it was the venue, and if it wasn't the venue, it was the equipment, and if it wasn't the equipment, it was the band itself. There were a million different ways things could go sideways.

I got the Hangmen a show with the Gun Club at the Variety Arts Center in downtown LA through my friendship with Jeffrey Lee Pierce and Brendan Mullen. I booked them a show at the Roxy with a band from England called the Godfathers, who had put out a record produced by a guy named Vic Maile, who recorded the Who's *Live at Leeds* and also did a run of Motörhead records and a handful of Kinks albums—there's no questioning the greatness of Vic Maile. Over a couple of months the Hangmen got better at playing together, the songs tightened up, and the band developed that thing you absolutely can't fake but you know it as soon as you hear it: an identity.

I was still doing the couch surfing thing over on Sunset Boulevard above Greenblatt's Deli, which was directly across from the Coconut Teaszer. After hanging out at the club I was able to get the Hangmen some shows at the Teaszer, and I'd invite people to come see them. One of those people, Rachel Matthews, worked at Capitol Records. She had moved down from San Francisco, where she'd worked for Bill

Graham's legendary management company. She was the young fresh face at the company, and after listening to the demo and seeing the Hangmen play, she was really excited about signing the band.

That's exactly what I wanted to hear. Things were looking good, so good, in fact, that I decided to take on another band . . .

THE NYMPH

I was at the Anti Club on a Monday night when the Nymphs took the stage. They were the opening band, and they deserved to be. They were sloppy and loose in a Velvet Underground–meets–the Stooges kind of way. Bobby Belltower and Manfred Hofer were guitarists who'd been members of the Leaving Trains with Falling James Moreland, and I love all of the characters who have come and gone out of that band over the years. A chubby Chicano cat who had a Charlie Watts thing going played drums, and he was just barely keeping it together, which I found very interesting. But it was the singer who got my attention.

Her name was Inger Lorre, and I was floored by her beauty and her band. If you want to throw this book across the room right now, be my guest. I won't hold it against you, because she had me hook, line, and sinker as soon as she stepped onto the stage. When Inger was performing, she had the kind of charisma that made you feel like you were the only person in the room. Granted, it being a Monday night, there were only about a half dozen people in the club, but still. I was broken into a thousand pieces.

Inger knew who I was, and after the show she didn't wait for an invitation.

She came up to me and we started a conversation. Even though I thought the band was a little sloppy, the songs were really happening, and she had superstar written all over her.

I told her what I'd been up to, and we quickly reached an agreement that I would help the Nymphs in much the same way I was helping the Hangmen. I called up Brett again, and this time we recorded the demo at West Beach 2, his second studio located behind Raji's on Hollywood Boulevard. Brett gave me another bro deal, I paid for the session, and we were on our way. During the recording I could tell Brett was impressed with the Nymphs. While we were doing the mixes he looked at me and said, "Keith, I want to sign Inger and the Nymphs."

I told Brett that I appreciated the offer, but expectations were sky high for the Nymphs. The bar had been set higher than any place I'd ever been as a musician. It was a crazy time in the music industry, when record labels were signing million-dollar-deals left and right. A label would go see a band on a Friday night and sign them to a seven-figure deal for four or five albums on Monday. Why not the Hangmen? Why not the Nymphs? Brett completely understood the situation, and there were no hard feelings between us.

All of a sudden I heard the sound of glass breaking outside the studio. It sounded like somebody had chucked a cinder block through a plate glass window or was getting ready to start World War III. We ran outside, and there was Inger, jumping up and down on the hood of a car, kicking in the windshield. She was freaking out about something, but I never did find out about what. That should have been a warning, an omen of some sort, but instead of running away, I rushed in to make sure she was okay.

The demo turned out better than I could have expected, and everyone was really pleased with the sounds. I had feelers out with various A&R people, and we sent the demos to all the record labels in town. These cassettes were accompanied by a stock letter Inger and I wrote stating that I would perform a blowjob on whoever signed the Nymphs. Of course, this was an attempt at humor, but we actually received a response from one of the A&R guys at Warner Brothers. He stated he didn't traffic in sexual favors and would only accept a brand-new car. Maybe he was joking, maybe not. I had a fall-back plan at

Epitaph, so why not go for the top floor? What was the worst thing that could happen?

INGER AND I STARTED A RELATIONSHIP. A nonbusiness relationship. I'd work with the Hangmen, and she'd work with the Nymphs, and afterward we'd meet up. We had midnight rendezvous all over the city.

I moved into Inger's place in Los Feliz, not far from where I live today. One night I was eating some Chinese food in the little kitchenette when Tony Kinman of the Dils walked in and asked me what the hell I was doing there, which was exactly what I was about to ask him. It turned out that Tony was Inger's ex-boyfriend and she'd pushed him out of their bedroom and onto the living room couch when she started seeing me. Tony didn't know about me, and I didn't know about Tony. If I'd known, maybe I would have proceeded more cautiously, but it was too late for that.

Tony wanted to strangle me, which was a shame because I'd known him since the early days of the Masque. Eventually he came around and told me I'd done him a big favor, and by then I knew exactly what he meant.

Predictably, my relationship with Inger led to jealousy between the two bands. Every time I did something for the Hangmen, Inger wanted to know why I'd excluded the Nymphs, and every time I did some something for the Nymphs, Bryan wanted to know why the Hangmen were getting the short end of the deal. It was a tug of war between the two bands, with me caught in the middle, and I'm no Stretch Armstrong. I was able to arrange for the bands to play together a few times, but it was difficult keeping them both happy.

Capitol Records treated the Hangmen like royalty to get them to come into their stable. When they could smell blood, they sent the Hangmen to see their lawyers to close the deal. I went to the meeting with them at one of the towers in Century City. The office had a view of the Santa Monica Bay from Palos Verdes to Malibu. The lawyer worked with Van Halen, and of course, he had their platinum records on the wall. The Hangmen guys were completely in awe. They were foaming at the mouth and jerking off all over this shit. The lawyer offered them a soft drink and a bottle of water, and even that impressed them.

I wasn't having any of it. I wasn't dazzled by these bogus displays of wealth. I'd been down that road and had learned the hard way that the only way people get that kind of money and power is by fucking over everyone who gets in their way. I was just there to listen to what the guy had to say. I think he might have even offered to take the band out on the golf course with him.

Afterward I told the guys that we didn't need to hire this shyster to review the contract. One, he was recommended by Capitol, so who do you think he's looking out for—you or the label? Two, there are hundreds of deals going down in Hollywood every day, and every one of them gets looked at by a lawyer. I wanted them to know that they were paying to have some rich dude fluff up their egos. I urged them to talk to some more people, and I convinced Bryan to meet with another lawyer. Predictably, he wasn't impressed with the guy I took him to: a working professional in a no-nonsense office. He'd already made up his mind. He wanted to follow Capitol's recommendation, and that was that.

I was hoping the Hangmen would seal the deal before I left town to go on tour with the Circle Jerks. With all the buzz they were generating, every promoter and club booker in town was approaching them. It was the perfect time for me to go on tour while the Hangmen were keeping busy in town.

"Guys, you're getting a ton of offers. You'll know who to play for and where to play because you've played a lot of these places before. You're not the opening band anymore. You'll be the middle-slot band. You're not the headliner yet, but we'll get you there. Use your heads. Pay attention. Keep your nose in your business."

Not long after I left town they called and told me that Rachel at Capitol had recommended a new manager for the band, someone she'd worked with when she was with Bill Graham's team in San

Francisco. I was blindsided by this development, but I should have seen it coming.

Of course they followed Rachel's advice. Of course the manager was Rachel's best friend. Of course she would be the one to collect the 20 percent from the deal. Of course I got screwed out of whatever I'd earned as their manager and was told we could still be friends.

Rachel knew who was going to be the Hangmen's manager and booking agent before the band did. It's what they do. The label always tries to bring in their own people. It's just sad that Bryan didn't have the balls to stick up for me or, at the very least, confront me before I left to go on tour and tell me to my face what was happening. Bryan could have said, "Keith, you've been really good and you really helped us out, but we can't work with you anymore."

It wouldn't have been easy and it wouldn't have been a conversation that either one of us would have enjoyed, but I would have appreciated the gesture and respected him for doing it. Instead, they just moved on as if I had to be sacrificed in their deal with the devil.

SCREWED

My relationship with Inger started to unravel when I got back from the Circle Jerks tour. I had a little money in my pocket and opened my wallet for the Nymphs. I paid the rent on the rehearsal space. I paid for gas. I paid for food. If the Nymphs were having a party, I was the one who went to the liquor store to get the keg and a couple of bottles of vodka. If there was an expense, I was the one footing the bill. I was determined not to let history repeat itself.

One evening Inger asked me to procure some substances, and I refused, which led to an argument. It had nothing to do with me being sober; I wouldn't do that for anyone—drunk or sober, friend or foe. That was probably a sign that my relationship with Inger needed to go in a different direction.

I put a lot of pressure on myself to get a record deal done as quickly as possible. As a result, I found myself talking to people I normally wouldn't be talking to, people I didn't like, people who made me scratch my head and wonder, *How the fuck did this person get this job?*

I took a meeting in the dark room at Geffen Records with an A&R executive who'd signed some big names. It was a very uncomfortable experience. His office was completely black with the exception of a couple of burning candles. Very freaky. Not what you'd expect from a top-floor executive in a one-story building. I thought I'd come across a pentagram on the floor splattered with animal blood. The conversation went something like this:

"I signed this band and I signed that band and we're doing this with this band and that with that band. We've spent all of this money on these bands and we're going to do the same thing with your band, whether you like it or not."

I wasn't feeling this guy as a human being on any level. He probably wiped his ass with thousand-dollar bills. I was hoping to have some kind of dialog about the band; instead, it was a barrage of his achievements in the industry. The suggestion was that he was going to get his way because he always did and resistance was futile. When he did talk about the Nymphs it was all over-the-top mumbo jumbo and empty rhetoric that he probably said to everyone who came into his office.

"We think Inger is one of the greatest rock stars we've seen. She's going to be huge!"

The problem with people who work at record labels is that they are constantly surrounded by artists and yes people. After a while they start to think of themselves as artists too. They put on the masquerade and like how it feels, and all the bobbleheads gather behind them. The bottom line is that these jobs are always about self-preservation and survival. Their job is the most important job in the universe, ergo no one is more important than them. That equates to a lot of backstabbing and an unbelievable amount of shit-talking.

It was an uncomfortable experience from start to finish. I left thinking, *If it were my band, I wouldn't sign with this guy in a million years.* It was an evil vibe from the get-go, and I was beginning to think it was contagious.

Not too long after that I came home one night, and Inger was sitting in the living room with my record collection spread all over the floor. She'd been taking the records out of their sleeves and flinging them across the room. That really upset me, which, of course, was exactly why she did it.

It was weird situation. I could see things weren't going to end well between me and Inger, but I needed the Nymphs' record deal to run its course so I could get paid for all of the work I'd put in as their manager.

Then the Sea Hags came to town.

The Sea Hags were a three-piece from San Francisco who I'd played with once or twice up in the Bay Area and were managed by my good friend Paul Rat, who was a promoter who got them shows with a lot of great bands like Killing Joke. When the Circle Jerks went up to San Francisco Paul always did a great job for us and was a fun guy to be around. He ended up getting the same treatment from the Sea Hags that I got from the Hangmen. When the Sea Hags cut their deal, they fucked Paul over and moved to LA. That was all I needed to know about the Sea Hags.

The Sea Hags got a lot of buzz when they came to LA. It didn't hurt that they were tall, good-looking guys who liked to party. They copied every single thing Guns N' Roses did in an effort to get those guys to notice them. I was there the night one of the members made a complete ass out of himself with Duff McKagan, the Guns N' Roses' bass player.

"We have to tour together, bro!"

It was like watching a guy with no intelligence try to carry on a conversation with Albert Einstein. But they had *something* going for them.

At a party after a show Inger disappeared with the Sea Hags' bass player. That was pretty much the end of my nonbusiness relationship with Inger Lorre. She basically blew me off for a pretty boy with a guitar strapped to his back. Nothing new or interesting about that story. Happens all the time.

I wanted to be angry. I was hurt and a bit depressed. She treated me like she'd treated Tony. Even after our falling out I was still managing the band. I went back to couch surfing and doing the things a manager does: booking shows, assembling guest lists, making a hundred phone calls.

I couldn't shake the feeling that it was happening again, that I was going to get screwed. And then it happened: the Nymphs signed with Geffen, and Inger replaced me with a slick new manager. She even asked me to go talk to my replacement, which I did. That's how desperate I was. I was hanging by a thread and would have done just about anything to stay in the picture. I was holding on to the hope that things between me and Inger would work out. My visit with the manager made it clear that wasn't going to happen.

The Nymphs' new manager had this huge house in the Hollywood Hills with twenty bedrooms, a swimming pool, a garage full of sports cars, and a view of the San Fernando Valley. His girlfriend was an insanely gorgeous young model who was at least thirty years younger than him. It was all kind of sickening.

IN SPITE OF CATCHING THE RIGHT BREAKS at the right time, things didn't really work out for the Hangmen or the Nymphs. Neither band found the success they were hoping would launch them into stadiums. Capitol Records shelved the Hangmen. The label took the record that was produced by Vic Maile, the guy I'd recommended they go with, and gave it to some headbanger to mix, and he completely ruined it.

For their big tour the label paired the Hangmen with a hair metal band called Dangerous Toys. That was the direction the record label wanted to push them in. Capitol was having so much success with Poison, they figured they'd have the Hangmen tease their hair with Aqua Net and buy some new cowboy boots. The label was in a hurry to get their record out the door and off the flight path because they had bigger jets waiting to take off. By the time the band realized what was happening, it was too late to stop it. They were flat-out fucked.

The Nymphs' situation was a lot more complicated. Geffen spent a ton of money on the band, but their relationship with the label was messed up. Geffen flew the Nymphs over to England to record with Bill Price, who had worked on a couple of Black Sabbath albums, and their first video was shot by Roger Pope, the guy who made all of the Cure's videos. This was at a time when radio stations followed MTV's lead, not the other way around. If your video was a big hit, it would get heavy rotation on the radio.

Well, it wasn't a hit and it didn't get a lot of airplay. When their record finally came out the only person left in the band from the first time I saw them that Monday night at the Anti Club was Inger. All of the original members were gone, which was really sad. They went from having this loose and loopy vibe to a much heavier approach, and it all came from the label. They were looking for a certain look and sound, and they weren't going to release the record until they got it.

As for the Sea Hags, I don't have anything good to say about them, and because two of the main guys in the band have overdosed and passed on, I'll just leave it at that. Paul Rat is also no longer with us. It's just a sad situation all around.

IF I HAD TO DO IT ALL OVER AGAIN, I would make sure I got commitments and responsibilities in writing before I did anything for either band. I would have gotten the lawyers involved, not that I could afford one. Inger and Bryan probably could have gone to their parents for the money. All the same, I understand why we didn't go that route. Who wants to deal with lawyers? Everything was done on a handshake. Empty promises and a slap on the back. I missed out on an opportunity that would have put me in a good position. With the money I got screwed out of, I could have bought a house. I'm not bitter about it and I don't regret it. You can't go through life afraid that you're going to be screwed over. You have to go where your passion takes you or you'll miss out on more than you'll ever achieve.

Still, it was a valuable experience for me. I've learned the hard way that you have to protect yourself in this business. You put your trust in people, and sooner or later they'll find a way to maneuver you over the trap door and pull the lever. Adios, Keith! Thanks for everything . . .

They did eventually thank me. I got a shout out on the back of both of their debut records. With the Hangmen I got a *special* thank you. Inger and I never rekindled the flame, so to speak. Once it was over, it was over. You don't go back and get burned. I'm still friendly with all of these people. I bump into Bryan and Inger from time to time. We talk on the phone. We chat on Facebook. They're both still hacking away, and I wish them the best of luck. I still love their music, which is why I got involved with them in the first place, but I very rarely listen to those albums.

That probably seems strange in other parts of the world, but that's just how it is in Hollywood. People get intoxicated by success, money, and fame, and it changes them. Things don't work out the way they think they're going to work out, and when the money's gone they go back to being who they really are. I've never had a lot of money, so I've never had that problem, but at least I've still got my good looks and effervescent personality.

BUG LAMP

After my experiences with the Hangmen and the Nymphs I was feeling pretty jaded about the music industry and decided to get out of Hollywood for a while.

I wasn't doing anything with the Circle Jerks. I'd had a fling with a Southern girl after my breakup with Inger, but it didn't really go anywhere. She was very stimulating on a physical level but not intellectually. Her idea of a good time was stealing pizzas out of the back of a Domino's Pizza delivery guy's car and watching *The Simpsons*.

I was fed up with LA, and while Greg was off doing something with Bad Religion, I decided not to wait around for him this time: Why not travel and explore a part of the world at my own pace and on my own terms instead of looking at it through the window of an eight-passenger van? Why the hell not? I decided to go to New York City.

I went to stay with a friend of mine on the Lower East Side. I didn't spend too much time in the apartment, which she shared with her boyfriend. I was constantly on the go, walking around, riding the subways, exploring the city. One of the things I loved about New York at that moment in time was you didn't have to go into stores to get what you needed. You could buy whatever you wanted on the street. It was like a giant swap meet. I amassed a small record collection just from buying records from people on the sidewalk. $5 here, $10 there. I even found a copy of my favorite Golden Earring album signed by all of the guys in the band. I think I paid $10, so I was totally psyched.

While I was in New York I developed a friendship with Daniel Rey. He was a guitar player and had been in a band called Shrapnel that would eventually break up and re-form as Monster Magnet. He was basically a staff producer and A&R guy for RCA Records. He'd produced a number of records, including a Raging Slab album and a Circus of Power album. He also cowrote the song "Pet Sematary" with Dee Dee Ramone, one of the Ramones' biggest hits. I think at one point Daniel was supposed to join the Ramones, but I don't know what happened.

I was hanging out with Daniel, and he had all kinds of recording equipment in his apartment. He was constantly riffing and jamming and coming up with these really great songs that stayed with me as I walked around the city. Every time I went back to his apartment I'd have lyrics to go with the songs. I must have been inspired by the change of scenery, because this went on for a while. Our attitude was, "Let's just do this and see where it goes."

We ended up recording fragments of about seven or eight songs. The stuff was a little poppier than what I'd been doing with the Circle Jerks. There was a Ramones quality to it, but it was a real departure for me in that I'd grown accustomed to a regimental beat. All those years in Black Flag and the Circle Jerks I was used to approaching songs in a way that was really aggressive, like a guy with an axe getting ready to chop down all of the trees in the forest and he only has a day to do it. This was snappier, a little bit more melodic.

One of Daniel's friends stopped by while we were working on some songs, and Daniel played him some of the tracks. He perked up right away.

"When you're ready to go, please come see me because I'd be more than happy to sign you guys."

It turned out that Daniel's friend was Michael Alago, the guy who signed Metallica to Elektra. All of a sudden my trip to New York was turning into something I didn't expect it to be. Normally the career of an A&R person at a record label is comparable to a career of a running back in the NFL: eventually even the good ones get chopped down to size. But if you bring an artist of the caliber of Metallica to your label, that opens the doors for a lot of other opportunities. Could this be one of them?

We continued to write songs and talk about what we were going to do with them. When are we going to get in a room with a drummer and a bass player? Are we going to do it on the East Coast or the West Coast?

My living situation in New York was starting to deteriorate. I noticed that my stack of records had shrunk. I fingered through my albums, and the Golden Earring record was gone, along with several others. My friend's boyfriend was ripping me off and using the money to buy heroin. I figured out what was going on because I would come back to the apartment at different times during the day and not be able to use the bathroom for hours at a time because the boyfriend had locked himself inside to shoot up and nod off. Not only was he stealing my records; he was also taking money out of my duffel bag. He'd go through my stuff and find whatever cash I had stashed in my bag. It was clear I couldn't stay in that apartment for much longer. My time in New York was drawing to a close.

I was ready to take the next step forward with our project, but Daniel Rey had to stay in New York to produce an album for Circus of Power. We agreed that I would go back to LA, put a band together, and Daniel would join us as soon as he could.

Before I left I came up with a name for the project: Bug Lamp. I had this vision in my mind of listeners being drawn to the sound of our music, wondering what was going on, and then getting zapped with something they'd never heard before like an insect getting fried by a bug lamp in a blast of lavender light.

I returned to LA, and the first thing I did was hit the music circuit to see who was out there, who was available. One of my favorite acts in LA at the time was a band called Laughing Sam's Dice (LSD for short). The main guitar player was Rob Stennet, who grew up outside of Dallas, Texas, where Johnny and Edgar Winter were from. He was a bluesy, rootsy, psychedelic guitar player with a fluid, colorful sound that I thought would balance out Daniel's more grind-it-out, pop-punk approach.

The drummer in the band was an old friend named Carlo Nuccio. He was from Metairie outside of New Orleans, and although he idolized John Bonham, he had the personality of Keith Moon: a wild man with a real feel for the drums. His style of drumming was truly unique: he played behind the beat, real swampy and murky. If you wanted a Ramones beat, good luck—you weren't going to get that from Carlo. One of the things that made him such a fascinating character was that he was close friends with Ivan Neville, one of the Neville Brothers' sons, and had grown up around all of these amazing musicians. He was tutored by the best in the business, so he had a really strong musical background.

Carlo also had a wild side. His dad was a boxer who'd gotten in the ring with Jake LaMotta, the Raging Bull, and had his ass handed to him. Carlo's dad owned a bar in New Orleans where all the transvestites hung out and danced. Rumor had it this bar was Led Zeppelin's favorite place to hang out when they were in that part of the world. Their song "Kashmir" was about one of their favorite exotic dancers at the club.

Despite the mindfuck of having managed the Hangmen and the Nymphs, if I had an opportunity to manage Laughing Sam's Dice, I would have jumped at the chance, but they were already on their way and had recorded demos for a handful of major labels around town. I loved the fact that Rob and Carlo were transplants with their own distinct styles. They weren't trying to bend to what they thought Hollywood wanted to hear, yet they were total pros who'd been around the block enough times not to get starstruck when a record company executive took an interest in what they were doing. I asked them if they wanted to get involved in my project, and they immediately said yes. I'd been to many of their shows and had expressed my excitement for what they were doing enough times that they knew who I was and what I was about.

Our bass player was Bruce Duff, who grew up in Riverside, California. He was a really good bass player who'd played in a bunch of bands. He was the most laid-back member of the band. He was a hap-py-go-lucky guy who was happy for the opportunity, which I really appreciated, because the other two guys, I would soon find out, were the opposite of mellow.

I was excited to get in a room and start bashing away at the songs Daniel and I had recorded in New York. During our first session to-gether Carlo said something not particularly encouraging about Rob's girlfriend, who happened to be an international fashion model. Rob promptly took off his guitar and threw it at Carlo. Carlo started taunt-ing Rob, and Rob came back with threats of violence. It was immedi-ately pretty clear I was dealing with some big, volatile egos—and they were best friends! I began to wonder whether I'd made a mistake put-ting these personalities together, that I was biting off more than I could chew. If this was how they acted now, how were they going to react when Daniel came to town?

There were other challenges. A top-notch drummer is probably playing in three or four bands, and that was the case with Carlo. He played with Billy Bremner, a guitarist in Rockpile, and Screaming Jay Hawkins. In addition to playing in Laughing Sam's Dice, both Rob and Carlo worked as sound guys at Raji's. It was challenging to get every-body in the room together, but when we did, good things happened.

Each member of the band contributed new elements to the songs. That's what was so great about the band: All of these different per-sonalities. All of these different colors. All of these different direc-tions. Everything came together pretty quickly, and we started to jell as a band.

Because of our connections, getting gigs wasn't a problem. We probably played about a dozen shows, and all of them were without Daniel. We played the Casbah down in San Diego. While we were loading in, Carlo noticed that the barback was emptying the fridge of King Cobra, some of the nastiest malt liquor on the market. It wasn't selling, so they were throwing it away to make room for something more palatable. Carlo drank about a case of free King Cobras before we'd even set up for sound check. I'd never seen anyone drink more than a six-pack of King Cobra without getting annihilated, but somehow Carlo held it together.

The show wasn't very well attended. No one knew who we were. We'd only been a band for a minute. At the end of the set, when we'd played all of the songs we had, Carlo kept playing and playing and playing until we realized it was the drum solo from "Moby Dick" on the second Led Zeppelin album. The crowd was treated to a John Bonham drum solo by a guy who loved him.

After a couple of gigs the guys started getting restless. When are we going to take Bug Lamp to the next level? Where was Daniel Rey? Does he even exist?

I called up Daniel to get some answers. "I'm not going to be able to come out and play with you," he told me. "I'm in the middle of this recording session, and it's going to be another couple of months."

He was still working on the Circus of Power album. He hadn't done his homework as a producer and checked in with the band to see how many songs they'd written. Before you go in the studio, you always want to make sure the band has enough material. But they only had a handful of songs. They were in a big hurry to book the studio and had to write the other half of the album in the studio. Daniel wouldn't be coming to Los Angeles anytime soon. To Daniel's credit, he didn't want to hold us back.

"Don't wait for me. Do what you've got to do. I'll get out there as soon as I can."

The rest of the guys weren't too happy about the situation. We'd been rehearsing and playing gigs, and everybody had itchy trigger fingers. The guys were ready. It's now or never. They felt it was time to put up or shut up. As far as the other members of the band were concerned, the window of opportunity was closing. What made Bug Lamp so interesting was this blend of different personalities, but at the end of the day everyone had his own agenda. When you're playing with musical mercenaries, whoever waves the bucks is king.

ZAPPED

I was living in Bob Forrest's old place up in the Cahuenga Pass with Rob and his model girlfriend, Twinkie. Rob would show up to Raji's wearing a $50,000 suit designed for him by Jean Paul Gaultier. Twinkie had fashion photographers following her around, and the guy who shot the Red Hot Chili Peppers video for "Give It Away" was staying with us. It was a nonstop party, a giant drug bust waiting to happen.

I was footing the bill for the band's expenses and a fair share of personal bills too. I'd pick up a rent payment here or a car repair there. A lot of bar tabs. I had some Circle Jerks income, so I figured I'd get my money back when we signed a record deal. I was getting in deeper and deeper, but I knew there was a payday on the horizon. I just needed to convince the rest of the guys that it would be worth sticking around for. It sometimes felt like everyone was invested in Bug Lamp except Bug Lamp.

I had cultivated some relationships at various record labels around town and was developing a bit of a rapport with some of these people. I had what I considered friends who worked at Chrysalis, Geffen, and Warner Brothers, and they were all interested in signing Bug Lamp. I thought one of the selling points for the band was that Daniel, Rob, and Carlo were not only talented musicians but experienced producers too. Our record was going to be mind-bogglingly great and wouldn't cost a fortune to make because of all the money we'd save on a producer. My friend at Geffen told me I needed to stop thinking like that.

When I told her I could get a record made for under $30,000 she laughed at me.

"That's not how we do things at Geffen." She told me that if I signed with Geffen, I could expect to pay $125,000 just for a producer.

If the labels were throwing around stupid amounts of money when I was trying to get the Hangmen and the Nymphs signed, it was absolutely ridiculous now. All of the labels were looking for the next Nirvana, and the competition was insane. Sometimes a label would overpay for a band just to keep them from going to another label. A lot of bands were getting signed out of ego. A band would get some buzz, and it became a competition to see who was going to throw the most money at them because they didn't want to get beat out by another label: *We've got more money than you.* They did it with bands they felt they had to have and with bands they didn't really care about—just to fuck over the competition. That was the stupidity of the record industry and one of the reasons why they find themselves in the position they're in now. I'm not saying it was good a situation for us. I'm not saying it was right. But it was a golden opportunity to buy a house in the hills where all of my friends could live rent-free with their girlfriends and pets. Welcome to the Morris Mansion, compliments of an industry that has no idea what's coming for them.

My first order of business was to find a replacement for Daniel. I brought in a guy who came highly recommended named Dan Root, who is now playing in the Adolescents. We got Dan up to speed, wrote more sounds, and recorded more tracks.

We had an opportunity to record a song for an Alice Cooper tribute album. Rob and Carlo produced the track—when they weren't arguing—and it turned out great. We did the song "Ballad of Dwight Fry" and appeared alongside bands like the Vandals and the Flaming Lips, one of my favorites.

There are a handful of other Bug Lamp tracks floating around. In addition to the Alice Cooper cover we did for the tribute album, we also recorded a track for a Ramones tribute album that Daniel Rey helped arrange. Bug Lamp is also featured on the soundtrack to *Road-side Prophets* alongside the Beastie Boys and the Pogues with a song called "El Dorado." El Dorado, by the way, is a mythical place filled with riches that is always just out of reach . . .

PREDICTABLY, WITH DANIEL REY out of the picture, Rob and Carlo were growing tired of the songs Daniel and I had written in New York. In fact, Rob hated the name Bug Lamp and was always trying to get me to change it to Bug Juice. They felt the new material they were writing was better. It was turning into a competition: "my song is better than your song" kind of deal. I tried to be as diplomatic as possible, but we had so many songs that I couldn't keep up with them all. Rob was also writing lyrics. I liked some of his lyrics, but I wasn't feeling them. I told him we could use his music but not his lyrics, and that's when things started to get edgy.

Chrysalis offered to pay for our demo. I knew I needed to get Daniel out to California so we could do the demo as soon as possible, but it was too late. Rob complained that things were moving too slow and quit the band.

I was under the impression that Rob was coasting through life on Twinkie's coattails. She was out working the runways and fashion shows and appeared on magazine covers and in music videos. She had it going on, and he was the rockstar boyfriend. I eventually found out that Rob came from money and was taking his time making it through the world. I'm not dissing Rob, because I still believe he was the greatest guitar player in LA at that time, but he just wasn't that interested in what we were doing.

With Rob gone, I felt like it was only a matter of time before his best friend Carlo followed. I told Daniel Rey that he needed to get out to LA as soon as possible. Daniel flew out shortly afterward, and we recorded the demo for Chrysalis with Daniel, Carlo, Bruce, and Dan Root. I learned an extremely valuable lesson from Daniel Rey: he believed that anytime you had an opportunity to go into the studio, especially on someone else's dime, you record like you mean business. You don't treat it like it's "just a demo." You treat it like you're laying down tracks for an album that's going to sit on a shelf among your favorite records.

The demo was excellent, and the buzz was starting to build. It was finally happening. I'd been waiting four or five months, but things were starting to take shape. A lot of bands sign on the dotted line and wait for the record label to do everything for them, but I had a plan for the production, a plan for publicity, and a plan for the tour. And then I lost my drummer.

I understood Carlo's situation. He was flat broke and was constantly getting offers to play with other bands. I'd spent more money on Carlo than any other member of the band. I told him, "Dude, I know you're in demand, but you need to be patient." When all was said and done I couldn't convince him to stay.

It couldn't have come at a worse time. Chrysalis wanted to know when they could come see us play. I stalled for time so I could find replacements for Rob and Carlo, but the label thought we were playing hard to get. Our demo was generating a buzz all over town, and my friends at Geffen and Warner Brothers wanted to get in on the act.

I replaced Rob with another Rob, Robbie Allen. His claim to fame was he was in the band Tender Fury with Jack Grisham of T.S.O.L. I recruited Michael Murphy from a band called Lions and Ghosts to play drums. Bruce and I were the only original members left, but we pushed on. Everyone learned the songs, and after a couple of weeks we finally had our big showcase for the major labels at Raji's.

The room was completely packed and as hot as a sauna. There were so many people in there, the walls were dripping sweat. It was an amazing show, and at the end of the night I was sandwiched between Barry Squire from Warner Brothers and Anna Statman from Geffen. Anna had played in the Red Lights with Jeffrey Lee Pierce. They'd seen what they came to see, and they both wanted to sign Bug Lamp.

"This band is amazing," Anna said. "Let's talk dollars and cents."

"Come into my office Monday," Barry said. "We'll sit with the president of the company and I'll write you a check for whatever you want."

I was standing there and listening in a state of depression because there wasn't a band to sign. Daniel was still in New York. Michael, the drummer, was starting a band with Dave Navarro that Rick Rubin was bankrolling. Dan and Robbie had decided to start a band together called One Hit Wonder that was creating unwelcome competition. I had not one but two offers to sign, but no band. Bug Lamp was no more.

I could have said, "I'll be there on Monday." I could have signed the deal and figured everything out afterward. I could have gotten the Keith Morris Band going. My ego is pretty big, but it's not that big. It wouldn't have been right. We didn't sign.

I did, however, take one more meeting with a woman who worked at Chrysalis. While I was sitting in the waiting room I thought of all the bands I knew who had signed with Chrysalis, guys like Henry Rollins and the Sea Hags, neither of which I felt particularly good about. An assistant took me in to see my friend, and she was sweet-talking me the whole time, which she didn't need to do, so what gives? The machinery in my mind started to clank and clunk.

I sat down with her, and she told me how much she wanted to sign Bug Lamp. She also casually mentioned that if I needed to talk to anyone about the label, I could just reach out to Henry Rollins, and he would be happy to share his experience with me. I told her I could do that, but in my mind I was wondering why she kept bringing up Henry. What does Henry have to do with Bug Lamp? She went on, saying that once Henry and I were both signed, the two of us could talk Ian MacKaye of Fugazi into signing with the label.

I nearly fell out of my chair. I'd heard the rumors—we all had. Every major label in the world wanted Fugazi on their roster. The only problem with that was Ian MacKaye had more integrity in his left testicle than all of the record industry insects in Hollywood combined. There was no way Fugazi was signing with a major. There was zero chance of me and Henry going to fly out to Washington, DC, to encourage Ian MacKaye and tell him how wonderful it was to be a recording artist with Chrysalis Records. It just wasn't going to happen.

I was finally able to see what the meeting was really about. They didn't care about Bug Lamp; they wanted to use me to get to Ian MacKaye—that's how much Fugazi was worth to them.

I declined the offer. I never considered signing, but the whole thing was so slimy that I left the building feeling as dejected as I've ever felt about the music business.

A WANDERING JEW

I was feeling pretty low about my situation, but to make matters worse, my dad's health was failing, and he was in a bad way. For years he had been grinding along with his bait-and-tackle business, keeping his nose clean, as he liked to say. Not too long after I got clean and sober, he was busted in a sting with two or three grams of cocaine. The feds weren't after him, but they wanted the guy he got the coke from. I don't know what went down. I never asked. We didn't have the kind of relationship where I could say, "Hey, Dad, what's up with those coke charges? You gonna beat it or what?"

My dad's dealer was under surveillance. He was this rich dude in Malibu who the feds were keeping an eye on. They were on his tip. I don't know if my dad turned informant or worked out a plea deal or if the feds just lost interest in him. I don't think my dad was the kind of guy who would sell out a friend. The cops must have known it was just a matter of time before the dealer made the wrong move. The weird thing was he was already rich. He didn't need to deal. My dad told me he thought the guy did it for the thrill. There are a lot of people who are more interested in procuring drugs than using them. For them, going to cop is much more exciting than actually doing the drugs.

I wasn't like that, and neither was my dad. He used all his life. A little of this, a little of that—whatever it took to get by. Eventually it caught up with him. He went into cardiac arrest when his esophagus started bleeding. They can't cut you open and replace your esophagus with a tube. When your esophagus goes, you go along with it.

That was only part of the story. My dad also had cirrhosis of the liver and hepatitis C. He didn't fit the profile of your raging alcoholic or drug addict, but he was a user nonetheless. He went about his business and fed his disease until his body couldn't take it anymore. Part of me wonders if the stress of getting busted was a contributing factor, that maybe he worried about it more than he let on and that sped up his demise. Long story short: his organs failed, his body shut down, and that was the last of Jerry Allen Morris.

We had a gathering for him at the Hermosa Pier where thousands of anglers had fished with bait and tackle they'd bought from my dad. All of his friends, customers, business associates, and acquaintances in the community came and told stories. When it was over, a handful of us went down to King Harbor, got in a boat, went out in the marina, and circled back up to Hermosa Beach. Once we were a couple of yards off the Hermosa Pier we sprinkled my father's ashes on the ocean. I think that would have made him happy.

I FIGURED IT WAS TIME TO TAKE A LONG, lengthy hiatus— not just from LA, but from music. I loaded up my backpack and bounced around for a little while. I took lonely walks though empty streets, kicked a can down desolate railroad tracks, whistled a tune as I hunkered down over a cup of coffee in bus station cafés. I was the proverbial wanderer, the wandering half-Jew.

My first stop was the flat lands of Edmonton, Canada—Wayne Gretzky country. I was seeing a girl named Jodi who was from there, and my plan was to move to Edmonton to be with her and live happily ever after. The Canadian authorities had something to say about that.

When I arrived in Edmonton I had to go through customs, and they kept me there for about four hours. They put me in one room and Jodi in another and asked me all kinds of questions about who I was, how much money I had in the bank, and what I planned on doing in Edmonton. Apparently all of my answers were incorrect, and they decided I wasn't going to be able to stay. They put me on the next flight back to Los Angeles, which was at 7 a.m. I spent the night with Jodi and we had an intense time together before I had to head back to the airport and say good-bye. So close and yet so far. Story of my life.

I was pretty broken up about the situation, so my mom invited me to come stay with her at my sister's house in North Carolina. She was living in Mount Holly, outside of Charlotte. The next city over was Gastonia, where the greatest basketball player of all time comes from: Michael Jordan. It was my mother, my sister Trudy, her husband, and their two sons. They had a huge house in the country, so another body wasn't going to make a difference. Jodi even came out for a visit. I spent three months with my family in the woods with the grass and the bushes and the trees.

I arrived in Charlotte just in time for the Island Records A&R tour. The label put a bunch of their young A&R people on a bus and sent them from city to city. They'd contacted some of the biggest clubs in Charlotte and told them they were sending representatives from their label to listen to the best bands in town.

It was a good deal for the bands because they got to play to a packed room and had a shot at getting the attention of a major label. It was also great for people like me who were scoping out the local musical talent. I had it in the back of my mind that I wanted to start a band in Charlotte. I changed my mind after I attended the showcase. Let's just say I was underwhelmed. I was like, *Are you kidding? This is the best your city has to offer?*

I met a few musicians in the grunge mold who played heavy music that was fast and loud. They were a bit ahead of the curve for Charlotte. The biggest band in town at the time was Fetchin' Bones. They made a bunch of records in the eighties but hadn't done much since—like the Circle Jerks—only their sound was a lot more radio friendly. I liked the band and enjoyed their music, but I wasn't going to leap off of a three-story building to go to one of their shows. I eventually came to the conclusion that there wasn't much going on in town. If I was going to start up another band, it wasn't going to be in Charlotte.

Eventually I made my way up to the city of Richmond in the commonwealth of Virginia, where I met up with an old friend. She had opened a new restaurant in town and had an extra room where I could crash and check out the city.

I thought Richmond was a strange and interesting place. A massive prison sat in the center of the city, the streets were named after Confederate soldiers, and the road that cut through town served as a racial divide between the blacks and the whites. I don't know if it's still like that, but that's how it was during my brief time there.

I liked Virginia. I enjoyed the slower pace. The people were friendlier. The weather was great, and Washington, DC, was just a few hours up the road. Having grown up in LA, it was cool to experience a different environment for a little while in a part of the world that had trees that actually changed color and water that fell from the sky. Weird.

I wasn't in Richmond for very long before I got the urge to be around music again. It was like a sickness, an addiction. I couldn't stay away. I had the songs I'd written with Daniel Rey and the Bug Lamp demo tape that Rob Stennet had recorded. I started to check out the local scene and went to some shows. A lot of interesting bands have come out of Richmond, but none more famous than GWAR.

Eventually I was introduced to the characters in GWAR, spent some time at their compound, and got to know Dave Brockey (RIP) and the rest of the band pretty well. I'm not a diehard fan of the band, but they're all really great musicians and put on a wild show. I couldn't listen to a GWAR album, but I love the spectacle. They do something you're not going to find anywhere else, and that's probably a good thing. I almost started a band with one of the members, but for whatever reason it didn't happen.

Then Bob Forrest showed up in Richmond, and things started to get weird. He moved in with me and got involved in a drug triangle with my friend, which caused all kinds of problems for everyone. I wasn't romantically involved with her, but everyone thought I was. She'd ask me what she should do, which put me in an awkward position. Eventually she started taking out her frustration on me and told me I had to leave.

I headed up north to Braintree, Massachusetts, where I crashed with Chris Doherty of Gang Green. We were going to start a band together but didn't get much further along than our initial conversation about it. Curtis Casella at Taang! Records in Cambridge hired me to work at the record store and the record label. Mudhoney came to town with Pearl Jam and invited me to their show. They asked me to perform "Fix Me." It was a huge rush to play in front of so many people in Boston Garden where the Celtics play. I got to hang out with Eddie Vedder. I was honest with him and told Eddie that aside from Pearl Jam's first album, I wasn't a fan of his music. He got a big kick out of the fact that I wasn't kissing his ass.

A friend gave me the keys to an apartment in the north end of Boston where I could crash for a while. The previous tenant was a mafia hit man who had strangled his girlfriend there. The place had a dark, heavy vibe. I didn't like it and had to get out. It was time to go home.

Some of the people I'd met while playing with Pearl Jam and Mudhoney asked me what it would take to get the Circle Jerks over to Europe to play some festivals. I called up Greg in LA and told him we had some unfinished business. We never made it to many of the places where we'd been invited to play. We couldn't find our asses with both hands, but the Circle Jerks weren't quite done with our reach-around.

THE LAST JERK OFF

After Green Day's *Dookie* sold more records than God every band who had been a part of the early punk rock community, whether they want to admit it or not, had their moment when they collectively thought, *Why not us?*

It went the other way too. The success of bands like Green Day and Offspring were causing A&R people at major labels to reconsider punk rock. Suddenly punk rock wasn't a dirty word anymore. Eventually our friend Bobby Carlton at Mercury Records inquired to find out if the Circle Jerks had written any new songs.

We hadn't.

Although we'd had a long layoff as a band, individually we'd been busy. While I was walking the earth, Greg had just finished recording a new album with Bad Religion. Zander had put together the Low & Sweet Orchestra with Mike Martt, who'd played in the Gun Club and Tex and the Horseheads. They had just signed a deal and were getting ready to go in the studio. Our drummer, Keith, had tax clients to satisfy and deadlines to meet. He was always busy.

I wasn't doing much of anything. In fact, I was the only guy in the band who depended on the Circle Jerks for an income. I was staying in a guest room in Greg's house up in the hills and riding my bike to Zander's place in Mar Vista, where we worked up some new material. Eventually we had enough to record a demo for Mercury Records, which we did. Mercury loved the songs, and we signed a long-term recording contract with them. Our sixth studio album would be our first with a major label.

It was almost too easy. After all of my struggles with major labels I was surprised by how quickly things fell into place. Of course, the label had the option to terminate our contract at any time, and if we didn't move enough product, they'd show us the door. If we wanted to earn out our contract we were going to have to hustle.

I don't remember the exact figures for the advance, but we split it equally, and we each got something in the neighborhood of $20,000. If I had gotten a deal like that ten or fifteen years earlier, it would have killed me. It would have gone right up my nose and everything would have come to a grinding halt. The advance allowed us to not have to worry about paying rent when the first of the month came around. Instead of worrying about what we could hock or how many CDs we could sell at Aaron's Records to make sure rent got paid, we could focus on what we were supposed to be doing.

But I was having a hard time getting the machinery moving again. Even though we hadn't put out a record in close to five years, everyone was so busy with side projects and side-side projects that getting everyone in the same room was a challenge. We were really scattered. I couldn't get an hour's worth of attention from anyone because there were so many things going on. So even though the band had been stagnant for years, we picked the worst time to get it going again. No one had the time. I was beginning to think the Circle Jerks wasn't a priority for the guys anymore. It had become the side project.

Then, the motivation to get our act together came from an unlikely place.

"Fellas," Greg announced. "I've got a schedule here. We have to get this recorded before Greg Graffin snaps his fingers."

Okay, maybe he didn't say it exactly like that, but the sentiment was the same. The whole situation had gotten ridiculous. We came up with some songs and agreed on a couple of covers. The three songs we wrote for the demo were the three best songs. The rest were just kind of mailed in. More than once I wondered, *Why are we even doing this?* It felt like the Circle Jerks' version of the *Great Rock and Roll Swindle*.

I chose Niko Bolas to produce the record because he was an engineer who'd worked on Neil Young's *Eldorado*, which features some of the loudest, noisiest music Neil ever recorded. In my opinion it's some of his best stuff. As the saying goes, be careful what you ask for. You just might get it . . .

ODDITIES, ABNORMALITIES AND CURIOSITIES is not a live record, but we recorded live, which was weird and kind of amazing. We didn't record our tracks individually; we were all in the room together at the same time, and I sang along with the guys while they played. I thought that was strange, but that's how Niko wanted to make the record.

Sometimes you hire a producer because he or she is a musician who can evaluate what you're doing and can make informed musical decisions—this note is too high, your bridge is too long, the intro is too slow. That wasn't Niko. He was a sound guy. Niko would be somebody who you would want doing your sound if you were playing live. I loved working with him and he has worked with some amazing musicians, but in retrospect I don't think he was a great choice for us.

That said, Niko was dating Debbie Gibson, every punk rocker's wet dream. His relationship with Debbie was how I talked her into singing on our cover of Robyn Hitchcock and the Soft Boys' "I Wanna Destroy You."

What was starting to happen with the music industry was you'd have the band go in the studio with a producer and record an album. The label would listen to the record and decide, "This is the first single, that's the second single," and so on. Then someone else would mix the songs the label had selected for the single. The guys mixing the songs would make as much money as the producer. Two or three different people mixed our record. This was all very alien to us. Why did we need all these people?

After the record came out we bought a giant recreational vehicle that could sleep eleven people. It had a kitchenette, a dining table—all kinds of stuff you'd need on the road. We pulled a trailer with all of our equipment and merch.

We purchased this monstrosity because we knew we were going to be out on the road for a while and it would help us save money on motels. It was a four-week tour that was split in half with a two-week break in between. I don't know who thought that up. Maybe it was because a couple of the guys were married and didn't want to be away from their wives and their kids and their dogs and their goldfish that long. I don't know. We went out and did the first two weeks, and it was extremely disappointing.

Apparently a new album by our label mates Bon Jovi had just dropped and wasn't doing as well as expected in the United States. The band was touring overseas, where the record was doing really well, so there wasn't much they could do about it over here. We were told that the president of the label basically told everyone in the company to drop what they were doing and pitch in on the Bon Jovi record.

As a result, the Circle Jerks were left to figure things out on our own. Usually when you go out on tour you try to make the most of your time in the city where you're playing. If you've got a gig at night, maybe you do an in-store appearance where you sign albums and shake hands. Personally, I like going to record stores. If it's a cool record store and the people who work there are knowledgeable and are into what we're doing, it can be a really nice experience for everyone. The store brings in fans, the fans get to see the band up close, and I bring home some new records.

Maybe you go to the local radio station for an interview and say, "We're playing tonight—why don't you come down? Here are a couple of tracks off the new record." Stuff like that. No one likes radio station interviews, but it breaks up the day. You roll into town, do your sound check, go do an interview, get something to eat, and come back for the show. It's part of the job. On this tour none of that stuff was lined up. It was all very disappointing.

I think our highest point of the tour would have been the night Chuck Berry was in the audience at Mississippi Nights in St. Louis and joined us onstage for "Roll Over Beethoven." After the show, after everyone had cleared out and gone home, the club owner pulled me aside and said, "Chuck Berry told me to tell you that you were one of the greatest rock and roll bands he has ever seen."

As a compliment, it doesn't get higher than that. Greg worshipped at the altars of Angus Young and Johnny Thunders, and neither of those guys would be playing if it weren't for Chuck Berry. If you're a guitar player on any level in any genre of music, you're going to have to hit some of those notes that Chuck Berry introduced to rock and roll. Without Chuck Berry there would be no Keith Richards, and with no Keith Richards we certainly wouldn't have Johnny Thunders, and if there's no Johnny Thunders, where would the rockers of today be? That night was one of the few good things to come out of that record.

THE LAST SHOW OF THE FIRST HALF of the tour was at St. Andrews Hall in Detroit. A couple of hours before the show we were all upstairs in what was considered the backstage area but was basically a smaller hall that could hold two or three hundred people. Greg gathered us up and said, "Guys, I've got something very important to tell you. Tonight's my last night. I'm leaving the tour."

He went down a list of excuses. My dog has worms. My mom has hemorrhoids. I need to fluff my girlfriend's pillow. Basically he was upset that the label hadn't done any of the things they told us they were going to do. Bon Jovi got all of the love, and we didn't get squat.

I understood Greg's disappointment. We were all disappointed. But he was in Bad Religion, and when they signed with Atlantic Records the label got behind the band in a big way. They played the Warped Tour and the festival circuit and were gone for months and months at a time. They had a very nice roll. They got the opportunities the Circle Jerks never seemed to get. He saw which side the bread was buttered and quit the band in the middle of the tour.

I was furious. I resented how, when push came to shove, the Circle Jerks played second banana to Bad Religion. But Greg was the only other cofounding member of the band. He'd been there from the beginning. We'd been doing this for fifteen years. Didn't that count for something?

Apparently not.

Greg may have quit, but I wasn't ready to throw in the towel. We had commitments to make, obligations to honor, rooms to rock.

"Guys, we're not going home," I said. "We're not turning around with our tails between our legs. We've got business to take care of. We've got to keep going, we've got to play out the tour. This is how we earn our living."

My plan was to keep going and drive to New York. I wanted to see if I could talk Todd Youth of Murphy's Law into finishing the tour with us. He knew all of the old Circle Jerks songs and was younger than Greg Hetson by six or seven years. He had a great deal of energy, and I knew he would jump at the chance. He would have been perfect, but my plea fell on deaf ears and I got voted down. Keith and Zander weren't interested in continuing without Greg.

"We're through."

That pretty much ended it. End of the tour. End of the band. The Circle Jerks had tossed off their last tour.

ODDITIES, ABNORMALITIES AND CURIOSITIES sold twenty-five thousand copies. Those numbers don't allow you to stay on a major label. Unless the president of the company is your best friend and thinks your band is going to be bigger than the Beatles, you don't stand a chance. Mercury put a stop to our long-term deal. I wouldn't be surprised if our A&R guy got fired.

In my opinion that record should have never been made. It has nothing to do with the quality of the recording but rather the collective lack of creativity put forth by the members of the band. In my opinion it's not even close to being a real album. Maybe two or three songs were worthy of being on a Circle Jerks album. I give the record a C-, and that's generous. When the most memorable song on the rec–ord is a cover with vocals by Debbie Gibson, you know you're in trouble.

The fact remains that I don't like the record, and I don't think I'm alone in that opinion. Everyone who worked on it should be ripped a new asshole, myself included.

DEVIL'S MESS

I was sleeping on the floor at Allison Dyer's house above Sunset Boulevard in Silver Lake for a couple of months. All during this time I wondered why I wasn't sleeping with her. She eventually broke the news that I wasn't her type. I got a place of my own at the top of Griffith Park Boulevard behind a Mexican restaurant called El Conquistador, which isn't there anymore. It was a tiny little studio apartment with a living area the size of a small office, a bathroom, and a kitchenette. The rent was $350. No deposit, no credit check required. The guy in charge of the building lived in a one-bedroom apartment with his wife and two teenage kids. I plopped down the money, he gave me the key, and I moved in the next day. Wham, bam, thank you, man.

I've never been much of a cook and have always preferred to eat out. Millie's Diner was so close to where I lived that if I started singing a Beatles song when I left, I'd be at Millie's before it was over. I was a fan of a dish called the Devil's Mess, and their French toast was amazing. When I would get on a financial roll, rather than prepare food at home, I would go and have a big breakfast at Millie's two or three times a week. At a certain point, being an upstanding member of the community and a loyal customer, I would get my meals for half price. The Keith Morris shuffle.

I don't remember how I came about working there. It was probably really busy one day and I offered to help or they asked me to pitch in and it became a regular thing. I was already going there every other day and knew all the people. Working there meant I'd be able to eat for free before and after each shift. Why not work at Millie's? How difficult could it be to pour coffee, take orders, and set silverware on the table?

Some might regard this as my "low period," but I don't see it that way. The truth was I had a lot of friends who worked at Millie's, and most of them were musicians. The manager was Charlie Hutchinson, the bass player from POPDeFECT. The waitstaff consisted of Aaron "The Moron" Donovan, who had played guitar in the Leaving Trains; Iris Berry, who is a poet and a writer; and Skot Morin, who was the vocalist in 400 Blows. Jean Le Bear was the cook, and his girlfriend, Sandrine, prepped. Bob Forrest worked there occasionally, if you can believe that, and future Circle Jerks drummer Kevin Fitzgerald was a waiter, as was a guy named Campbell who was in a band called Ferocious Suck. There was a dishwasher named Johnny, who was in Anus the Menace, and a cook named Bill, who was in a band called UFO Gang. Patti would sometimes cook, even though she owned the place. There was this whole crew of people who worked at Millie's, partied at Al's Bar, and played music every chance they could get. I loved it.

It was a really creative environment, and in some ways it was just as much a scene as Al's Bar, where they all hung out afterward. For a while I was dating one of the bartenders at Al's Bar. Hope Urban made me feel as though I was with Sofia Loren's youngest sister.

My assignment at Millie's was to take drink orders. I worked weekends when it was busiest. The whole idea was to get people in there, get their orders, get them served, and get them the fuck out. We had a high turnover, which led to high volume. We got to the point where we went from having $1,000 Saturdays to $3,000 Saturdays and Sundays. A good Saturday paid the rent. If Sunday was as good as Saturday, I had all of my expenses for the rest of the month covered with tips. Everything after that was a bonus. I would get the customers their coffee as soon as they sat down, and then it was off to the races. There would be people lined up and down the sidewalk waiting to get their grizzle on.

There was a lot of crossover among the staff, a lot of multitasking. I was doing some prep and mistook my thumb for a tomato and sliced it open. It was fucking ugly. I should have gotten stitches, but I just wrapped it in tape—that was the end of my prepping days. I washed dishes. I bussed tables. I took orders. I did whatever needed to be done.

I started as the Saturday and Sunday busboy/server and added a few more shifts during the week. Between my pay and my tips I was able to cover my rent, put shoes on my feet, and buy some music here and there.

Occasionally Iris would organize what amounted to staff talent shows. After the restaurant was closed and the floors were cleaned we'd have a little party. Someone would take some of the tip money and go buy some beer, and people would stick around to drink. One night I did a spoken-word thing with Craig Grady, who at the time was in a relationship with the owner. Craig had this giant palm branch that had blown off of a tree, and he brushed it back and forth across the room in a rhythmic motion. Jean Le Bear had his saxophone with him and started to improvise, and I told stories over the music they made.

It wasn't all good times. I went to work and two of the kitchen workers were no shows. Bill was a cook and Johnny did prep and washed dishes. It was eight o'clock, and the first wave of people was starting to filter in. It was time for somebody to cut the fruit, make the granola, and all that other stuff. The orders were starting to come in, and we didn't have a cook.

Bill and Johnny were crashing out in the same building I was living in, and Iris sent me over to knock on their window and wake them up. I went and was very loud and very obnoxious, but there was no response. I tried to peek in the window, but I couldn't see anything. Knowing them, they were probably in a drunken stupor and dead to the world.

I went back to Millie's. Iris was frantic. The orders were coming in fast, and she could pour only so much coffee. She sent me back to their apartment and told me not to return without them. I banged on their window and door and still couldn't get a response, so I went to the guy who ran the building to see if I could get him to open the door. I told him they were my friends and I needed to wake them up for work. The manager got the keys, and we went and opened the door to their apartment. I could tell right away that things weren't right. Johnny was face down in a pillow, and Bill was wrapped up in a rug on the floor. He was half in and half out of the bathroom, and his face was beet red and caked in purple vomit.

I went inside and poked Johnny, but he wasn't moving. I called 911 and told them what I was dealing with. The woman on the other end of the line told me to go into the kitchen and get a plate to hold in front of their faces to see if they were breathing.

I told the lady that Bill definitely wasn't breathing. I rolled Johnny over and put the plate under his nose but there was nothing happening, No breathing or any other signs of life.

The paramedics got there and saw what I'd failed to see: there was a suicide note on the table next to the bed. They had gotten a hot batch of heroin. Bill overdosed in the bathroom and Johnny freaked out, thinking, *What am I going to do with the body?* He tried to roll him up in a rug. When he realized there wasn't anything he could do, he shot up the rest of the hot batch and overdosed. It was really sad because neither one of them were hardcore heroin users. If they had been, they would have known to not cook up as much as they had. They both had been in relationships that had ended badly and were severely depressed, and now they were dead.

When I didn't come back to Millie's, Iris called the manager, and Charlie came over to the apartment to see what was going on. I was sitting on the stairs outside the apartment in shock, and when I told him the news Charlie broke down in tears. We were all pretty shaken up.

It was sad because they were friends, but the fact of the matter was they were musicians, and everyone in this business has lost a lot of friends this way. On one hand, it was a tragic waste because they were grown men who didn't have to die like that. On the other hand, when it happens it feels almost inevitable. In this kind of life, there's just no escaping it. It's really unfortunate, but there's nothing you can do about it. There's a list I go through whenever I hear about a friend, acquaintance, or colleague who's lost his or her battle with drugs and alcohol, and it never fails to bring me to the realization that I'm psyched to be here and able to carry on . . .

DOWN

After I'd been working at Millie's for about a year I got really sick. I came down with a summer cold that wouldn't go away. Two weeks, three weeks—I couldn't shake it.

I was always cold. No matter what I did, I couldn't stay warm. I walked around the neighborhood in the middle of summer, wearing two pairs of socks, long underwear, a T-shirt, a sweatshirt, and a coat. Nobody dresses like that when it's 90 degrees outside. Normally I'd be sweating like a pig at a luau. I'd walk up the stairs to my apartment, bury myself under six or seven blankets, and lie there shivering and soaking in sweat. Something was wrong.

The walls in the apartment were paper-thin, and I could hear everything that was going on around me, all night long. Foot traffic, arguments, doors opening and closing. There was a guy who'd bring back transvestite hookers to his apartment a couple of nights a week, and I could hear him slapping them around. I'd hear all this commotion and things breaking and furniture falling over. Screaming and crying and carrying on, and nobody ever complained. I just wanted to lie there in peace and try to get some rest, but I couldn't do that.

I was losing weight, and I couldn't go anywhere without someone commenting on it.

"Keith, are you okay?"

"Keith, you look terrible."

"Keith, you should go see a doctor."

I told them it was just a cold, a cold that was stretching into its second month. I didn't know what else to tell them. My shifts at Millie's took everything out of me. I was too tired to stick around to eat. I'd go to the dollar store on the way home and stock up on two-liter bottles of soda and packages of cookies. Every time I woke up I'd chomp on a cookie or guzzle some soda, and this would go on through the night.

Bob Forrest and Michael Kelly came to see me. I'd dropped down to about eighty-five pounds, and they were really concerned.

"Morty," Bob said, "you look like shit."

"You look like you have cancer," Michael said.

"Let us take you to Cedars Sinai for some tests," Bob said.

I told them it wasn't necessary, that I'd been through a rough patch but was feeling better. I wasn't, but I didn't want them to worry about me. About a week later I was going across the street, and instead of crossing at the crosswalk, I decided to jaywalk and tripped over a small mound of unfinished asphalt. When I fell, I twisted and somehow landed on my back. I was absolutely fucking blindsided with pain. The next day it felt even worse. Convinced I'd crushed another vertebrae, I went to Toluca Lake to see my chiropractor, John Ciambotti, who had played bass on the first two Elvis Costello albums.

"Keith," John said, "you need to step into the bathroom and stand in front of the mirror for about ten minutes and then come back and tell me what you see."

My response was, "I know I'm a fairly handsome guy but . . . "

"That's not what I'm talking about. You look like you're getting ready to fall over or blow away in a good strong wind. You look like you're ready to die."

It was true. I didn't look so good. I looked like somebody who'd just escaped from a Nazi concentration camp.

"I've got a registered nurse here. She's going to draw some blood, we're going to do a blood panel, and we'll get to the bottom of this."

"Okay," I said. "Let's do it."

It turned out my back wasn't broken; I'd only bruised some ribs. Painful but manageable, but I couldn't cough or laugh for weeks.

When the lab results came in, my chiropractor called me back and told me the news. "No AIDS. No hepatitis. Your blood is perfect all the way across except for your glucose. At 345, that's through the roof."

I told him that didn't sound so bad.

"It should be between 70 and 120. You're a diabetic! Now you've got to go see a real doctor and deal with it."

He made me promise to get it straightened out and start taking care of myself. He scared me with stories about diabetics going blind, losing limbs, falling into comas they never came out of. I promised him I would go see a doctor and get this taken care of. That bit of advice probably saved my life.

The first doctor I went to see said, "You're going to eliminate sugar."

"What does that mean? Can you give me a list?"

He started rattling things off at the top of his head: no fruit, no nuts, no bread, no soda. A lot of that made sense to me. But give up fruit? Fruit's one of the healthiest things you can eat. How was I going to eliminate fruit? What would I put on top of my pancakes and French toast?

My doctor sent me to a diabetic class over at USC. The first question the nurse leading the class asked was, "What do you think is the major cause of diabetes?"

"Sugar," I responded.

"Wrong. The number-one cause of diabetes is stress."

That got my attention. I'd been in an extremely stressful situation. Money was tight, and I was working in a restaurant during the busiest time of day. It wasn't rocket science, but it was go, go, go from start to finish. An eight-hour shift wasn't just stressful; it was insanity.

While I was working at Millie's I developed a pattern of bingeing on carbonated beverages. Where before I might have had a can of Dr Pepper or a cream soda a couple of times a month, now I had access to the soda machine during my shifts. I was easily drinking six to eight large soft drinks per shift, over a hundred ounces a day. That's some of the worst stuff you can put in your system, and I was bingeing on it like a horse with a bendy straw.

So the stress coupled with the soda, my addictive nature, and the fact that Millie's was so close and convenient added up to a bad situation for my personal health and well-being. Over the course of my tenure at Millie's I must have had 126 pieces of French toast slathered with maple syrup and chased with 175 glasses of orange juice and soft drinks. Sugar upon sugar upon sugar on top of a shitload of stress. So yes, I blame my diabetes on the habits I developed at Millie's.

MIDGET HANDJOB

Midget Handjob emerged from the work parties we had at Millie's. While everyone was filling the ketchup bottles, sugar pourers, and salt and pepper shakers, they would have a couple of beers. It was easier for my coworkers to mop the floors and wipe down the counters when they knew there were a couple of cold ones waiting. The manager knew what he was doing. These guys were all drinkers, and he supplied them with the right motivation.

After a couple of these shows I was contacted by Chris Bagarozzi, who was the lead guitar player in Clawhammer and Down by Law. He invited me over to his place in Silver Lake for jam sessions with a loose collective of my coworkers at Millie's. Jon Wahl and Jean Le Bear would blow on various size saxophones. Tony Malone, who played in Detox and Thelonious Monster and was dating Iris Berry, played guitar. Kevin Fitzgerald, a drummer who was playing with the Geraldine Fibbers, was our drummer, if you can call it that—we never had a full drum kit. Sometimes we'd have a kick drum and a high hat, but more often than not we'd use a bucket of chains, a five-gallon bottle filled with screws, and a can full of coins. We'd use anything to get crazy effects. A plastic tube that made a whirring sound when you whipped it around your head. A piece of aluminum siding that sounded like something out of *The Wizard of Oz* when the tornado sets down. We made noises with all kinds of strange stuff. We were an unconventional band.

I don't know at what point we started to think of ourselves as a band. The name was slang for an unscrupulous political arrangement, a dirty deal inspired by my experiences with the music industry.

After a while we started to book shows and play out in public because it was a lot more fun to play to a group of people than in Chris's living room. Whenever I booked a show I would call up all the participants and say, "This is the date and venue of the show." Whoever showed up that night, that was the band. We weren't going to cancel a gig because one of the players didn't show up: "Oh no, the guy with the bucket of chains isn't here! What are we going to do?"

There was none of that. Because of our connection to Al's Bar, Clawhammer, POPDeFECT, and a dozen other bands, we had a lot of opportunities to play around town. We played with Solid Eye, which is Rick Potts from Human Hands, at Spaceland. We played the Echo. We played at the Troubadour and opened for Caustic Resin, Brett Netson's band when he wasn't playing guitar with Built to Spill. We played the Knitting Factory a couple of times, and at one of the shows we opened for the Fall. Mark E. Smith loved Midget Handjob.

"You guys are amazing! You have to come on tour with the Fall."

For what we were doing, it didn't get much better than that. Actually, it did get better: we opened for John Frusciante at the Roxy, playing in front of a bunch of love-struck teenage girls who wanted to hear Red Hot Chili Peppers hits. Andy Kaulkin, who was in charge of Anti Records, ended up playing keyboards with us one night. That's the kind of disorganized musical organization we were.

We had a blast doing our thing. The people who came and saw us got a kick out of it. There were a few raised eyebrows at the beginning of the performance, but then people would get into it. It was different. I was in no kind of shape to memorize all of the words I was speaking, so I'd read out of a newspaper with all the lyrics pasted inside. Sometimes it was *Playboy*, *Flipside Fanzine*, *Hustler*, the *Los Angeles Times*, or whatever.

Maybe Andy got in Brett Gurewitz's ear and told him he should sign us. Maybe Brett had heard I had diabetes and wanted to do something to help. I don't know, but Brett reached out and said, "I'll give you a deal here at Epitaph." He didn't have to do that. No one else was going to give Midget Handjob any kind of record deal. He did it to light a fire under my ass, to keep me from giving up and going under. I'll never be able to thank Brett enough for all he's done for me.

When word got out that I had diabetes, a lot of my friends came to my rescue. They organized benefits on my behalf. One featured performances by the Weirdos, X, and Thelonious Monster; film clips by Penelope Spheeris; and was emceed by Gibby Haynes. Recreational Racism played punk versions of country western songs—or maybe it was vice versa. Another benefit at the Whisky, which donated the space, had Fishbone, Pennywise, and the Vandals. That one was organized by Bob Forrest. I may have pissed a few people off during my wild years, but people who knew me understood where I was coming from. I'm not a bad person, I don't screw people over, and I try to treat people the way I would want to be treated. I have an ego and a temper and every now and then I blow my stack, but for the most part I have a lot more friends than enemies in this town, which isn't easy to do when you've been a part of the scene for as long as I have.

Brett offered Midget Handjob a contract, and I split it evenly with everyone who committed to playing on the record. It wasn't one of those deals where I took the cash and everyone worked for free; I wasn't about to pass out scraps. We ended up recording *Midnight Snack Break at the Poodle Factory* at Rancho de la Luna in Joshua Tree with Fred Drake and our friend Tom Grimley from Poop Alley. Fred's no longer with us—RIP. He was one of the co-owners at Rancho de la Luna, which is right up the dirt road from where Graham Parsons died in the little hotel. That studio is also where the Desert Sessions were recorded, Josh Homme's collective of musicians like P. J. Harvey, Mark Lanegan, and Chris Goss, who happens to be one of my musical heroes.

So many great musicians have passed through Rancho de la Luna. It's basically a four-room house, and everyone just sets up and records. It was a perfect situation for Midget Handjob. We had two guitar players, two sax players, two percussionists, and myself. Petra Haden played violin while we were recording vocals and overdubs with Tom Grimley above Al's Bar at the American Hotel.

The album featured an image of a poodle with a boner that was painted by Aaron Donovan, aka the Moron. I'm not sure if the image inspired the title of the album or vice versa, but that's what we went with. The painting rests on my mantle in my Los Feliz apartment.

BELIEVE IT OR NOT, MIDGET HANDJOB went on a US tour. The booking agent played up the fact during his sales pitch that it was a spoken-word tour: "Like Henry Rollins with saxophones!" That's not something I would ever want to hear, but I thought it was funny.

The tour wasn't long and was fairly mellow by Circle Jerks standards, but it had to be. As a diabetic, I couldn't handle the rigors of the road. I couldn't put my body through the stress and strain like I used to. I had to take it easy, keep my diet regular, and get plenty of rest.

We'd start each show by hauling these milk crates filled with shakers and maracas and bits of metal and broken tambourines and all sorts of stuff people could bang on. We'd just dump it in front of the stage and invite the audience to play along with us—cacophonous audience participation added to our festivities. We weren't trying to turn it into a drum circle or anything like that—world beat has never been my thing—but we wanted people to know they were in for something that was a little out of the ordinary, a little peculiar, and they were welcome to join the fun.

Unfortunately the shows were not very well attended. We were on the road for about three weeks, and it was very underwhelming.

One of the most memorable nights was in Atlanta, but it was memorable for the wrong reasons. We played upstairs in this really cool ballroom, and there was absolutely nobody there. No paying customers. Not one. We played anyway because we're pros and had a good time playing with ourselves (pun intended). As we were packing up our gear, two girls came running up the stairs. They wanted to know if they could buy a couple of our T-shirts. I was kind of taken aback but was happy to sell them some merch. Maybe we'd make enough money to pay part of our bar tab.

"Out of curiosity," I asked, "what prompted you to purchase these T-shirts?"

The girls responded, "We were at another show, but we liked the name of your band, so we wanted to get a T-shirt!"

At least they liked the name. Not everyone did.

We played a youth center in Tucson, Arizona, and my mom was in the audience. There were about seventy-five kids there, and they were all getting their picture taken with my mom. My mom stole the show that night. She was wearing this outfit with paisley print on her matching jacket and parachute pants.

Our last show of the tour was at a nightclub located in downtown Hollywood—Bill's Disco Paradise or some other silly shit. There were maybe sixty people there, including Epitaph employees and guests. One of the people who showed up was Andy Kaulkin, the president of Anti Records, and he said, "When do you want to put out your second record?"

I was like, "Are you kidding me?"

Although the tour was nothing to write home about, our guarantees paid for the recreational vehicle, we stayed in hotels, and everybody got a per diem. So it was a good experience for everyone, especially for some of the guys like Jean Le Bear, who'd never been in a touring band before. Let's go see America!

Our last two shows we played back to back on the same night. The first show was at Spaceland, and it was a really fantastic show with a full complement of performers. Then we packed up our gear and headed down to Long Beach to play at DiPiazza's on Pacific Coast Highway. That show didn't turn out so well in that we only had Kevin on drums, Chris playing guitar, Jon Wahl on sax, and me doing spoken word, which completely defeated the whole purpose of what we were supposed to be doing. In that configuration we resembled a regular band, and what's so special about that? The final performance of the band was disappointing and deflating.

Epitaph was able to sell only five hundred copies of *Midnight Snack Break at the Poodle Factory*. They couldn't give the CDs away. At one point I got a call from the guys at the Epitaph/Anti warehouse stating the CDs were going to be destroyed and I could come down and take what I wanted. I grabbed a bunch of boxes. I probably still have some shoved in the back of the closet.

I've also got a stack of royalty checks from Epitaph for *Midnight Snack Break at the Poodle Factory*. I've got about seven or eight of them that come to a grand total of twelve or thirteen dollars. Hell, it costs more to pay somebody to do the books and cut a check than the payments are worth. I guess it's good they treat everybody the same, but it's not like I'm going to be sitting down on my front porch waiting for the mailman to deliver the next one.

V2

Keith Clark was too busy with his tax clients for the Circle Jerks' increasingly infrequent appearances, so he bowed out of the band and we replaced him with Kevin Fitzgerald, whom I knew from the Midget Handjob experience. I was also a huge fan of his work in the Geraldine Fibbers, who sounded like Sonic Youth attempting to play country music.

Our booking agent put together a nice two-week tour for us, and Greg was available, so we headed out there. You might think Greg and I were through after he quit on us during the Oddities tour, but it was one of those deals where we never really made up because we'd never really broken up. There was still resentment. Sometimes it was directed at Greg, sometimes it was directed at Bad Religion. But I was in no position to point the finger because I never used the time when he was gone to push the band forward. I could have booked a rehearsal space or borrowed one of my friend's spaces to work on new material, but I never did. I never thought that way. You would think I would be the guy spearheading the charge, racing down Sunset Boulevard in a slowly dying Toyota. The Charge of the Circle Jerks Brigade! But it wasn't like that. Why do that when I can be a bitter, grouchy guy? Instead of staying positive and being creative, I submerged myself in negativity.

We went on tour and made more money in two weeks than we had in an entire year. Kevin, our new drummer, started seeing dollar signs and hearing cash registers and was ready to familiarize himself with all of the female tellers at the local bank. I had to explain to him that I was a diabetic. I couldn't go out on the road for months at a time like I used to. I could barely get through two weeks, and there were no plans in the works to do it again anytime soon. That was the limit for me, the new normal.

Epitaph loved Midget Handjob and wanted to do a second album, even though *Midnight Snack Break at the Poodle Factory* was the worst-selling record in the label's history. The advertising campaign was going to be: "You too can be a part of the worst thing we've ever done!"

It was time to do something else. My good friend John Sidel had been an A&R guy at Interscope and was getting involved in different projects and business ventures, and he would sometimes have odd jobs for me. John was responsible for Power Tools, a secret underground club held in various warehouses around the city. The club got so big that it eventually moved to Park Plaza next to MacArthur Park in what used to be the Elks' Lodge, where the infamous St. Patrick's Day massacre took place.

Power Tools really took off and became a magnet for all kinds of celebrities. Madonna would show up with her entourage. The guys from Run-D.M.C. or the Beastie Boys would hang out and, next thing you know, they would be up on stage in the main room doing an impromptu rap session. Due to press and word of mouth, people would wait in line for hours to get in. It got to a point where three or four thousand people would come through the building on a Saturday night.

Sometimes I'd go with Bob and Pete from the Monster, Flea and Anthony from the Chili Peppers, maybe some of the guys from the Butthole Surfers and Fishbone. If you knew people, you could drink for free all night. It was a great place to score cocaine. I was no longer a participant, of course, but an amused observer, and there was always something to see.

I saw some great shows in that space. I saw a really amazing Red Hot Chili Peppers performance while Hillel Slovak was still alive. He would rock back and forth with incredible force like something out of the Three Stooges. I have no idea what was holding that guy up. I saw the Dickies, the Legendary Pink Dots, and Wire in that room. When Power Tools had run its course the club shut down and turned into the Scream, another popular LA nightclub.

John moved on to Smalls, the little bar over on Melrose and Gower, and I was invited to be the celebrity barback. On opening night it got so busy I was asked to bartend. I made up drinks on the spot—Sex on the Harpoon, Rusty Greyhound. My invention was vodka with a splash of cranberry, grapefruit, and orange juice and it became really popular. I called it Give Me a Good Tip Or Get the Fuck Out of Here, but most people just called it Keith's Special. They loved me there, which was weird, as I didn't drink. A lot of people would show up just because I was working there. I served Joe Strummer when he was in town playing with the Pogues, and he gave me a compliment that I'll never forget:

"I think your body of work with Black Flag and the Circle Jerks is great!"

I mixed drinks and opened beers for the Black Crowes, the Replacements, R.E.M.—all sorts of people. A lot of these bands come to LA to record an album, so they'd be in town for a month or so. They'd be in the studio all day, and when the session was over they'd need a place to unwind where they could relax without being mobbed. One night after last call a couple of Pixies, Kim Deal, and Frank Black convinced Joey Santiago to get up on the bar and dance naked.

The other owner, John's business partner, didn't like me. He thought I was giving away too many drinks, which was probably true. I worked the Friday shift. Small's opened at 7 p.m. every night except for Friday, when we opened at 4 p.m. to cater to the record company and show business people. Smalls was the place these freaks would come to finish out the week or start their weekend. John had friends at all the labels, and the women who worked at them would come in on Friday and get smashed. I'd make $500 in tips in three hours. That raised eyebrows. I got into a confrontation with John's business partner over that.

Sometimes John and I worked together on creative projects. For a while I was DJing two nights a week in the meatpacking district in New York City. It was the same kind of deal as Power Tools, but a lot more obvious—a playground for rich kids, tourists, and the occasional slumming celebrity. I produced a demo for his band Fudge Factory Incorporated, with John on guitar and vocals. He and I did all kinds of things together. We understood each other and enjoyed each other's company. He accepted an offer to get back in the record company world with happy-go-lucky billionaire Richard Branson and asked me if I wanted to work with him. I didn't see how I could say no.

Sir Richard Branson is, of course, the owner of Virgin Airlines. He's the guy who wants to fly around the world in a balloon and take people to the moon. He started Virgin Records but sold the company to EMI after a twenty-year run. Branson has a long and complicated history in the music business, with companies and subsidiaries and offices all over the world, and I'm not the guy to tell it. All I know is he got a wild hair up his ass to get back in the music business and started up V2. He hired somebody who hired John Sidel to work in LA, and John hired me as his assistant.

John had brought some really great bands to the label like the White Stripes and Burning Brides, and there were some interesting bands on the roster who I would come to dig on, like the Icarus Line and the Datsuns. John didn't ask for a résumé, and I didn't ask for a job description—it was a learn-as-you-go type of deal. He hired me because of my musical experience and knowledge of how the business really works. I was basically the A&R boy. I'd scout the newspapers and magazines. I'd go out to see shows and talk to bands. We were constantly listening to music to find the next group who could tickle our testicles.

The advantage I had over everybody else at the label was I wasn't paying attention to managers and lawyers and publicity people. I wasn't getting my music through the industry pipeline; I was actually going to clubs and seeing live shows. There was a point in time while I was managing the Nymphs and the Hangmen when I was at Cathay de Grande or Raji's or Coconut Teaszer or the Whisky five or six nights a week. The beauty of the situation for me was I'd been a part of the scene for so long that when I went to these places everybody knew who I was.

"That's the dude from Black Flag."

"That's the guy from the Circle Jerks."

"He was in the first punk rock band I ever heard."

I had clout, and Andy Gershon, the president of the label in North America, knew it. He'd worked at Virgin Records when the Nymphs signed to Geffen. He'd tried to sign them and knew about my involvement in managing the Nymphs. When I met him for the first time after a roundtable discussion at South by Southwest in Austin, Texas, he said to me, "Keith, if you were to come into my office right now, you would see on my desk a demo that you recorded." He told me that if he'd signed the Nymphs, he would have used the demo Brett Gurewitz and I made. He would have remixed it first, but those recordings would have been part of their debut album.

"It's the best demo I've ever heard."

After all I'd been through with the Nymphs, it was really gratifying to know that at least some of my hard work had meant something to someone. It also made me feel good about the path I'd chosen. I felt like I was in the right place. Like maybe, just maybe, it was meant to be . . .

HEART OF DARKNESS

In 2003 the Circle Jerks were playing with Cypress Hill at the Smoke Out, which was held in the parking lot of the LA Coliseum, a place where I had many fond memories of watching the Rams in the sixties and the Raiders in the nineties.

I was cruising around, checking things out like I always do, when I ran into Rick Van Santen and Paul Tollett, a couple of concert promoters from Goldenvoice who would go on to start a music festival called Coachella. They told me they were organizing a Black Flag reunion at the Hollywood Palladium and wanted me to be a part of it.

"You were one of the founding members and we can't do this without you!"

Being the kind of guy who leaps before he looks, I was ready to take the plunge. No arm twisting required. The thought of reuniting with the guys for an all-out, sweat-drenched scuzzfest filled me with excitement. What better way to let out all the anger and frustration of the last twenty-five years since we'd parted ways than by getting together and bashing out some old-school punk rock? It would be better than therapy.

I'd had a handful of interactions with Greg Ginn over the years, and they hadn't all been bad. I filled in for Ron Reyes for a couple of shows at the Fleetwood in Redondo Beach and Mabuhay Gardens in San Francisco way back in 1980. More recently, three or four years prior, I'd gone down to Greg's rundown recording studio in Long

Beach to discuss getting Black Flag back together. I even had a set list all worked out. I had this idea of playing "Paralyzed" from *In My Head*, as that was my favorite Rollins track, Dukowski's "My War," and "You Bet We've Got Something Personal Against You!" which was the last song on the *Jealous Again* EP and was directed at me after I walked away from Black Flag. This was my idea of humor, a joke at my own expense to lighten the mood.

We talked for a bit in an attempt to reestablish our long lost friendship. I played him a handful of my tunes, which he dug, and then he blasted some of his new music. You need to understand that Greg is one of my all-time favorite guitarists, and I have no problem putting him on the same mountaintop alongside Chuck Berry, Jimmy Page, Link Wray, Wayne Kramer, Pete Townsend, and a handful of others. He's earned the right to do whatever he pleases, but this six-string skrunk he was jamming was pretty much unlistenable. I didn't want to piss him off, so I bit my tongue and told myself to be patient. I figured we'd pay that toll when the time came. At the end of our meeting he said he'd call me, but he never did, and for that I was grateful.

A couple of years later I ran into Greg at a club in Hollywood called the Dragonfly. Some friends invited me to play with them and I said sure, but little did I know I'd be participating on a bill with the Greg Ginn Band. At the show Greg caught me off guard by asking me if I'd join him onstage for a couple of Black Flag songs. I told him I'd be happy to if he'd cut me a check for $75,000 for past-due royalties. He looked at me as if I was an escapee from an insane asylum.

I'd heard reports about Greg's performances, and they weren't very encouraging. Most were of the "two thumbs down" and "no stars out of five" variety, but I needed to witness it for myself. Greg's band more than backed up the bad criticism and offered a good excuse to vacate the premises. His intensity was a dozen notches lower than the last time we'd played together, and the tempos were even slower. The bassist struggled through the songs, and the barefoot drummer pounded on a kit covered in fur. Not only did he look like he was Barney Rubble from the Flintstones, but he played like it too! No crack. No whack.

This painful experience was like watching a wheelchair race at a retirement home. Greg Ginn delivered the exclamation point of the night when he started to sing. Greg is a genius guitarist, but he has absolutely no business playing and singing at the same time. Maybe in an acoustic unplugged punk rock troubadour setting, but this was an unadulterated downer.

So when the guys at Goldenvoice told me about the reunion at the Palladium, I was stoked but skeptical. The next day I called up Greg to feel him out, and he seemed jazzed. Usually when you talk with Greg, it's really hard to get a read on him. There's no emotion in his voice, but this time he sounded genuinely interested in having me be a part of the reunion, and that got me psyched. We set up a rehearsal, and it was all downhill from there.

I jumped into my beat-up Mercedes and headed south on the freeway to Greg's SST compound. Greg smiled as he welcomed me in, and I nearly went into shock as I checked out his new space. It was like a club with a fancy little coffee area and a bar set-up. There were pool tables, couches, and a stage with a full-size PA system, lighting rig, and a massive video screen. There was easily enough room in the space for three or four hundred people. The stage was bigger than the one at CBGB's, the old 9:30 Club in Washington, DC, or even the Whisky. It was huge, and I hadn't even seen the recording studio, SST Records, and the area where he told me Korn stored their equipment, which doubled as their practice space.

We talked about the music we were listening to. I'm always listening to new music from lots of genres. I rattled off a dozen bands from Queens of the Stone Age to Turbonegro. Greg mumbled a single word: Korn. I'd been to one of their shows and couldn't get down with their mediocre tuneage. To me they sounded like a horrible nu-metal version of the Red Hot Chili Peppers, but the chain wallet thugs in wife-beaters who'd come to see them loved it. I should have taken that little revelation as a bad sign.

Greg was playing a karaoke CD of Black Flag songs. I barely recognized them because they were slower than slow. I looked at the boom box, thinking the batteries were dying, and noticed it was plugged into the wall. Bummer! I asked Greg what was wrong with the tempo?

He replied, "Keith, when we first recorded these songs we were playing them way too fast!"

That's not what I wanted to hear. In an attempt to liven things up and add some energy I suggested we cut loose and bang out some songs. Greg agreed, but as soon as we mounted the stage the drummer stuck the Black Flag karaoke CD into the PA system, and the same track started up. We all stood around trying to figure out which song we were listening to, and after a while Greg and the drummer started to jam along to the CD. This was how they rehearsed!

After what felt like an eternity, I asked if I could take the CD home and make a track listing and a set list so everyone would know what we were listening to. Made sense, right?

Greg got pissed off and blurted an angry, "No!"

I backed off and asked him if Chuck was going to rehearse with us, and Greg told me he hadn't talked to him yet.

I drove back to Los Feliz seriously bummed out, but I told myself that we still had three months to get ready. That was plenty of time to get into playing shape and do some damage.

Two nights later I made the journey back down to Long Beach, thinking it would be much more rawking this time. Boy, was I in for a completely messed-up surprise. We "practiced" the same way we'd muddled through a few nights before, only this time Dale Nixon, Greg Ginn's alter ego, made a special guest appearance on bass guitar. Greg started noodling around on his bass, and the glop coming out of his bass gear wanted to be free jazz but it wasn't even close to anything Black Flag had ever recorded. It sounded like a pair of eight-year-olds at Guitar Center playing different songs. Fuck, it was awful!

After about half an hour I called a timeout and explained to Greg that I couldn't make out the songs. I never cued off the bass. It was always about the guitar riffs and drumbeats.

Greg wasn't sympathizing with me: "You need to lock in with the rhythm section."

I thought, *What rhythm section are you talking about? This mucky ear sludge? Are you out of your mind?*

It was just too much. I was seriously worried now. These songs mean a great deal to a lot of people—you can't just go out there and half-ass it. If we were going to promise the fans Black Flag, then we'd better deliver. If this reunion was going to go down, I needed to get Chuck and Robo involved.

Goldenvoice was billing the concert as Black Flag: The First Four Years. To me that meant Greg Ginn, Chuck Dukowski, Robo, Ron Reyes, Dez Cadena, and myself. I left Bryan Migdol out of the equation due to the fact that I'd had a phone conversation with him wanting to put Black Flag back together. I knew this was not going to happen because when I asked him what he was up to, he explained that he was playing his country music hit, "Play That Country Music Cowboy," which completely threw me for a loop. He and his wife had rewritten Wild Cherry's "Play That Funky Music White Boy." Further in the conversation he stated to me that he was also playing in Cheap Trick, and he was completely serious. So I scratched him off the list for the reunion. But where were Chuck and Robo?

I knew Chuck was interested because I'd played a show with him at Amoeba Records for the release of the Rollins Band Black Flag tribute to raise money for the West Memphis 3. He lit up when I told him about the reunion Goldenvoice was planning because that meant we'd finally get paid. I was lining up calls when Greg rang me up out of the blue and told me not to talk to any of the guys. He said it wasn't my job to organize things and that I needed to stop spreading rumors.

Rumors? What rumors? I tried to defend myself but realized it was pointless. As far as I was concerned, Greg was on a power trip again. Maybe he never got off the old one. Maybe he was smoking a lot of pot that was making him paranoid. To put the icing on the cake, he told me that Chuck didn't want to be a part of the reunion, which I knew was not true. What the hell was going on?

Things got even weirder when, outside of a club in Silver Lake, I ran into Duff McKagan, who'd just removed himself from bass-playing duties with Guns N' Roses. He asked me if I was going to sing in the Black Flag reunion. I was dumbfounded. How did he even know about the show?

Duff said that Dez had told him about the show. Dez invited Duff to play bass on a couple of songs, which Duff didn't feel right about because he couldn't see how he fit in.

That made two of us. I was starting to have visions of the Black Flag reunion turning into some kind of celebrity rock star jam session.

All was not well. Not even close. Rick from Goldenvoice was getting restless, grinding on me to give him details about how the lineup was shaping up. After being chewed out by Greg, I didn't have anything to say. If I told him what was going on in Long Beach, Rick would have reached through the phone and strangled me and Greg would give me shit about it later. I was getting pummeled on both sides.

The reason I quit Black Flag was because of all the mind games and ego tripping, and here I was, stuck in the skullduggery again. From my perspective, Greg was planning something that had nothing to do with the band's first four years. I considered it a complete rip-off, a total scam, and Rick had no idea what was really going on. The guys at Goldenvoice expected me to make it right and keep them in the loop, but there wasn't a loop to keep them filled in on. I felt like I was reenacting Martin Sheen's character Captain Willard in a punk rock version of *Apocalypse Now* with some *This Is Spinal Tap* tossed in to add to the hilarity. Goldenvoice gave me my orders to drive down the 710 Freeway into the heart of Long Beach and kill Colonel Ginn with all the knobs turned to 11 . . .

It finally came down, as it almost always does, to money. I'd heard Greg wanted the show to be a benefit and the proceeds to go to an animal shelter in Long Beach. I'm a lover of kittens, puppies, ponies, squirrels, goldfish, and the rest of the little critters on our wonderful planet, but I wasn't in a financial position to give up my time and energy so I could drive my car with a cracked windshield and a busted head gasket to play Black Flag karaoke for a charity. I was in on this reunion scenario because it was Black Flag, and that wasn't something

I should have to validate. If Greg wanted to donate money to a charity, he could use his own cut of the dough.

I asked Greg about the guarantee and how he was going to divide it up. His response was, "We'll talk about that after the show." In my opinion, this raised some serious red flags.

I took my concerns to Rick at Goldenvoice and told him I wasn't going to go through with this insanity without being compensated. Rick's solution was to give me an earful of shit.

"We've sold out the first night and we're going to sell out the second. Greg says you're not cooperating. Your services are no longer necessary. There's no reason for you to be at the Palladium!"

As I listened to Rick's rant I honestly didn't know if I should break out in laughter or tell him to fuck off. This flaming shit-show was turning into a Hollywood sign–sized embarrassment. He was actually doing me a favor by sparing me from being involved in what would have been the biggest bummer of my career. The irony wasn't lost on me. After all these years Greg finally got his revenge by kicking me out of Black Flag, except it wasn't Greg who fired me but a friend.

About a week before the concert Rick called me up to tell me he was putting me on the VIP guest list and if I felt like jumping up on stage to sing a few songs, I could do that. I thanked him and told him that wouldn't be necessary because I wasn't planning on going anywhere near the Palladium that night. Rick got the message, and that was that.

Although I didn't attend the show, I know plenty of people who did, and they had nothing good to say, which wasn't surprising but was still disappointing. Rick called me up again after the show to apologize for putting me through Greg Ginn's torture chamber and for talking to me the way he did. I accepted his apology, and he asked if he we were still friends. I told him not to worry, that we'd always be friends, which was true right up until he passed away. I just felt bad for the fans who were promised Black Flag's first four years and were treated to a mucked-up mess that bore no resemblance to the band we used to be. That night I believe Greg did some serious damage to Black Flag's reputation.

BLACKOUT

Like any job, working at V2 had its ups and downs. I'd worked in an office before, but this time I had more responsibilities. I had to figure out how to operate the photocopier and the fax machine and to make sure there was ink and paper in the printer. I answered the phones. All that lame office stuff.

My second or third week on the job I got a call from someone who said he was calling from India. This guy wanted me to know all about the band he was managing. They were coming all the way from India to LA and I absolutely had to see them. I was still new at the job and had no idea how to get him off the phone. Instead of hanging up on him, I took down all of his contact information and the name of the band and promised I'd look for the CD in the mailroom. Managers were always calling us up, asking if we'd listened to the CD they may or may not have bothered to send. It was exhausting.

I would later find out that Bob Forrest had talked Maynard Keenan from Tool into calling and pretending to be the manager for India's biggest band.

Another time I had the manager of a metal band call me about his band, but he didn't ask if I'd listened to it or would consider listening to it; he told me I'd *better* listen to it, and if I didn't, he was going to come down there and beat the crap out of me.

The job had plenty of perks. If the Circle Jerks had a tour lined up, I was always able to go. In fact, the label encouraged me to tour because then I could scout bands on the road. I'd go into record stores and talk to the people behind the counter and ask all kinds of questions.

"Who's that you're playing?

"What are you listening to?"

"Who are the kids going ape-shit over?"

I'd come back from a two-week tour with stacks of CDs to listen to.

During my run with V2 I scouted tons of bands and played a role in a couple of them getting signed. I was really big on an Australian band called Neon, kind of a mix between Nirvana and Cheap Trick. They had some hits in Australia, and their managers also managed some big bands like Jet and the Vines. Unfortunately Neon's vocalist/guitarist wasn't built to go out and play every night; he wasn't physically equipped for heavy touring. A label can throw money at a band, they can provide tour support, they can even buy a van for them, but it's up to the band to get out there and play and develop a following.

For me a live show is the ultimate test. There's only so much music you can listen to before you have to go out and listen to it live. You've got to be able to feel the energy when a band gives it their all and the crowd is really into it and gives it right back. You know when this happens; it can't be faked. There are lots of reasons why it doesn't happen: faulty equipment, bad sound, poor attendance, lousy promotion. Maybe the bass player had a bad burrito, or perhaps the singer picked that night to resume her heroin habit. But when something special is happening, everybody in the room knows it. You can't get that from listening to a track on your computer or reading a press release.

I liked scouting bands, but I wasn't a hype man. I was never going to be one of those guys who'd tell someone they were the greatest of all time just to get them signed on the label. I wasn't going to do that. That wasn't me. Skip the bullshit.

One of my assignments was to go and see the Raveonettes play a showcase with the Used at the Troubadour. They're a Danish indie rock duo in the Jesus and Mary Chain mold, and there were a lot of people talking about them. The Troubadour was at full capacity. There were so many people packed in there, I couldn't turn around, and it's not like I take up a lot of space. I watched the band do their thing and thought they were really cool. They put on a great performance, and I could definitely recommend them. I wanted to talk to the band, see what the Raveonettes were like in person, but every record company schmoe and schmoette was lined up in front of me. I could see by all the interest they were attracting that it was going to turn into a bidding war. So I bailed. I wasn't going to wait in line for an hour or so with a bunch of industry people I didn't like for a chance to shake someone's hand and blow smoke up their ass for thirty seconds. No way. I was out of there.

I didn't need to love a band to be able to tell if they would be a good fit for the label. Some of my best friends have been in bands who I thought were just all right. I don't have to like your band or music to like you as a person. Working as V2's A&R boy, I didn't have the luxury of keeping my opinions to myself, but it also made me aware of the fact that my opinions aren't always in step with everybody else.

Another one of my assignments was to see the first LA performance of Vampire Weekend. One of the uppity ups from New York asked me to go, and I was the low man on the totem pole, so I told him I'd be happy to check them out. I knew the history of the band and how they'd all met at some rich-kid music academy on the East Coast. I didn't hold that against them. If they were a happening band, it wouldn't matter where they met or who they were attached to. Good music is good music. I went to the show, they started playing, and I wasn't feeling it. I thought they sounded like Paul Simon's backing band when he discovered world beat.

My rule of thumb for when I'm going to see a band live is I'll give them three to four songs. If they start off with a slow song and they're stumbling and bumbling around, maybe they'll pick up the pace and things will get better. It didn't get better. It got worse. I wasn't buying what they were selling, and I couldn't get out of there fast enough.

THERE WERE NIGHTS IN HOLLYWOOD when I'd start at the Viper Room, go across the street to Whisky, and then head up to the Roxy. Silver Lake was the same way: I'd hit Spaceland, the Fold, and the Echo all in one night. One night I didn't make it to the show.

It was a night like any other. I was driving my beat-up Mercedes through the hills, navigating the twists and turns on Mulholland Drive as I made my way down into Hollywood to see a show at Amoeba Records on Sunset Boulevard. What I would do in those days is measure my glucose and do my insulin procedure before I left work. Then I'd get in my car and head to wherever I was going and stop and get something to eat along the way.

I was thinking about the show and the people I might see and all the things I needed to do before work the next day when I just drifted off and went into a diabetic blackout. It's not like an alcoholic blackout, where your body keeps going and your brain has no memory of what happened. A diabetic blackout is more like a seizure that results in a temporary loss of consciousness. I basically passed out behind the wheel, and when I came to, my face had smashed into the steering wheel and I was bleeding from my mouth. The weird thing was the car was still moving, slowly drifting through a red light and into the intersection during the middle of rush-hour traffic.

I slammed on the brakes and backed up the car. A few inches more and I would have been scrunched up like an accordion. I pulled over next to the Jack in the Box directly across the street from Amoeba and got out to assess the damage.

I knew I'd hit something, but I had no idea who or what I'd hit. I went back and looked for broken glass, but I couldn't find anything. Did the other driver drive off? What the hell happened?

It was the strangest feeling. I was jittery and out of sorts and completely soaked in sweat. I was supposed to go see Jeremy Enigk that night, who was the main guy from Sunny Day Real Estate, who I do not like, but I love Jeremy Enigk's solo stuff. It has this grand, dark, weird, I've-been-tortured vibe. There was a lot going on in his work. I was going to see him play live and decide whether I wanted to give him the double thumbs up. But I couldn't remember any of that at the time. It had been completely wiped from my memory. All I knew was that I was headed to Amoeba, so that's where I went.

I got back in the car and drove across the street and parked in the Amoeba employee parking lot. While I was walking inside it started to dawn on me how lucky I was that I didn't black out until I was half a block away from where I was going. If I'd blacked out while I was up in the hills, I'd be dead. I would have crashed into somebody's garage, plunged into a swimming pool, or driven right off a cliff.

A couple of my friends who were working at Amoeba knew something was wrong as soon as I came through the door. I was in bad shape. White as a ghost and shaking like a junkie. I knew I was at Amoeba and was there for a reason, but what was it? Why did I come here?

"Keith, what's wrong?"

"I don't know. I think I hit something."

I explained that I was a diabetic and that I wasn't feeling well, and they sent me upstairs to their green room where there were snacks left over from Jeremy Enigk's performance.

I went upstairs and ate some chocolate and drank some juice and started to feel like myself again. The better I felt, the more I worried about what had happened. I'd left the scene of an accident. I had to go back and make sure everything was all right.

One of the guys came with me, and we did some exploring while I told him what happened. We looked for broken glass, smashed plastic—any leftover debris from a car wreck. I'd convinced myself that I'd run into a newspaper stand, but there wasn't one in the vicinity. We went up and down the street in case I'd hit a parked car. But there was no evidence of an accident anywhere except the damage to my car. There was no way to write a note or leave my number to explain what had happened—not that I had car insurance. It was all so confusing.

After the accident I made sure I took my insulin immediately before eating. Not a half hour or an hour before, but right before my meal.

Two weeks later I got a call while I was at work. It was an agent from an insurance company who wanted to talk to me about a claim. A woman was driving her boyfriend's brand-new Mercedes when I hit her. She got my license plate number and drove away, which was a pretty shitty thing to do, given my medical condition.

"Okay, how much damage did I do?"

It wasn't a lot of damage, but it was a Mercedes. I explained that I didn't have any insurance and that I'd had a diabetic blackout at the time of the accident. I wasn't playing on his sympathies, but I wanted him to know the full situation, that technically *she* was the one who left the scene of an accident. Neither one of us wanted to get the courts involved, so we agreed that I would send a couple of hundred dollars every month for three or four months. I sent four or five checks and never heard from them again.

OSLO COMA SITUATION

My time as an A&R boy came to an end when the world's happiest billionaire decided he needed some cash. Sir Richard got into a predicament with some of his business partners and needed to come up with 8 million bucks. You would think he wouldn't have a problem coming up with that kind of cash, that his financial people would be able to take care of it without having to shut down an entire operation, but that's what he did. I don't know, maybe that's why I'm not a billionaire, but it was 2007, and a lot of screwy shit was going down with the global economy, and I was one more person without a job.

At least I'd had pretty decent health insurance for a while, and I did manage to get a $3,000 colonoscopy out of it. That's when they stick a tube up your ass to see what you've got going on up there. Trust me, it hurts a lot less when you're not the one paying for it.

My health was as good as it had been in years. I thought I had a pretty good handle on my diabetes. In fact, I'd stopped measuring my glucose before every meal. I'd gotten lazy. I'd been dealing with it long enough that I could feel if it was up or down. As long as I did what I was supposed to do, I didn't need to worry about it.

After my scare when I blacked out on Sunset Boulevard, I felt like I'd been through everything that life could possibly throw at me except an atomic bomb blast, and I was still standing with human-sized roaches. But I was wrong. There was one thing I hadn't experienced: Turbonegro. And they nearly killed me.

In the summer of 2008 I had an opportunity to play with Turbone-gro at the Oya Festival: Norway's biggest rock band on Norway's big-gest stage. Happy-Tom, Turbonegro's bass player, reached out to me. He's always been a big fan of Black Flag and the Circle Jerks and a big supporter of the SoCal punk rock scene. Turbonegro was headlining on the last day of the festival and had this idea to bring over some guys from bands they'd love to have play with them. Nick Oliveri from Queens of the Stone Age was already on board. Would I be interested in playing?

"Why not?" I said. "Circle Jerks aren't doing anything."

They booked me a ticket, and off I went to Oslo. It all happened in a hurry. One day I'm kicking around Hollywood, and the next I'm in Norway. The flight took about a day. From LA I had to fly up to the North Pole and back down to England for a stopover in Heathrow. Being a diabetic, whenever an airline offers me food, I usually just go ahead and eat it. It's all about maintaining a consistent energy level and keeping my glucose up. That's the gas that runs the engine.

The key to living with diabetes is sticking to a schedule. I try to eat every four to five hours so I can regulate my insulin intake. Flying makes that tricky. Sticking to a schedule is next to impossible when you're crossing multiple time zones.

I didn't have time to eat at Heathrow, but on the flight to Oslo the flight attendant offered me a chicken sandwich. I took a couple of bites and knew something wasn't right. It seemed like it wanted to be fresh, but it wasn't. I got some bad chicken, and that was bad news. Luckily I didn't eat enough to get sick, but it completely turned off my appetite.

When the plane touched down in Oslo a driver took me and Nick to the hotel where most of the musicians from the festival were stay-ing. It was a madhouse. The lobby was packed with people, and the bar was overflowing. I had enough time to check in and drop off my bags before we had to take off again to rehearse with Turbonegro. I don't know if it was time for lunch or dinner back in California, but I was starving.

The driver told us he was taking us to a club where Turbonegro was waiting for us, and off we went. I thought about asking the driver to pull over so I could get something to eat, but I was feeling strangely anxious about the rehearsal and didn't want to be late. I figured it wouldn't be far and there would be something at the club. Maybe there would be a pizza joint or something nearby, but that idea went out the window when we got on the highway and put Oslo in the rearview. I don't know how many miles—I mean kilometers—we traveled, but it took us about an hour and a half down a two-lane road to get to the spot. It was way off in the middle of the woods next to a beautiful lake, and there wasn't a restaurant, market, or convenience store in sight. Fuck me.

The club turned out to be a lodge on a lake that had a massive pro sound system with a big stage and a kitchen, but it was closed. When I saw that, I knew I was in trouble.

Happy-Tom introduced Nick and me to the rest of the band. There was Hank Von Helvete, the vocalist, and Knut "Euroboy" Schreiner and a couple of other guys whose names I didn't catch because I was distracted by my hunger.

"Guys, do you have any snacks? We didn't get a chance to eat at the hotel, and I'm starving."

"Sure," Happy-Tom said, pointing to the closed kitchen, "right over there."

I was thinking maybe there was a deli platter or a bowl of fruit, but there was nothing of the sort. There was a bowl of M&Ms and a coffee machine. That's it. This was the biggest band in Norway with a reputation for partying. Where were the exotic dancers? Where was the coke dealer? Where the fuck was the *food*?

There was none of that. Turbonegro was all business. They weren't even drinking. They cranked up their amps. It was time to show them what I could do.

I got up on stage, but I wasn't feeling very good and broke out in a cold, clammy sweat.

They wanted me to sing, "Good Head." I knew the words, had them down—I'd only listened to it about seven hundred times—but that wasn't the problem. *I* was the problem. I was brutally off. We went through the song a few times, and I wasn't even close to good. My energy level was so low, I couldn't get it together. The guys were looking at me and looking at each other, and I could tell they weren't happy with the situation.

"I haven't eaten all day," I explained. "I'm not feeling well, and there's nothing to eat here."

Hank was pissed. *We flew this guy all the way over here for this?* He didn't say it to my face, but he didn't need to. I got the message loud and clear.

"Guys," I said, "Let me take a quick little walk. I'll collect my thoughts. I'll get my energy back up, try to get to a place where I need to be. I just need to eat some M&Ms and drink some coffee and I'll be fine."

I went for a walk in the woods. It was late afternoon. Even though it was August, it felt a little chilly outside. Some guy was water skiing on the lake, going around and around the lake in pointless circles. I was super-depressed. *What am I doing here?* I thought. *What am I gonna do? What's gonna happen to me?*

I was sweating and shaking and freaking out. I thought the problem was food, but maybe it was a bad case of nerves . . .

Back in the late nineties, when I was first learning how to deal with my diabetes, I had a few hypoglycemic episodes. I knew the symptoms: heart palpitations, drowsiness, shaking, and sweating. Been there and through that before.

This was different. These symptoms were *mental*, meaning they didn't feel like symptoms. When you're feeling anxious and upset, you don't recognize them as symptoms of something. It feels like you've gotten yourself in a really shitty situation and you don't know how to get out. I couldn't shake the feeling that something terrible was going to happen if I didn't get my act together.

For the first time in a long time I felt like I had to justify myself, to prove to these guys that I could do this, that they didn't throw their money away by bringing me all the way to Norway. That was something I'd never felt when I was with Black Flag, Circle Jerks, Bug Lamp, or Midget Handjob.

I went back to the club. I drank some more coffee and ate some M&Ms. Turbonegro had their shit way dialed in. They were loud and rocking. Nick ran through his song a half dozen times, and it sounded great. I wanted them to be psyched about the show the next day. I didn't want to ruin the energy. I didn't want to let them down.

I got up on stage, grabbed the mic, and gave it my best shot. It wasn't bad, but I knew I could do better. We played the song a couple of more times, and I put all that bullshit about proving myself out of my head and just yelled my brain out. It got louder and better each time until we were all satisfied.

"That's the reason we flew him over," Happy-Tom said to Hank.

Euroboy weighed in as well, "If he's half that when he gets up on stage tomorrow, we're going to destroy the place!"

Of everyone in the band, Euroboy was the most sympathetic. He was a cancer survivor and had lost a ton of weight due to chemo, but he was back with the band and starting to get his legs underneath him again. Everybody was walking around, like, "Yeah, this is totally going to rule!" They knew what was up. I was finally starting to get stoked about the show. We were going to close out the festival, and it was going to be amazing.

Everybody said their good-byes and went their separate ways. Nick and I got in the van that was going to take us back to the hotel. I was completely spent. Rehearsal had taken a lot out of me, and I didn't have much energy left. I closed my eyes and thought about all the pizza and pastries I was going to eat when I got back to the hotel.

By the time we got to the hotel I barely recognized the place. The hotel was overrun with people associated with the rock festival. The lobby was packed with drunks and drug addicts, musicians and people from record labels. People were lounging around, smoking and drinking and carrying on. It was a total party.

I was starving. I was so hungry I could have gotten down on my hands and knees and started gnawing on the furniture. So I went to the front desk and asked the concierge where I could get some food. He gave me the bad news.

"The kitchen is closed."

It was ten o'clock on a Saturday night and I was shit out of luck. The hotel bar was open, but they didn't serve food to help the drunks soak up all the booze. The concierge insisted there was nothing to eat at the hotel. I was starting to think I was in some kind of bizarre world. What was it with Norwegians and food? Did they ever eat? He told me I might be able to find a $300 pizza.

"I need some food," I said, trying not to sound like the ugly, whiny American.

The concierge explained that the hotel was connected to the train depot, and whatever food I was going to find would be up there. I wanted to know what was up there, but he brushed me off. A diabetic punk rocker was the least of his worries.

I went up some stairs and walked around a bit, and by the time I came to the depot I was famished and exhausted. There were two options. 7-11 and the Norwegian version of 7-11. I chose 7-11. I don't know if it was because it was the end of the week or if they were about to close—did 7-11s in Norway actually close at eleven?—but the pickings were slim. There was some over-ripened fruit, stale pastries, and packages of pasta covered in this brown muddy-looking muck that looked like something I'd stepped in. To add insult to injury, it was all super-expensive. No way I was eating that. Just looking at it made me lose my appetite.

I was having a hard time making up my mind. I'm looking at the pastries. I'm looking at the fruit. I thought I'd get a couple of pastries, a couple of pieces of fruit, and bump myself up with enough insulin to cover me. Then I came up with a brilliant idea. It's late. I'm tired. I'll get a few bottles of water, go back to the hotel, put on a movie, fall asleep, get up really early and eat the best breakfast I've ever had in my life. A breakfast fit for the King of Norway.

It was one of the worst decisions I've ever made.

I grabbed three bottles of water, shuffled back through the train station, made my way through the pandemonium in the hotel lobby, went up to my room, and got myself into bed. I turned on the TV and drank some water while watching a Will Smith movie. I don't remember which one, but it had subtitles and I was having trouble focusing because I was so tired. After the movie was finished, I didn't feel so good. I went to the bathroom and threw up.

Whoa, I thought, *that was random.*

I drank more water and got back in bed. Fifteen minutes later I threw up again. I couldn't figure out what it was that was making me sick because I hadn't eaten anything except a couple of bites of a bad chicken sandwich and some M&Ms, and that was exactly the problem. Because I didn't eat, I didn't take any insulin. For a diabetic, that's one of the worst things you can do. I didn't know this because it had never happened to me before. What I'd done was kickstart ketoacidosis. Ketoacidosis is when the acidity in your system builds up to a level where it starts feeding on itself because there's no sugar. First it feeds on your fat, then your organs, then you die. So now all of a sudden the acidity in my system is rising, which causes my glucose to spike to combat the acidity. There was a battle going on in my system, sugar versus acid. That's why I was vomiting and vomiting and vomiting.

Like clockwork, I vomited every fifteen minutes. The room was tiny. Just a bed, a bathroom, and a TV. At least it was a quick trip to bathroom. I went back and forth every fifteen minutes all night long.

I kept drinking water just so I'd have something to puke up. My stomach was empty. I was past the bile. I needed something else or I'd just dry heave, which was even worse. At some point I got a call. It was Ebbot Lundberg, the lead singer from one of my current favorite bands The Soundtrack of Our Lives.

"We're coming to get you, Keith! Be outside the hotel in fifteen minutes!"

"I can't," I told him. "I've been up all night puking."

"Meet us outside!"

"I have to hang up right now because I have to vomit."

I went and vomited. They called back.

"We're outside the hotel."

"I can't do it."

"We need you here."

"I can't."

I don't remember much else about the conversation. I don't even know if I hung up the phone. I was slumped in bed with half my body on the bed the other hanging over the side with one foot on the floor and one arm hanging down. I'd stopped vomiting, but I no longer had the energy to move.

I was in my boxers and the room felt really cold, like being in a freezer. I couldn't pull the covers over me. I couldn't move my arms or legs. All I could do was look around the room. I was paralyzed. It wasn't like the movies, where my mind was racing but my body was stuck in neutral. I wasn't coherent. I wasn't thinking clearly. I knew what was going on, but only barely. I was cold, and I knew I was cold—I felt like a popsicle—but I couldn't do anything about it. I couldn't help myself, I couldn't move, but at least I wasn't puking anymore.

As strange as it might sound, I wasn't freaked out. I was operating on a more primal level of existence. I never passed out, never lost consciousness or blacked out, but I was so exhausted, so used up and spent, that there was almost nothing left. I just laid there in a daze, drained and dehydrated, panting and gasping for air like I had been running as fast as I could for twelve hours and was completely gone. I was done.

At some point the cleaning lady came in. She probably took one look at me and thought, "Oh great, here's another drunk." Everyone at the hotel was partying and fucked up. In the condition I was in, I blended right in, even though I hadn't had a drink in nearly twenty years.

About an hour later the cleaning lady came back. This time she came all the way into the room to have a closer look at me. Maybe she was attracted by my good looks. I don't know, but she knew something wasn't right. It was freezing cold, and I was almost naked on the bed in the exact same position she found me in an hour ago.

She peeked into the bathroom where there was vomit on the floor from when I missed the toilet. All of my syringes were on the counter above the sink. She put two and two together and said in her native tongue, "Something's not right here." Then she went down and got the manager.

He came up right away. He took one look at me and started asking the cleaning lady questions. They were speaking in Norwegian, so I had no idea what they were saying. Maybe he was saying, "Shit, we need to do something about this immediately!" Or maybe he was saying, "Fuck this guy! I don't like these rock and roll assholes! They're all just a bunch of drug addicts!"

Who knows what they were saying, but shortly after he arrived the paramedics showed up. There were only three, but the room was so small it felt like thirty of them. They were checking out my medical bracelet, trying to figure out what it meant. They kept asking me questions, but I couldn't answer them. I was still panting and gasping, panting and gasping. I was in survival mode. My system was focused on keeping me alive. That's all it could handle. Everything else felt like it was happening to somebody else.

When we got to the hospital they wheeled me into the emergency room. The nurse told me she could speak English and they were going to help me. Now that I was out of that freezing room and wrapped in some blankets I started to get really thirsty and was barely able to speak.

"Water," I whispered.

"We can't give you any liquids until we do a blood panel and find out what's wrong with you."

I didn't have to wait long. They spread my legs open and jabbed a giant needle in my thigh right near my sack. I started to come back to life after that.

The blood panel told them what they needed to know, and they gave me a cup of freezing cold water—aaahhh—and stuck a couple of IVs in me to bring the acidity down and get me hydrated again. After they balanced me out they went to work on my glucose levels. They bumped me with a couple of units of insulin here, a couple of units there, until everything was back to normal, but it took a while.

They told me I'd gone into a coma, which didn't make sense to me because I never went under—I was conscious the entire time.

"When they brought you in, you were comatose."

"Really? But my eyes were open the whole time. I remember everything."

"You were completely unresponsive."

The doctors explained that I'd gone into a diabetic coma and my system was slowly starting to shut down. They said the thing that saved me was the water. If I hadn't kept hydrating, I would have gone into a coma a lot sooner, and by the time they found me it would have been too late.

EVEN THOUGH THEY'D GIVEN ME NUTRIENTS intravenously, I was starving. I couldn't wait to eat. But I was less than thrilled with the cuisine at the hospital in Oslo. The first solid food they gave me was a chicken breast. I don't know if it had been roasted or fried or what they did to it, but it was a crispy burnt-orange red. It looked like someone had painted it with mercurochrome and blasted it in the microwave for an hour and a half. It might not have been chicken. All I knew was I wasn't eating it. I gave it to the guy in the next bed. The only English he knew was, "Are you going to eat that?"

They kept me in the hospital for observation. They wanted me to eat three meals a day, monitor my blood, and smooth out all the peaks and valleys.

I didn't have anywhere to go. I was supposed to leave the day after the festival, but I'd already missed my flight. Where would I go? Back to the meat locker? Find a new hotel? I didn't have the wherewithal for any of that.

The next day I didn't feel any better. My outlook didn't improve when I saw what was for lunch: shrimp paste in a tube. If I had an extra toothbrush, I could have brushed my teeth with it. It was brutal. Shrimp in a tube came with this gray thing that was shaped like a cracker but had the consistency of a Brillo pad. If you took a white sponge and wiped your floors with it, that's what this thing on my plate looked like: a filthy brownish-gray sponge. I don't know if it was my diabetes or the food they served me, but my recovery was slow.

Luckily Rune, otherwise known as Rune Rebellion, came to visit me on the second day in the hospital. He told me the band felt really bad when they heard I'd been in a coma.

"Keith, is there anything you need?"

"Yeah!"

"What is it?"

"Get me some real food!"

I told him that, being an American, I wasn't down with his country's culinary course of action. It wasn't working for me. I asked him if he could get me some fruit, juice, and candy bars, and he did.

My second day stretched into a third and then another and another. I was there for seven days. Whenever an administrator came around to ask about my financial arrangements, I'd point at Rune or Happy-Tom. I have no idea if the bill was ever paid. I know they have socialized medicine over there, but it's also one of the most expensive places to live in the world and the food is terrible. That doesn't sound like a great deal to me.

I don't know who paid for my medical expenses or if, being a foreigner, I got the same deal as the Norwegians did, but I never saw a bill. I just sat in my bed, reading a book about the history of the CIA that Happy-Tom had brought me and surviving on sweets that I wasn't supposed to eat.

That week in the hospital in Norway gave me a lot of time to think about all the damage I've put myself through over the years, all the experiences I wasn't supposed to walk away from. From car crashes to comas, I'd been extremely lucky. I don't think I'm here for a reason or that my experience on this planet is any more or less meaningful than anyone else's, but the coma was a reminder that I wasn't going to live forever, that my time was limited, maybe even more limited than most.

I'd come close to death before, but this was different. My body was in shut-down mode. I was checking out, slowly slipping away, and there was nothing I could do to stop the process. When you think of someone being in a coma, you think of them as being in a vegetative state. Maybe someone's there, maybe not. For me and for lots of other diabetics, slipping into a coma was a sneak peak at the worst-case scenario, a glimpse of where my disease could take me if I didn't take care of myself.

I wasn't ready to go. I still had some things I wanted to do. I had a lot more damage to do, but if I wanted to stick around, I needed to stop bringing it on myself.

OFF!

One of the most important relationships I developed at V2 Records was with Dimitri Coats, the guitar player for Burning Brides. I was really impressed with his songwriting ability and energy on stage. He would get aggro with his guitar playing. He wasn't a punk rock guy, and he knew very little about hardcore, but some riffage in one particular song ("Glass Slipper") reminded me of Greg Ginn. I never thought I'd work with Dimitri, but out of nowhere he approached the Circle Jerks about working with us as a producer.

One of the things the Circle Jerks never had when we went into the studio was a producer who could write and play our style of music. In the beginning we didn't know what we were doing. We were just playing by ear, coasting along, and getting by. But as the years went on we kept ending up in situations where we weren't following a creative vision so much as making the best of whatever situation presented itself and calling it a record. I put a lot of that on me, not being a leader, but after the clusterfuck that doomed *Oddities*, I was determined not to go through that again.

I had a vision for how the next record would be made. We were going to take our time and do it right. We would develop the songs organically, let the record become what it wanted to become, and when the time came we'd record the album at some grimy, low-digit, hole-in-the-wall studio where scuzzballs go to tape their noise. It didn't work out that way.

Instead, once again, we had a deadline created by Greg because he was getting ready to go out on the Warped Tour with Bad Religion. "We've got two months before I go on tour. We have to record the album before I leave."

All of a sudden we were in a time crunch. We had to get this stuff done as soon as possible. We no longer had the luxury of taking our time.

We all got together to hash out what we had and how we were going to proceed. Dimitri and I had written some songs, and we had a lot of great ideas for the new album. Working with Dimitri brought me back to my roots. The songs we were writing were as aggressive as anything the Circle Jerks had done, which was interesting because Dimitri was into bands like Black Sabbath and Nirvana. The Melvins were about as hardcore as it got for him.

The rest of the guys, however, weren't receptive to Dimitri's contributions for a couple of reasons. One, they were bitter and old and stuck in their ways. Two, Dimitri was young, brash, and had a hard-on up to his chin that made the rest of us look like a bunch of limp dicks. This combination proved to be especially combustible when Dimitri told the guys that the music they were creating wasn't good enough to be on a Circle Jerks album. He flat-out told them their ideas weren't cutting it, which did not go over well. When he challenged them to bring something better to the table, they weren't having it.

If we were going to record the album according to Greg's timeline, we needed to come up with another half dozen or so songs immediately. Not whenever or eventually, but right away. Dimitri held firm. "We're going to meet in Keith's living room and write every day. We're going to hash this out."

Dimitri and I went back to work and wrote some more songs, but nobody else made an appearance. Zander showed up once and then disappeared. Kevin did the same thing. Greg came over for an hour one day and left. His excuse was he had to go pick up a computer he'd ordered online that was sitting in the Long Beach post office; he was afraid it would get swiped. The whole thing was spiraling into a big fat zero. No work ethic. No creativity.

Dimitri and I worked in my living room. He'd sit and strum his guitar as we worked out riffs. One day he started to play some guitar lines, and we looked at each other, knowing that something clicked. He stood up and started slashing away a bit more. That was the first time he'd done that. From that moment the energy level intensified and took me back to the Church.

I told Dimitri we had to come up with a Plan B. I knew what was going to happen. We'd write all the songs, and when the work was done and it was time to record, one of the guys would figure out a way to put a screeching halt to the proceedings, which was pretty much what happened.

Greg was especially complimentary when we played him the CD. "This is great! This is going to be such a great album! Dimitri, you've finally got Keith to sing real choruses!"

No offense to Greg, but I felt that the recordings he'd been involved with over the years all had a degree of predictability. Familiarity is good. Like when you hear a Ramones' song, you recognize it right away. A lot of younger bands have this mentality: make it safe, make it predictable, and maybe we'll make it on the radio or a video game or a car commercial. You see a lot of that kind of brainwashing on the Warped Tour. I'm not dissing the Warped Tour—it's important, it has its place, and it's boosted a lot of careers. Kevin Lyman is a totally stand-up character, and I have nothing bad to say about him. But when you go to the Warped Tour you're not going to have many curveballs thrown your way. It's become a playground for kids. Mom pulls up in the minivan and drops off a load of teenagers. "You take care of them for the next seven hours!" Daycare for a portion of America's new youth. When the Warped Tour is your steak and potatoes and you're surrounded by a bunch of boy bands and their fans, you take on that personality, and I wasn't going to have anything to do with that.

We had a deal with Dimitri. We were going to pay him a fee to produce the record. Dimitri had just had his first daughter, and he had no income. I didn't think it was fair for Greg to assume that these songs were for the new Circle Jerks album. The fact of the matter was that Dimitri and I had gone to a place beyond the Circle Jerks, a place the rest of the guys weren't willing to go. I was done with the status quo. I didn't want Greg to take the songs and turn them into what the CJs had become. I didn't want songs that were fat, puffy, and overproduced. I didn't want a sing-along. I wanted something that made a statement: fuck you, here we are, now get out of our way.

That's when OFF! was born.

WHEN DIMITRI AND I SAT DOWN TO TALK about filling out the rest of the band he suggested I make a list with two columns. In one column put all the drummers I'd want to start a band with and all the bass players in the other. I did that, and at the top of the list were Mario Rubalcaba and Steven McDonald.

I called Mario first. He is a former professional skateboarder from San Diego who has been in some amazing bands: Rocket from the Crypt, Hot Snakes, Earthless—and that's just the tip of his iceberg. What's really impressive to me is that each of those bands has a distinct sound but stylistically they're all very different. I asked him if he was interested. He said, "Of course I'm interested."

Shortly afterward I went to see the Entrance Band play at the Center for the Arts in Eagle Rock. I was at the show and looked over to my right, and there standing next to me was Steven McDonald. We chatted for a bit after the show, and he said he was going to go outside to smoke a cigarette.

"I'll join you," I said. "There's something I want to run by you."

I explained what was happening with me and Dimitri and asked him if he wanted to be a part of it. He was very skeptical at first, and I don't blame him. I've known Steven since he was eleven years old and playing in the Tourists. He was leery of me after everything that had gone down with Greg Hetson and Red Cross/Redd Kross. Why wouldn't he be? But I had a demo in my car. Dimitri and I had recorded the guitar parts to four or five songs through a little amp in my living room. I wrote my phone digits on the CD and gave it to Steven. He called me up a couple of days later.

"When are we getting into a room to rehearse?"

We met up at ABC on San Fernando Road, where Redd Kross rehearses. Mario and Steven learned the songs very quickly, which was really impressive. The songs took on new life and sounded great, but it wasn't quite what I imagined. I felt it was almost too heavy. As I was driving away, I had my doubts. The songs made me imagine what Black Flag would have sounded like if we had paid more attention to Led Zeppelin. That's when I had my epiphany. These guys are some of the best players in the business. They didn't need me telling them what to do. I shouldn't be trying to bring them down to my level—I should by striving to reach theirs. I knew playing in a hardcore band at my age and in my physical condition with supremely talented musicians who were all younger than me wouldn't be easy, but I was up for the challenge.

WE KEPT REHEARSING AND FLESHING OUT the rest of the songs, and eventually we made a CD. I played it for Brett Gurewitz at Epitaph to see what he thought of it, and he almost fell out of his chair.

"Keith, this is the best music I've heard in four or five years. You sound like you're eighteen years old."

After everything we've been through, I knew Brett wasn't just blowing smoke in my ears. He'd helped me when I was down and wouldn't lie to me. He asked me what we wanted to do, which wasn't an easy question to answer.

The one thing I knew I didn't want to do was go on the Warped Tour, which was what the marketing guy at Epitaph suggested. Aside from how I personally felt about the kind of music the Warped Tour promotes, I wouldn't have been able to handle the rigors of a long summer tour. My medical issues make it impossible to hit the road for extended periods of time.

The rest of the guys in OFF! felt we owed it to ourselves to let some other people listen to what we'd done and see how they felt about it. Steven knew one of the founding fathers at VICE. They're an interesting company in that they do a lot of different things, and although their record label was fairly small, they had the assets to get behind us and the creativity to support some of the unusual things we wanted to do.

For instance, I didn't want to record an album; I wanted to release a series of EPs, just like the old days of punk rock. I also wanted Raymond Pettibon to do the artwork as a way of announcing to the world that we were going all the way back to the beginning of American hardcore. I also made it clear that we wouldn't be touring for six months out of the year and no stretch could be longer than two or three weeks due to the fact that we have three dads with four kids, three wives, and two dogs. A lot of labels would have said no dice, but VICE was behind us 100 percent.

HAPPY ENDING

They say you can't go home again. That's certainly true of Hermosa Beach. Hermosa Beach has changed since I lived there. They've just destroyed the place. It's like any beach city in Florida now. Spring break every day. You used to be able to drive down Pier Avenue all the way to the beach. Not anymore. They've closed off the street and added a bunch of bars and clothing stores and mediocre restaurants. All the personality has been stamped out. This was an amazing place to grow up in. Now on the weekends it gets inundated with frat boys and party people. It's horrible.

I've visited a few times since I left but never for very long. I came back about ten years ago with a girlfriend for Valentine's Day. My romantic interlude turned into a bro-down on Pier Avenue, which was packed with drunken, self-important, me-before-yous. There were fights breaking out all over the place. I couldn't walk down the street without someone getting in my face, telling me I didn't belong here, which is probably true. Hermosa Beach has become a giant, brightly lit urinal.

All the things I used to love about Hermosa Beach are gone. The Church isn't there anymore. They leveled it and turned it into a mini mall. I never knew the address when I lived there, so good luck finding it now. Down by the Mermaid there's a mural that presents the history of Hermosa Beach. There's a section dedicated to music, and there are some punk icons preserved for posterity. One of the figures is Jim Lindberg of Pennywise and the other is Henry Rollins. They could have picked one of the founding members, someone who actually grew up in Hermosa Beach, but instead they chose Black Flag's fourth vocalist who was born and raised thousands of miles away. The place is so screwed up, they can't even get their own history right. A small part of me misses the way Hermosa Beach used to be, but that place doesn't exist anymore.

For most of my run in Black Flag all of the members were on the same page. We joked around with each other and had fun. Guys would get upset at each other from time to time, but that happens with every band. Today it's a little different. I don't talk to Bryan Migdol anymore. Raymond and I are bros. I'll always have his back and he'll always have mine. I have no idea what happened to Kansas. Spot and I have remained friends through the years. I'll always love Robo, and I have the utmost respect for Chuck. As for Greg, I respect him as a guitar player, but the nicest thing I can say is that when he turned in his paperwork to be a member of the human race they rejected his application.

I'VE BEEN SOBER SINCE 1988. I've never relapsed.

Sobriety worked for me because I knew that I wanted to quit. I'd already done everything that I wanted to do. Those days are over for me. I don't regret them, but I don't miss them either. I know I'm not going back to where I was before. All of that stuff is in the past.

When I was younger and was around drugs and alcohol all the time, I'd see what other people were doing and figured, "They're doing it and they're having a good time, so I'm going to do it too." I was always afraid I was going to miss out on something. I was a follower. Now I go my own way.

Of course, I'm still surrounded by it. In the music business, drinks and drugs come with the territory. I now have the wherewithal to be able to say, "No, thanks." I already did all of that. I don't need to get any higher. I don't need to get any lower.

I'm happy to talk about my sobriety, but I don't like to get too preachy about it. It's all up to the individual. What's hardcore to you might not seem hardcore to me. What works for me might not work for you. I'm not going to hold your hand. I'm not going to give you a list of things to do to stay sober today. If you want to go out and drink and wreck cars and create all kinds of damage, that's what you're going to do. There's nothing anyone can do to stop you. You have to make that decision for yourself by yourself. Then you're ready for help.

I couldn't really make a clean break with the past and hit the reset button without apologizing to my family, and my dad was at the top of the list. I haven't read a ton of recovery literature, but I know when you fuck up, you apologize to the people you've hurt. It's just common sense. I didn't have to do a lot of soul searching to figure out what I needed to do. It was pretty obvious what needed to happen next.

I'VE HAD DIABETES FOR ALMOST twenty years. You'd think I would have figured it out by now, but I haven't. I'm much more rigorous about recording my glucose levels and insulin procedures. The thing with the diabetes is that each case is completely different. It affects each person differently, and each body responds in its own peculiar way. No two cases are ever the same. It's something each diabetic has to figure out. No one can do it for you.

I've come to terms with the fact that I'm never going to beat diabetes. That's the wrong mindset. You don't beat diabetes in much the same way that you don't beat alcoholism or drug addiction. You manage it.

I don't live in a perfect world. In fact, my world is highly irregular. I'm always making up for this or overcompensating for that. For instance, as I write this, I'm suffering from hypoglycemia because I'm trying to adjust to a new rehearsal schedule. I'm rehearsing in between breakfast and lunch, which I eat at the same time every day, and that raises my glucose level. The intensity of the music creates stress and brings my glucose level up. So before I eat, when I check my glucose, I see that it's high, and that impacts the amount of insulin I take and the amount of food I eat. I took some extra insulin in the morning to compensate for the spike in my glucose level during rehearsal, but it didn't work and now I'm feeling hypoglycemic.

It's all a big balancing act with a million different factors: stress, rest, travel, exercise—even the weather. There's always something I'm trying to get a handle on. If I could just figure out how to mellow out a little bit more, I'd be in great shape.

That said, my diabetologist told me that even though I have diabetes, I haven't done any permanent damage. I haven't messed up my internal organs. I haven't lost any feeling in my fingers or toes, hands or feet, arms or legs. My vision is pretty normal. All I need to do is get my food levels and insulin levels to where they need to be and I'll be feeling like a million bucks.

IN 2011 GARY TOVAR PUT TOGETHER a three-night show to celebrate the thirtieth anniversary of Goldenvoice at the Santa Monica Civic. Gary wanted Chuck Dukowski to give a speech, which Chuck wanted no part of. Instead, he called Billy Stevenson with the idea of getting a bunch of guys who'd been in Black Flag to play together. He knew the Descendents were headlining and Billy had played drums in Black Flag and Stephen Egerton had learned to play guitar listening to the records. There wasn't money to fly Dez or Ron in, but Chuck was available, and he knew I was down.

Chuck went back to Goldenvoice and let them know that former members of Black Flag were going to play a secret set on the last night of GV 30, and they started spreading the word. We went on between the Vandals and the Descendents, and we played the *Nervous Breakdown* EP. We blasted through the songs, and people went ape-shit. The vibe and energy and excitement were through the roof. We would have been stupid to not to want to do it again.

We generated such a buzz that Greg Ginn started playing as Black Flag with the people he was playing with, which is fine, and then he took us to court, which I can't talk about and isn't worth discussing anyway, but FLAG will continue to play, and nothing else needs to be said.

We never set out to create a competition, but it turned into one. We all played those songs. We played a role in recording them and making them what they are. We fulfilled the promise Black Flag had made during the First Four Years shows at the Palladium. Everyone who has come to see us play as FLAG knows we mean business, and we're going to keep doing it as long as people want to hear the songs the way they're supposed to be played.

OFF! HAS CHANGED EVERYTHING FOR ME. I'm much more energized, especially from a creative standpoint. I'm in constant lyric writing mode. I'm a slow reader, but when I read a book, a sentence will jump off the page and grab me by my eyes or kick me in the head. All of a sudden I've stopped reading, and now I'm focused on something completely different and have to go pick up my pen and start scribbling my thoughts.

Before, I used to write only when I had to. Now I write bits and pieces every day. Most of the time I don't know where it's going or how I'm going to use it, but I do it, and it's been extremely rewarding. Not only am I enjoying songwriting again, but I like the creativity. I used to move on from a song pretty quickly. I'd make up some lyrics, hash out the song, put it on a record, and then it was on to the next thing. But I'm genuinely moved by the songs we've written with OFF! and look forward to playing them. I really like "Poison City," which is about 9/11, and "Jeffrey Lee Pierce," my tribute to an underrated punk rock icon and a true friend. J. L. P. RIP.

I have a lot more opportunities to express myself than I ever did before. The videos we did for a couple of tracks on OFF!'s third album, *Wasted Years*, with Jack Black are a great example. We all got to do some acting. I didn't have a lot of lines, but I ended up fighting a grizzly bear. It was a lot of fun, but it was hard work. We worked for three days on that shoot, but we got to work with Jack Black.

As soon as the video was released all of the haters showed up online, the punk rock ethics committee. "Why would you work with Jack Black? Fuck that guy!" People get online and rail on this guy and that guy. "I met him one time and he was a total asshole!"

He can come across as overbearing on camera. A lot of actors and comedians are that way. They have to put themselves out there with their performance, and when they're in the zone you don't want to mess around with that. Off camera you're not going to find a sweeter, nicer, more generous guy than Jack Black. We had dinner at Fatburger and didn't talk about the shoot or the band or Hollywood bullshit. We talked about his kids, ate our burgers like a couple of regular dudes, and enjoyed the fine cuisine.

One of the things people don't understand: when we first started playing music all I wanted to do was party. Playing in a band was our fun. Every show was a thrill. Then it started to become work. We'd get in the van and drive around the country for months and months playing two shows a night. I'm not complaining—that's what we jumped on board for. That was our job. But it took a toll and became a grind.

Now I'm having fun again. What's interesting is that being older and dealing with diabetes makes being in a band a lot harder than when I was younger. Sometimes it can be grueling, but I'm really enjoying it. I'm going to places I thought I'd never get to see and meeting people I never would have met. Although I can be a grouchy old man at times, I'm a people person.

At the end of the day we're all just human beings. We have good days and bad days. I'm very fortunate in that I'm well known on a cult level, which means a lot of people know who I am, but the big-time ultra-mega break never happened for me. I don't get to live on an island or in a mansion. I'm fine with that. I'm more than fine. I walk these streets, and people honk and yell, "Hey, Keith!" And sometimes I nod and wave, and sometimes I don't based on a million different things. Have I had my coffee? Did I eat? How's my blood sugar? Am I late for a meeting? Is someone waiting on me? Am I thinking about a song lyric or worrying about my bills?

The fact of the matter is if people are going to take time out of their life to ask me to give up the same amount of time for an autograph or a picture, I feel I owe it to them. That said, some people seem to think I'm supposed to stop dead in my tracks and fulfill every little request. I can't stop and chat with everybody who asks me how I'm doing and what movies I'm watching and what was the last book I read and how's my love life and who are my favorite bands. I don't even have time to do that with my friends. If I'm walking down the street it's because I'm actually going somewhere.

I'm pretty accessible, but I have to tell you that the worst fucking invention in the world besides the gun, the jet, and the car is the fucking cell phone. Everybody and their goddamn motherfucking entire family can corner you and get their photo taken with you. I actually had a guy follow me in his van not too long ago. All he wanted was his picture taken with me, but how do I know that? It's not a good feeling to be tailed by a stranger in a van who knows you but you don't know him. I went inside a bookstore, and next thing I knew the guy in the van was next to me in the store and wanted to take a selfie with me. No skin off my ass, but then he asked the guy working behind the counter to shoot the picture for him, which meant he was taking time away from his customers to take a picture of me, and that's not cool.

I've had a lot of people say, "Keith, you're cool, but so-and-so is a real asshole." Why is that? Because you approached a musician immediately after they got through playing for an hour? Maybe they just wanted to go backstage and dry off, drink some water, and collect their thoughts while they got their shit together and came back to a normal state of mind. They just gave everything they had and left it on the stage, but that's not enough for you? You need more? I would say *you're* the asshole.

It happens to me all the time. People come up to me seconds after I get off stage. "Dude, you look like just got through running the LA marathon, but come have a smoke with me." Or "I know you're clean and sober, but you look thirsty so let's drink a beer together. I've got some wine. Would you like to smoke a pipe? Bang some smack? Come with me outside—I've got some questions for you."

I know that sounds absurd, but you wouldn't believe the requests I get. The next time you go to a show and you bump into your favorite musician, instead of crowding around, give him or her a little space, and instead of asking that person to give more of their time and energy, show some appreciation. You wouldn't believe what a boost it is to hear a fan say "Thank you" after the show.

I don't know what's next for OFF! or what will happen in the future. I can tell you that I'm having a lot more fun as a member of OFF! than I ever did as a member of Black Flag or the Circle Jerks. For the first time I'm able to make the most of the opportunities presented to me because all the members in the band are in agreement 80 percent of the time. That's pretty damn good.

With OFF! I've been able to do a lot more traveling to faraway places. We've packed so much action and adventure into such a short period of time. We've only been a band for about five years. We've put out three studio albums and a few live records. We've been to South America, Japan, Australia twice, and Europe three times. We're doing everything the Circle Jerks weren't capable of doing.

We opened up for Pearl Jam and Black Rebel Motorcycle Club at an outdoor venue in Milton Keynes about sixty miles up the road from London, and it was one of the biggest shows I've ever played. We played in Mexico City, and that opened some doors for us to tour in more places in Mexico, like Guadalajara and Oaxaca, which would be totally amazing. We get invited to play at music festivals all over the world.

I think this means you won't be seeing the Circle Jerks doing anything in the near future. Some of the guys have been trying to get me to write songs with them, approached me about reunion shows with this lineup or that lineup, but I'm not concerned with the CJs right now; I've got too much to look forward to.

As for OFF! we're going to make another album or two or three and hopefully write a movie soundtrack. That means I'll be able to start gambling in the Mediterranean, hanging out in Rio during Carnival, and buying up British Petroleum and Monsanto stock. We're all going to have our own private jets. We might even have helicopters and jet skis. It's going to be so fucking great.

Acknowledgments

Keith Morris: Working on this book has been a blast and wouldn't have happened without a few old pals and a couple of new friends. Jim Ruland sat in my living room, grilling me for several dozen hours over the course of a year. Ben Schafer, our main man at Da Capo who we swindled into publishing this book, kicked down the digitalis for the breakfasts and lunches. Marc Gerald, my literary agent at United Talent Agency, wrangled Ben in, and Andy Somers at the APA Agency, who was and still is the booking agent for some of the bands I'm in or I've been in, was the one who started this mess by going to Marc in the first place. Of course Joseph M. Sofio Esq., more commonly known as Joe Sofio, gets a big thank you for making sure all the paperwork was kosher, and Raymond Pettibon cannot be thanked enough. I owe him a burrito.

I also need to thank the crew at Los Angeles Fire Station 35 for the two bumps of dextrose. While I'm on the dextrose tip, I've got to give a shout out to those freaks in Turbonegro and the Norwegian medical system. Hooray for socialized health care! A Hollywood sign–size acknowledgement to my two biggest influences; my dad, Jerry Morris, R.I.P., and John Jancar, R.I.P., who taught fine art at Mira Costa High School and instilled in me an attitude of go for it and be fearless!

Now I'm going to rattle off a bunch of friends in no particular order, Jeffrey Lee Pierce, R.I.P., Pete "Grandmaster Butterfly" Weiss, Sean "Peachfuzz" Carlson, Jon "Sidealer" Sidel, Bob "Buckskin" Forrest, Louie "The Hedge" Mathieu also known as "Oscar," Michael Piper, R.I.P., Doug Williams, Dick Rude, Jeff Migdol, R.I.P., Martyn LeNoble, Kenny Shiffrin, the cast and characters that make up or made up Black Flag, Circle Jerks, Spanking Monkeys, Bug Lamp,

Midget Handjob, OFF!, FLAG, The Tourists, Red Cross, Redd Kross, Thelonious Monster, X, Red Hot Chili Peppers, Fishbone, Chris Doherty and Gang Green, Wasted Youth, Social Distortion, Bad Religion, Vandals, TSOL, Pennywise, Maynard James Keenan and his Recreational Racism, Weirdos, Top Jimmy and the Rhythm Pigs, Plugz, Alley Cats, Last, Adolescents, Descendents, Nick Razor's GFI, P, Hangmen, Nymphs, Motorcycle Boy, Laughing Sam's Dice, Gibby Haynes, Penelope Spheeris, Gary Hirstius, Dream Delon, Gary Tovar, Paul Tollett, Rick Van Santen, B. Otis Link, Sal Jenco, Brett "Starbolt" Gurewitz, Sosie Hublitz, Anne Dagnello, Ed Colver, Gary Leonard, Glenn "Spot" Lockett, Cathy Rundell of FIZ magazine, Brian and Nikki Tucker of FER YOUz, Bruce Kalberg and Ewa (pronounced Eva) Wojciak of NO MAG, Rooh Stief, Chris D., BJ Papas, Glen E Friedman, Greg Allen, Antonio "Willy" Garcia, Joby Ford of the Bronx, Rodrigo Melleiro, John Ciambotti, R.I.P., Patty Peck, Iris Berry, Aida Ruilova, John Roecker, Exene Cervenka, my sister Trudy Ann Morris Van Winkle Guyton, Jonathan Pink, Dr. Ann Peters, the crew at Vida Coffee for fueling this, and the females that have propped me up and crushed my heart over the years, including Karen Jensen "REEEEEEEEEEEEEEEEET!!!!", Alexandra Root, Jody Shenkarek, Inger Lorre, Hope Urban, Jennifer Ballantyne, Amy Nicoletto, Rachel Haden, and Janelle.

And the last people I'd like to give a shout out to are the fans who have stuck around and paid attention to all of my condescending rants and tirades throughout all of this! Everybody enjoy yourselves, have fun, be well, and THANK YOU!

Jim Ruland: Thanks to Peter McGuigan and Ben Schafer, without whom this book wouldn't exist, Pete Weiss for the insight and inspiration, Flea for the digs, Raymond Pettibon for the captive chains, and Steve McDonald for setting the record straight. Additional thanks to Todd Taylor and Michael T. Fournier for dropping knowledge and editorial acumen, and the Razorcake familia for doing your part. I owe a debt of gratitude to the late Brendan Mullen for consenting to an interview long ago and who has been whispering in my ear ever since. Special thanks to my wife—Nuvia Crisol Guerra—and my daughter—Annie McKenna—who endured a steady diet of punk and hardcore and never complained. Lastly, thanks to Keith Morris, whose dedication, enthusiasm, and integrity is an affirmation of everything good about the music I love.

About the Authors

Keith Morris is an icon of American hardcore music. He is a cofounding member of Black Flag, the most recognizable name in West Coast punk rock, and the Circle Jerks, which cemented his reputation at the forefront of hardcore vocalists. He has recorded over fifteen albums, appeared on countless albums and compilations, and has a half dozen film credits to his name. The intensity of the music produced by his latest bands, OFF! and FLAG, are equal to his best work from the seventies, eighties, and nineties and add to a legendary career that is still being carved out one gig at a time. A native of California, he has lived in Los Feliz for over twenty years.

Jim Ruland caught the punk rock virus when his mom took him to see the Ramones when he was fifteen. He has been writing for punk rock zines like *Flipside* since the early nineties and has written for every issue of *Razorcake*, America's only nonprofit independent music fanzine. He is the author of the award-winning novel *Forest of Fortune* and the short story collection *Big Lonesome*. He is the curator of the Southern California–based irreverent reading series Vermin on the Mount. He lives in San Diego.

Index

AC/DC, 38

Adam and the Ants, 115

Adolescents, 100, 101, 103, 209

Aerosmith, 26, 82

Alago, Michael, 203

Alcoholics Anonymous, 178

Alexandra (girlfriend), 165,
    176–177, 178

Alice Bag Band, 114

Alice Cooper, 26, 209

Allen, Robbie, 211, 212

Alley Cats, 49, 52, 61, 75, 78

Allman Brothers Band, 18, 153

Alva, Tony, 82

Alvin, Dave, 156, 172

A&M Records, 125–126, 127

Amber (Circle Jerks manager), 132

Amoeba Records, 1, 250, 256, 257

Anderle, David, 125–126, 127

Andretti, Mario, 168

Angry Samoans, 90, 97, 109

Anka, Paul, 136

Anthony (from Red Hot Chili
    Peppers), 155, 168, 172, 242

Anus the Menace, 227

Arena rock, 56

Arnaz, Desi, 99

Association, 136

Avengers, 109

Aykroyd, Dan, 119

Back Door Man (zine), 26, 61, 106

Bad Religion, 75, 159, 186, 187, 188,
    202, 219, 223–224, 241, 272

Bad Seeds, 95

Bag, Alice, 64, 114

Bagarozzi, Chris, 235, 236, 239

Bags, 63, 109

Baker, Chet, 29

Ball, Lucille, 99

Balzary, Michael. *See* Flea (Michael
    Balzary)

Bangles, 56, 175

Barbarians, 9

Barrett, K. K., 76

Bateman, Bill, 172

Bators, Stiv, 51

Beastie Boys, 210, 242

Beat, Nickey, 109, 175

Beatles, 103, 224, 226

Bell, Michelle Gerber, 100, 139

Bellson, Louie, 89

Belltower, Bobby, 191

Belushi, John, 119

Bentley, Jay, 75, 159

Berry, Chuck, 223, 247

Berry, Iris, 227, 228, 229, 235

Bessy, Claude (Kickboy Face), 61, 62, 64

Big Boys, 34

Big Wow, 74

Biggs, Bob, 113

Bill (at Millie's Diner), 227, 228–229

Bingenheimer, Rodney, 51

Biscuits, Chuck, 138–139, 141, 147, 148–149, 155, 157, 158

Bla-Bla Café, 69–70

Black, Frank, 243

Black, Jack, 281–282

Black, Kara Ella, 76

Black Crowes, 243

Black Flag, 1, 12, 34, 82, 84, 102, 110, 124, 138, 203, 243, 245, 263, 284

    artwork and album covers, 45, 60

    birth and naming of, 45, 90

    and Bomp!, 59, 100

    Cathay de Grande show, 122–123

    and celebrity from touring, 139

    contrast with Circle Jerks, 95, 96, 97, 99

    and cops, 77–81, 83–84

    court case, 280

    and Decline of Western Civilization, 113–114

    difficulty booking shows, 82, 84

    Dukowski's and Ginn brothers' contributions to, 36, 45

    Everything Went Black album, 46

    and "Femme Fatale" dispute, 48

    first real show (1979) and other early shows, 49–55

    as FLAG, 280–281

    and Flea, 155

    frustration as root of, 59, 68

    and Goldenvoice show, 280

    and Happy-Tom, 260

    and Hermosa Beach dedication, 278

    internal dissension and conflict in, 84–87, 94, 96

    Jealous Again EP, 122, 247

    and the Last, 56, 57

    and Led Zeppelin, 275

    logo, 45

    and lyrics, 46–47, 48, 96, 97, 99

    and the Masque, 62, 65–66

    and members afterward, 278

    Morris leaves, 84–87, 88, 91, 94, 113, 121, 247, 251

    Morris's relations with and views of after leaving, 94, 113, 121–123

    In My Head album, 247

    Nervous Breakdown EP, 45–46, 47, 59–62, 100, 280

    and new wave of punk bands and fans, 82–84

    Panic predecessor of, 31–45

    parties, 75–76

    Polliwog Park show, 73–76, 77

    promoting shows, 72

    reputation as thugs, 64–65

    reunion, 246–252

and Reyes, 86, 88, 121

and Rollins, 86, 94, 122, 123

and screw-ups and bad venues
    and situations, 67–72

and second wave of LA punk,
    108

seeds of, 25–30

Stardust Ballroom show, 117

starts being taken seriously,
    61–62

Valencia joins, 59

"White Minority" song, 46–47

Black Hearts, 66

Black Oak Arkansas, 54

Black Rebel Motorcycle Club, 284

Black Sabbath, 15, 82, 199, 272

Blasters, 96, 106, 156, 172

Blotzer, Bobby, 31, 57

Blow, Joe, 65

Bob (grandfather), 10, 54

Bolan, Marc, 19

Bolas, Niko, 221

Bolder, Trevor, 16

Bon Jovi, 222, 223

Bonham, John, 138, 205, 207

Boon, D., 52

Bow Wow Wow, 133

Bowie, David, 111

    and Crash, 116

    and Hong Kong Café, 71, 72

    poster, 19

    and Raw Power, 16

    and "Waiting for the Man," 48

    and Ziggy Stardust, 16–17, 116

Branson, Richard, 244, 259

Bremner, Billy, 206

Brockey, Dave, 217

Bud Club, 155, 156

Bug Lamp, 1, 263

    early challenges and gigs,
        206–207

    end of, 212

    formation and naming of,
        204–206

    and record labels, 208–209,
        210–213

    tracks and demo tape, 209–211,
        217

Built to Spill, 236

Burnett, Chester, 175

Burning Brides, 244, 271

Butthole Surfers, 154, 184, 242

Buzzcocks, 72, 100

Cadena, Dez, 280

    and Black Flag parties, 76

    and Black Flag reunion, 250, 251

    and first Black Flag show, 51

    and Morris friendship, 12, 122

    and Polliwog Park Black Flag
        show, 75

    as vocalist, 122

Cage, Nicolas, 78

Cale, John, 33

Capitol Records, 170, 189, 193–194,
    199

Capone, Al, 5

Captain & Tennille, 136

Carlton, Bobby, 219

Carpenters, 136

Carroll, Jim, 107

Casella, Curtis, 218

Caustic Resin, 236

CBGB, 63, 248

Celebrity Rehab (TV show), 164

Cervenka, Exene, 106

Chai, Diane, 75

Chaplin, Charlie, 133

Cheap Trick, 250, 254

Cheifs, 69, 99

Chelsea, 132

Chenier, Clifton, 106

China White, 117

Chrome, Cheetah, 120

Chrysalis, 208, 210, 211, 212–213

Church (rehearsal space and house),
    39–42, 75–76, 77, 84, 86, 88,
    273, 277

CIA, 130, 269

Ciambotti, John, 232–233

Circle Jerks, 1, 194, 196, 202, 203,
    216, 238, 243, 245, 263, 284
  at After Everything Else, 175
  audition for new bassist, 159–161
  and Biscuits, 138–139, 141, 157,
    158
  and Clark, 158–159, 162, 181–
    184, 241
  and Coats, 271–274
  contrast with Black Flag, 95, 96,
    97, 99
  and Crash's death, 115
  and Decline of Western
    Civilization, 113–114,
    118–119, 125
  and drama, 124
  dud shows, 182
  early shows and activity, 94–97
  and Europe, 218
  and Far Out Management,
    133–134, 136–137, 139, 147,
    152
  and Fitzgerald, 227
  and Flea, 155–156, 159
  formation and naming of, 89–90
  and Ginn's involvement with
    Bad Religion, 187, 223–224,
    241
  Golden Shower of Hits album,
    136–137, 139, 146
  Golden Shower tour, 146–153,
    155
  and Goldenvoice, 165
  Group Sex album, 98–101, 102,
    119, 125
  and Happy-Tom, 260
  and Hirstius, 125, 127, 132
  and income, 182, 208, 219, 220
  and Ingram, 131–132, 137
  and I.R.S. Records, Faulty
    Products, and Miles Copeland,
    125–126, 130–132
  and the Last, 57
  and latest wave of hardcore
    punk, 108
  logo and image, 101
  and lyrics and songs, 96–97, 98–
    99, 109–110, 125, 127, 131,
    134, 136–137, 141, 162, 183,
    219, 220, 221, 272, 273, 274

and Mercury Records, 219–220, 224

with Morris in body brace, 173

and Morris's father, 131

and Morris's V2 Records job, 253–254

New York shows, 119–120

and Oakland festival, 158

Oddities, Abnormalities and Curiosities album, 221–222, 224–225, 271

Oddities tour, 222–224, 241

and partying, 94, 99, 101, 117, 124

and possible reunion shows, 284

and Rat, 198

and Red Hot Chili Peppers, 155

and Repo Man, 141–144

and Rogerson's departure, 139–140

scattered and busy members of, 219, 220

and Schloss, 161, 162

shows after Wild in the Streets release, 128–129

and Sid and Nancy, 144–145

and Slash, 95, 102

at Smoke Out, 246

Stardust Ballroom show, 117

and summer barbecue, 106–107

two-week tour, 241–242

and van, 146–147, 148–149, 150–152

VI album, 181–182, 183

VI tour, 183–184, 186

weird shows, 102–104

Wild in the Streets album, 127–128

Wönderful album, 162–163, 181

Circus of Power, 203, 204, 207

Clark, Keith, 158–159, 162, 163, 181–184, 219, 224, 241

Clash, 27, 160

Clawhammer, 235, 236

Club Lingerie, 154, 156, 175

Coats, Dimitri, 271–274

Colver, Ed, 100

Combat Records, 162

Controllers, 63

Copeland, Ian, 130

Copeland, Miles, 130, 131, 132

Copeland, Stewart, 130

Costello, Elvis, 232

Cox, Alex, 141, 143, 144–145

Cramps, 65, 95

Crash, Darby, 37, 64, 79, 110–111, 114, 115–116, 118, 132

Creeping Ritual, 95

Criterion Collection, 144

Cro Mags, 119

Croucier, Juan, 57

Crowd, 100

Cruzados, 132, 133

Culture Club, 169

Cure, 200

Cypress Hill, 246

Dangerhouse, 49

Dangerous Toys, 199

Danzig, 138

Datsuns, 244

Davies, Dave, 17

Davies, Ray, 17

Davis, Miles, 29

Dead Boys, 51, 120

Deal, Kim, 243

The Decline of Western Civilization (movie), 113–115, 118–119, 125, 175

Deep Purple, 26

Denny, Dix, 64

Descendents, 34, 52, 280

Desert Sessions, 237

Desjardins, Chris, 106, 110, 155

Detox, 173, 235

Dickies, 63, 85, 243

Dils, 65, 193

Ditko, Steve, 93

DOA, 109, 138

Doe, John, 106, 110, 155, 156, 165, 175

Dogtown, 82

Doherty, Chris, 218

Dokken, Don, 57, 58

Donovan, Aaron, 227, 238

Doobie Brothers, 57

Doors, 64

Down by Law, 235

Drake, Fred, 237

Dream Syndicate, 160

Droubay, Marc, 31

Drug, Doug, 101

Du Plenty, Tomata, 156

Duff, Bruce, 205–206, 210, 211

Dukowski, Chuck, 121, 278
    and Bla-Bla Café show, 69
    and Black Flag reunion, 247, 249, 250
    and Black Flag set at Goldenvoice show, 280
    and Black Flag's first show, 50
    and Circle Jerks, 97
    and Decline of Western Civilization, 113
    as heart and soul of Black Flag, 36
    and New Masque, 79
    and Panic, 36–38, 39, 40
    and practice, work ethic, and strictness of, 36, 38, 84–85, 86
    rift with Morris of, 84–87

Dutch (doorman), 58

Dyer, Allison, 226

Eagles, 44, 57, 135

Earth Wind and Fire, 163

Earthless, 274

Egerton, Stephen, 280

Einstein, Albert, 198

Either/Or Bookstore, 42

Electric Hippie, 175

Elks' Lodge Riot, 78

Enigk, Jeremy, 256, 257

Entrance Band, 274

Epitaph, 188, 193, 237, 239, 240, 242, 275

Eyes, 63

Fall, 236

Fancher, Lisa, 100

Far Out Management, 132–134, 136–137, 139, 147, 152

Faulty Products, 125–126, 130, 132

F.B.I (booking agency), 130

Fear, 63, 64, 65, 71, 103, 114, 117, 120, 155, 167

Ferocious Suck, 227

Fetchin' Bones, 216

The Fire of Love (album), 96

Fishbone, 155, 167, 237, 242

Fitzgerald, Kevin, 227, 235, 239, 241–242, 272

Five Torches, 96

Flaming Lips, 154, 209

Flanagan, Harley, 119

Flea (Michael Balzary), 155–156, 159, 167, 168, 169, 172, 242

Fleetwood Mac, 44, 59, 73, 74, 163

Flesh Eaters, 106, 125, 132, 155

Flipside (fanzine), 76, 78, 236

Flyboys, 100

Forrest, Bob, 208
   and After Everything Else, 175
   and benefit at Whisky, 237
   and Flea and Anthony, 172
   and Keenan, 253
   and Millie's, 227, 232
   as Morris's roommate, 169–170
   and Replacements, 164, 165, 166
   in Richmond, 217
   and Thelonious Monster, 155, 164, 167

45 Grave, 103

400 Blows, 227

Fowley, Kim, 17, 18

Foxx, Red, 96

Frampton, Peter, 58

Frances (aunt), 9–10, 91

Frontier Records, 100, 101

Frusciante, John, 236

Fudge Factory, 244

Fugazi, 212–213

Gallego, Tim, 159

Gang Green, 218

Gautier, John Paul, 208

Gazzarri's, 71–72

Gears, 67, 69, 75, 99, 114

Geffen Records, 196, 199, 200, 208–209, 211, 245

Generation X, 175

Geraldine Fibbers, 235, 241

Germs, 37, 63, 71, 78, 88, 101, 109, 114, 115

Gershon, Andy, 245

Geza X, 121

Gibson, Debbie, 221, 225

Ginn, Erika, 25–26

Ginn, Greg, 137, 271
   and Bad Religion, 186, 187, 202, 219, 223–224, 241, 272
   Band, 247–248
   and Biscuits, 157
   and Black Flag court case, 280
   and Black Flag internal dissension and Morris's departure, 85–87
   and Black Flag reunion, 246–252
   and Bryan Migdol, 59
   and business, 27–28, 29, 59–60

Ginn, Greg, (*continued*)
  and Circle Jerks, 89–90, 96–97,
    119, 147, 152, 157, 162, 183,
    187, 218, 220, 223–224, 241,
    272, 273, 274
  and dad, 95
  and Decline of Western
    Civilization, 113
  described, 27–28, 32
  and early Black Flag show, 51
  and "Femme Fatale," 48
  guitar playing of, 27, 31
  and lyrics, 48, 96, 97
  as member of human race, 278
  and naming of Black Flag, 45
  and Nervous Breakdown, 59–60,
    62
  and New Masque, 79
  and Panic, 31–35, 36, 39, 40, 41
  and Polliwog Park Black Flag
    show, 73
  quits Black Flag, 89
  and Repo Man, 141
  as reputed mastermind of Black
    Flag, 36, 45
  and Reyes, 88
  and screw-ups and bad venues
    for Black Flag shows, 67, 69
  and seeds of Black Flag, 25–30
  and singing, 248
  SST compound of, 248
  and stolen marijuana tree, 34
  temping of, 130
  and "White Minority," 47
  and Young and Thunders, 223

Ginn, Raymond, 33–34, 45, 60, 79
  See also Pettibon, Raymond
Glasscock, Aaron, 158
Go-Go's, 78, 85, 109
Godfathers, 189
Golden Earring, 202, 204
Goldenvoice, 155, 165, 246, 248,
  250, 251, 252, 280
Goldstein, Jerry, 133
Goss, Chris, 237
Grady, Craig, 228
Graffin, Greg, 220
Graham, Bill, 189–190, 194
Grant, Cary, 167
Grass Roots, 16
Grateful Dead, 9, 26, 27, 41, 58,
  137, 153
Green, Peter, 59
Green Day, 219
Gretzky, Wayne, 215
Grillo, Brian, 76
Grimley, Tom, 237, 238
Gueneri, John, 125
Gun Club, 61, 98, 114, 189, 219
Guns N' Roses, 189, 198, 251
Gurewitz, Brett, 188, 192, 236–237,
  245, 275
GWAR, 217

Haden, Petra, 238
Hagar, Sammy, 170
Haizman, Todd, 109–110
Hangmen, 186–190, 192, 193–195,
  198, 199, 200, 202, 205, 209, 245
Happy-Tom, 260, 261, 263, 269

Harvey, P. J., 237
Hawkins, Screaming Jay, 154, 206
Haynes, Gibby, 184–185, 237
Henley, Rob, 100
Hetson, Greg, 76, 88, 97, 115, 155,
        165, 183, 224, 274
Hirstius, Gary, 125, 127, 132, 164
Hofer, Manfred, 191
Hollywood Bowl, 18
Homme, Josh, 237
Hong Kong Café, 70, 71, 85, 96, 107,
        109, 110, 111
Hot Snakes, 274
Howie (father's uncle), 7
Howlin' Wolf, 9
Human Hands, 236
Hurley, George, 52
Hüsker Dü, 34, 134
Hutchinson, Charlie, 227, 229

Icarus Line, 244
Ice-T, 92
Idol, Billy, 175
Iggy and the Stooges, 16, 26, 29, 48
Ingram, John, 131–132, 135, 137
I.R.S. Records, 125–126, 130
Island Records, 216

Jacobs, Hap, 12
Jam, 100
Jan and Dean, 126
Jazz, 28–29, 89, 163
Jefferson Airplane, 41, 50
Jesus and Mary Chain, 254
Jet, 254

Jim (roommate), 107
Jodi (girlfriend), 215–216
Johnny (at Millie's Diner), 227,
        228–229
Jones, Cliff, 38
Jones, Elvin, 29
Jones, Texacala, 107
Jordan, Jill, 76
Jordan, Michael, 181, 216
Journey, 25, 26
Juicy Bananas, 142

Kane, Arthur "Killer," 17–18, 119
Kansas (bass player), 34, 278
Kaulkin, Andy, 236, 239
Keenan, Maynard, 253
Kelly, Michael, 176, 177, 232
Kerri, Shawn, 101
Ketoacidosis, 265
Kid Congo, 95
Kiedis, Anthony, 156
Killing Joke, 197
Kinks, 17, 189
Kinman, Tony, 193, 199
Kirby, Jack, 93
Kirk, Don, 132
Kirwan, Danny, 59
KISS, 19
Knack, 56, 70
Knievel, Evel, 149
Korn, 248
Kramer, Wayne, 247

LaMotta, Jake, 205
Lanegan, Mark, 237

Last, 52, 56, 57, 61, 70, 75

Laughing Sam's Dice (LSD), 204, 205, 206

Le Bear, Jean, 227, 228, 235, 239

Leaving Trains, 191, 227

Led Zeppelin, 17, 143, 205, 207, 275

Lee, Arthur, 9

Lee, Bruce, 6

Legendary Pink Dots, 243

Lehrer, Chet, 95, 103

Lehrer, Lucky, 94, 95, 97
 and Circle Jerks, 89, 99, 102–103, 124, 130
 and Crash, 116
 and drumming, 88–89, 131, 138
 and girlfriend's stolen car, 119
 and Whisky, 108

Lennon, John, 116

Lewis, Jerry, 143

Liberty, Earl, 139, 141, 147–148, 149, 155

Lighthouse, 28–29

Lindberg, Jim, 41, 277

Link, B. Otis, 155

Lions and Ghosts, 211

Little Kings, 107

Lock Up, 76

Lockett, Glen (Spot), 34–35, 45, 75, 278

Loren, Sofia, 227

Lorre, Inger, 191–193, 196–201, 202

Los Lobos, 96, 109

Love, 9, 64

Low, 206

Low & Sweet Orchestra, 219

Lundberg, Ebbot, 265–266

Lyman, Kevin, 273

Lynch, David, 78, 132

Lynott, Phil, 26

Mabuhay Gardens, 121, 128, 246

MacKaye, Ian, 120, 212–213

Mad Society, 158

Madame Wong's, 70, 109

Madonna, 242

Maile, Vic, 189, 199

Malone, Tony, 235

Martin, Dean, 142–143, 164

Martt, Mike, 219

Masque, 58, 61, 62, 63–66, 83, 96, 114, 125, 193

Matthews, Rachel, 189–190, 194–195

Mau Maus, 65–66, 71

McDaniel, Gary, 36–38
 See also Dukowski, Chuck

McDonald, Jeff, 74, 75, 76, 88, 89, 97

McDonald, Steve, 74, 75, 76, 88, 89, 97, 274, 275

McKagan, Duff, 198, 250–251

McNeely, Big Jay, 154

Meat Puppets, 34

Megadeath, 158–159, 162

Melvins, 272

Mentors, 103

Mercury Records, 219–220, 224

Metallica, 57, 203, 204

Meyers, Michelle, 175

Midget Handjob, 1, 235–240, 241,
    242, 263
*Midnight Snack Break at the Poodle
    Factory* (album), 237–238, 240,
    242
Migdol, Bryan, 31–32, 34, 43, 59, 60,
    250, 278
Migdol, Jeff, 31–32
Minor Threat, 120
Minutemen, 34, 52, 117, 134, 167
Misfits, 34
Mitchell, Joni, 25
Mommymen, 121
Monroe, Marilyn, 167
Monster Magnet, 203
Moon, Keith, 138, 205
Moreland, Falling James, 191
Morello, Tommy, 76
Morgan (neighborhood boy), 8
Morin, Skot, 227
Morris, Chris, 165
Morris, Jerry Allen (father), 8, 10,
    32, 60, 91
    attempted mugging of, 12
    and bullying of son in
        neighborhood, 6
    and Chevy Impala, 25
    and Circle Jerks, 131
    conservatism of, 93
    description, background, and
        work of, 3–4, 5, 7, 11–13, 15,
        22
    divorce of, 24, 179
    and drugs and alcohol, 7, 16, 22,
        214–215

and "fags," 19
failing health and death of,
    214–215
and fire, 13
and Lighthouse, 139
and music, 12, 19, 28–29, 131,
    179
nature of relationship with son,
    179, 180
and son's drug use and drinking,
    21–23, 177–180, 279
and Watson, 93
Morris, Keith
    and alcohol, 2, 15–16, 21, 22, 29,
        33, 44, 49, 58, 74, 85, 95, 103,
        106, 111, 135, 150, 155, 163–
        166, 167, 170, 172, 175, 176,
        178–179, 180, 183–184, 278
    and art, 23–24
    and bad behavior at shows, 83
    and Black Flag, 1, 25–30, 45–55,
        59–62, 64–66, 67–72, 73–76,
        83, 84–87, 88, 91, 94, 113, 121–
        123, 203, 246–252, 263, 278,
        284
    and Bug Lamp, 1, 204–207, 208–
        213, 263
    and business and responsibility,
        60
    and car crashes, 1–2, 21, 256–
        258, 269
    childhood of, 4–24
    and Circle Jerks, 1, 89–90, 94–97,
        98–104, 106, 118–120, 124–
        129, 130–135, 136–140,

Morris, Keith
  and Circle Jerks, (*continued*)
      146–153, 156, 158–161,
      162–163, 173, 181–185, 194,
      196, 202, 203, 208, 219–225,
      241–242, 263, 271–274, 284
  and Club Lingerie, 154–155
  and community college, 32
  and cops, 77–81, 111–112
  dark period of, nearly destitute,
      163–164
  and Decline of Western
      Civilization, 113–114
  and diabetes, 1–2, 231–234,
      236–237, 238, 242, 256–258,
      259–270, 279–280, 282
  and dress and look, 58–59
  and drugs, 1–2, 15, 16, 18,
      20–23, 25, 32, 55, 58, 65, 87,
      95, 111, 133–135, 137, 150,
      163–165, 167–169, 170, 172,
      174–180, 183–185, 278
  and drums, 28–29
  and dumpster incident,
      108–109
  and early musical experiences
      and influences, 7, 9–10, 15–19,
      25–30
  and fire, 13
  and Flea and Anthony,
      167–169
  and gangbangers on bus,
      105–106
  and girls, 95
  grandparents of, 91–93, 94
  and Hangmen, 186–190, 192,
      193–195, 198, 201, 202, 205,
      209, 245
  height and weight of, 27, 65
  as heroic vocalist, 68
  Hollywood Hills house of, 133
  in hospital, 171–173, 267–270
  in jail, 81, 112
  as Johnny Bob Goldstein, 38, 183
  and Karen (KJ), 95, 106, 107
  as lone wolf on the road, 146
  and the Masque, 63–66
  and Midget Handjob, 1, 235–240,
      263
  at Millie's Diner, 226–230, 231,
      232, 233–234, 235
  mother as ally of, 93–94
  nature of relationship with
      father, 179, 180
  in New York City, 202–204
  and Norway and Turbonegro,
      259–270
  and Nymphs and Lorre, 191–193,
      196–201, 202, 205, 209, 245
  and OFF!, 1, 32, 274–276, 281,
      284
  as outsider, 28, 59
  and Panic, 31–45
  and partying in Hollywood,
      Chinatown, and Beverly Hills,
      108–112, 167, 174–177
  as poster boy for downward
      spiral, 137
  and public recognition and
      attention, 282–284

and Repo Man, 141–144

and Reyes and Cadena
  friendships, 122

rift with Dukowski of, 84–87

and Rubicon record store, 25–26

and second-guessing songs and
  records, 127

and Sid and Nancy, 145

at Smalls, 243–244

sober, 180, 183–184, 186, 196,
  198, 214, 278–279, 283

and songwriting, 46, 96, 97, 134,
  136, 183, 281

and sports, 10–11

stealing from father's store by,
  179–180

at Street Scene music festival,
  170–171

and suicide victim, 8–9

and surfing, 20–21, 28, 47

at V2 Records, 244–245,
  253–256, 259, 271

as wandering half-Jew, 215–218

and Westerberg and
  Replacements, 164–166

working for father, 11–12, 15, 22,
  24, 28, 32, 37, 86, 130–131,
  179, 184

Morris, Maudena (mother), 8

and bullying of son in
  neighborhood, 6

description and background of,
  3, 4

divorce of, 24, 179

family of, 91

and Frances's party, 10

and Howie, 7

and Midget Handjob, 239

quits Los Angeles Times job, 94

and Repo Man, 143–144

as son's ally, 93–94

and son's drinking, 15–16

and son's hospitalization, 172

and son's stay in North Carolina,
  216

Morris, Saul (grandfather), 4, 5

Morris, Trudy (sister), 7, 8, 24, 92,
  93, 177, 216

Morrison, Jim, 125–126

Mötley Crüe, 108

Motörhead, 57, 189

Mott the Hoople, 48

MTV, 200

Mudhoney, 218

Mullen, Brendan, 61, 62, 65, 66, 121,
  154, 189

Murphy, Michael, 211, 212

Murphy's Law, 224

Mustaine, Dave, 158

Napoli, John, 131

Narcotics Anonymous, 178

Naughty Sweeties, 70

Navarro, Dave, 212

Necros, 119

Neon, 254

Ness, Mike, 110, 128

Netson, Brett, 236

Neville, Ivan, 205

Neville Brothers, 205

New Masque, 65, 79, 80, 154, 162

New York Dolls, 17, 27, 88, 108

Nicks, Stevie, 25, 59

Nirvana, 209, 254, 272

No Crisis, 103

Noll, Greg, 12

Nolte, Dave, 56, 75

Nolte, Joe, 56, 70, 75

Nolte, Mike, 56, 75

Nuccio, Carlo, 205, 206–207, 208, 209, 210, 211

Nugent, Ted, 26, 82

Nymphs, 191–193, 196–200, 202, 205, 209, 245

October, Gene, 132

OFF!, 1, 32, 274–276, 281, 284

Offspring, 219

Oliveri, Nick, 260, 261, 263

One Hit Wonder, 212

Page, Jimmy, 247

Panic, 31–45

Parsec, 71

Parsons, Graham, 237

Pasadena Art Center, 23–24

Patterson, Phast Phreddie, 61

Pearl Jam, 211, 218, 284

Pennywise, 41, 237, 277

Perry, Steve, 26

Pettibon, Raymond, 33–34, 45, 60, 75, 79, 90, 276, 278

Pierce, Jeffrey Lee, 75, 106, 156
    and Black Flag and Circle Jerks, 95

and Bud Club, 155

and Club Lingerie, 154

and Creeping Ritual, 95

and dumpster, 108

and Gun Club, 61, 98, 189

and Red Lights, 211

and Slash, 61, 95

as songwriter and performer, 95–96, 98

and Tex and the Horseheads, 107

as underrated punk icon, 281

Pink Floyd, 18

Pink House, 91, 94, 95, 96, 103, 104, 105–107, 135

Piper, Michael, 25–26

Pixies, 243

Plimsouls, 46, 56, 109

Plugz, 52, 78, 114, 119, 125, 132, 137

Pogues, 210, 243

Poison, 199

Police (band), 130

Police (cops), 77–81, 83–84, 111–112, 117, 118

Pop, Iggy, 126

POPDeFECT, 227, 236

Pope, Roger, 199

Potts, Rick, 236

Power Tools, 242–243, 244

Presley, Elvis, 10

Price, Bill, 199

Procol Harum, 18

Prog rock, 26

Punk rock, 85, 103, 146, 164, 175, 248, 264, 271
    and Bell, 139

and Biscuits, 138
black, 65
and Black Flag, 45, 50, 88, 245, 246
and Blasters, 156
and the blues, 95
in California, 27, 56, 59, 63–66, 67, 70, 82–83, 101, 108, 109, 118, 260
and Club Lingerie, 154
and cops, 80, 117, 118
and Dangerhouse, 49
and EPs, 276
fashion, 58–59
and Flea, 155
fury, 46
and Gibson, 221
grapevine, 126
and Green Day, 219
hardcore, 25, 45, 83, 108
and heavy metal, 183
houses, 40
manual, 28
and Masque, 61, 63–66
and media, 116–117
and medleys, 136
and new wave of bands and fans, 82–84
Oakland festival, 158
original Hollywood, 82, 83
parties and party people, 83, 101
and Pierce, 281
and prior music, 143
and Repo Man, 143, 144
scene in New York, 26

second wave of LA, 63, 108
and slam dancing and stage diving, 82, 117
and spitting, 102
variety and depth of, 96
and violence, 116–117, 125
See also particular bands and people
Pure Hell, 65

Queens of the Stone Age, 248, 260
Quintana, Charlie, 119, 132, 133

Rage Against the Machine, 76
Raging Slab, 203
Raji's, 167, 174, 192, 206, 208, 211, 245
Ramone, Dee Dee, 203
Ramones, 24, 27, 57, 58, 186, 203, 205, 209, 273
Rat, Paul, 197, 200
Ratt, 31, 57
Raveonettes, 254–255
Reactionaries, 52
Recreational Racism, 237
Recycled Records, 107
Red (hippie), 40–41
Red Cross, 88, 89, 97, 110, 274
Red Hot Chili Peppers, 155, 159, 167, 169, 208, 211, 236, 242, 243, 248
Red Lights, 211
Redd Kross, 88, 274, 275
Reed, Lou, 48
Relativity Records, 162, 181

R.E.M., 243

Replacements, 164–166, 243

Repo Man (movie), 141–144, 161

Rey, Daniel, 203–205, 206, 207, 208, 209, 210, 212, 217

Reyes, Ron, 206, 246, 280
    becomes Black Flag vocalist, 86, 88
    and Black Flag parties, 76
    and Black Flag reunion, 250
    and Decline of Western Civilization, 113
    and first Black Flag show, 51
    and Jealous Again EP, 122
    and Morris friendship, 122
    and Polliwog Park Black Flag show, 75
    quits Black Flag, 121
    and Red Cross, 88

Reynolds, Burt, 147

RHCP, 167

Rhino 39, 49

Rhythm Pigs, 174

Rich, Buddy, 89

Richards, Keith, 223

Roach, Max, 29

Robyn Hitchcock and the Soft Boys, 221

Rocket from the Crypt, 274

Roessler, Paul, 76

Rogerson, Roger
    and Circle Jerks, 90, 97, 99, 103–104, 109–110, 119, 124, 130, 131, 136, 137, 139–140
    drug overdose of, 138

and girlfriend, 95, 103–104, 139, 140

Rolling Stones, 186

Rollins, Henry, 86, 94, 122, 123, 139, 212–213, 238, 247, 250, 277

Ronson, Mick, 16

Ronstadt, Linda, 25

Root, Dan, 209, 210, 212

Rose, Donny, 78

Roth, David Lee, 174–175

Royal Loyal Order of the Water Buffalo, 155

Rubalcaba, Mario, 274, 275

Rubicon record store, 25–26

Rubin, Rick, 212

Ruby Records, 106

Rudd, Phil, 38

Run-D.M.C., 242

Runaways, 17

Rune Rebellion, 269

Saccharine Trust, 139

Santana, 171

Santiago, Joey, 243

Saturday Night Live, 119–120

Schloss, Zander, 142, 161, 162, 183, 219, 224, 272

Schreiner, Knut "Euroboy," 261, 263

Scott, Bon, 38

Scratch, Derf, 64, 65, 117, 155

Scream, 243

Screamers, 76, 114, 156

Sea Hags, 197, 200, 212

Seeds, 64

Sex Pistols, 27

Sham 69, 19

Sheen, Martin, 251

Shorty (truck driver), 153

Shrapnel, 203

Shrine, 41, 43

Sid and Nancy (movie), 144–145

Sidel, John, 242, 243–244

Simon, Paul, 255

Simpletones, 69, 75

Sin 34, 176

Sinatra, Frank, 143, 164

Skaterdater (movie), 9

Skunkhead, 78

Slash (magazine), 59, 61, 64, 95, 102, 106, 107, 113, 114

Slash Records, 113

Slayer, 156

Slovak, Hillel, 243

Sly and the Family Stone, 163

Small, Bryan, 187, 188, 193, 194, 195, 200, 201

Smart Pills, 66

Smith, Mark E., 236

Smith, Will, 265

Smokestack Lightning, 9–10

Snowden, Don, 95

Social Distortion, 110, 128, 138

Solid Eye, 236

Somers, Andy, 181

Sonic Youth, 241

Soundtrack of Our Lives, 265

Spencer, Jeremy, 59

Spheeris, Penelope, 113–114, 118, 237

Spicoli, Jeff, 34

Spinal Tap, 156

Spinal Tap (movie), 159, 251

Springsteen, Bruce, 25

Squire, Barry, 211–212

SSD, 167

SST Records, 34, 59, 248

Standells, 64

Starland Vocal Band, 136

Statman, Anna, 211–212

Stennet, Rob, 204, 205, 206, 208, 209, 210, 211, 217

Steppenwolf, 16

Stevenson, Billy, 280

Stimulators, 119

Stinson, Bob, 165

Stone, Sly, 163

Stooges. *See* Iggy and the Stooges

Strangeloves, 133

Street Scene (outdoor LA music festival), 170–171

Stretch Marks, 173

Strummer, Joe, 243

Subhumans, 121

Suicidal Tendencies, 101, 167

Sunny Day Real Estate, 256

Survivor, 31

Tarling, Dave, 46

Ted and Dave (twins), 15

Tex and the Horseheads, 107, 155, 219

Thelonious Monster, 155, 158, 164, 167, 176, 235, 237, 242

Thin Lizzy, 25, 26

Three Dog Night, 16
Thunders, Johnny, 223
Tollett, Paul, 246
Tool, 253
Top Jimmy, 174–175
Tourists, 74, 75, 76, 89, 274
Tovar, Gary, 165, 280
Townsend, Pete, 247
TSOL, 101, 103
Turbonegro, 248, 259–263
Turner, Ike, 96
Turner, Tina, 96
20/20, 159
Twinkie, 208, 210

UFO Gang, 227
Underwood, Chuck, 13–14, 21
Urban, Hope, 227
Urinals, 103, 114
Used, 254
UXA, 66, 67

Valencia, Julio Roberto Valverde
    (Robo), 59, 60, 79, 250, 278
Vampire Weekend, 255
Van Halen, 174–175, 193
Van Santen, Rick, 246, 251, 252
Vandals, 155, 173, 209, 237, 280
Vedder, Eddie, 218
Velvet Underground, 48, 191
Ventures, 129
Verbinsky, Gore, 107
VICE, 275–276
Vicious, Sid, 58, 144–145
Vidal, Mark, 139

Village Voice, 26
Vines, 254
Ving, Lee, 155
Virgin Records, 244, 245
Von Helvete, Hank, 261, 262, 263
V2 Records, 244–245, 253–255,
    271

Wahl, Jon, 235, 239
Waits, Tom, 175
Waller, Don, 61
Walton, Mark, 160
WAR, 133, 136, 137
Warhol, Andy, 132
Warner Brothers, 165, 192, 208,
    211
Warped Tour, 223, 272, 273,
    275
Wasted Years (album), 281
Wasted Youth, 95, 103, 159
Watson, Art, 93
Watt, Mike, 52
Watts, Charlie, 191
Weber, Dewey, 12
Weirdos, 63, 109, 114, 175, 237
Weiss, Pete, 155, 158, 167, 172
Westerberg, Paul, 164–166
Weston, Doug, 57
Whisky, 16, 33, 38, 58, 61, 85, 89,
    108, 237, 245, 248, 256
White Stripes, 244
Who, 189
Wild at Heart (movie), 78
Wild Cherry, 250
Williamson, James, 16

Winter, Edgar, 19, 204
Winter, Johnny, 204
Wipers, 78
Wire, 243
Wonder, Stevie, 163
Woodmansey, Mick "Woody," 16
Wray, Link, 247
Würm and Würmhole, 36, 37, 38,
    39
Wynette, Tammy, 136

X, 67, 78, 106, 125, 155, 169, 237

Yardbirds, 9
Young, Angus, 38, 223
Young, Joe, 37
Young, Malcolm, 38
Young, Neil, 221
Youth, Todd, 224
Youth Brigade, 173

Zappa, Frank, 45
01 Gallery, 174–175
Zeros, 78
Zincavage, Diana, 100